AF352445

# UNDERSTANDING LAW FOR THE SOCIAL SCIENCES

# Understanding Law for the Social Sciences

DENNIS BAKER AND BYRON SHELDRICK

UNIVERSITY OF TORONTO PRESS
Toronto Buffalo London

© University of Toronto Press 2025
Toronto Buffalo London
utppublishing.com
Printed in Canada

ISBN 978-1-4875-9334-6 (cloth)     ISBN 978-1-4875-9335-3 (EPUB)
ISBN 978-1-4875-9333-9 (paper)     ISBN 978-1-4875-9336-0 (PDF)



**Library and Archives Canada Cataloguing in Publication**

Title: Understanding law for the social sciences / Dennis Baker and Byron Sheldrick.
Names: Baker, Dennis (Lecturer in political science), author | Sheldrick, Byron M., author.
Description: Includes bibliographical references and index.
Identifiers: Canadiana (print) 20250154692 | Canadiana (ebook) 20250154730 | ISBN 9781487593339 (paper) | ISBN 9781487593346 (cloth) | ISBN 9781487593353 (EPUB) | ISBN 9781487593360 (PDF)
Subjects: LCSH: Law – Canada – Textbooks. | LCSH: Law and the social sciences – Canada – Textbooks. | LCGFT: Textbooks.
Classification: LCC KE444 .B35 2025 | LCC KF385.ZA2 B35 2025 | DDC 349.71 – dc23

Cover design: Val Cooke
Cover image: istock.com/Stefan Ilic

We welcome comments and suggestions regarding any aspect of our publications – please feel free to contact us at news@utorontopress.com or visit us at utppublishing.com.

Every effort has been made to contact copyright holders; in the event of an error or omission, please notify the publisher.

We wish to acknowledge the land on which the University of Toronto Press operates. This land is the traditional territory of the Wendat, the Anishnaabeg, the Haudenosaunee, the Métis, and the Mississaugas of the Credit First Nation.

University of Toronto Press acknowledges the financial support of the Government of Canada and the Ontario Arts Council, an agency of the Government of Ontario, for its publishing activities.

Canada

*As learners and students, we have been fortunate to have been inspired and mentored by so many incredible minds and generous individuals. We owe them all a huge debt and are eternally grateful. There are always, however, those who stand out.*

*For Dennis: Rainer Knopff, who will always be my model of what it means to be a scholar, and Janet Ajzenstat, who sparked my first interest in the relationship between law and politics.*

*For Byron: Margaret Ogilvie, whose Introduction to Law course inspired me to go to law school, and Leo Panitch, who showed me how to critically interrogate everything, yet remain optimistic and hopeful.*

*For both of us, our hope is that we can pay our debt forward and motivate our students to critically engage both with ideas and with the world around them.*

*So, in the end, this book is dedicated to our students, past, present, and future.*

# Contents

## Part Two: Fields of Legal Doctrine and Practice

# Preface

As two legally trained political scientists, we have observed in our teaching and research several difficulties in approaching law in an interdisciplinary fashion. While we remain steadfast in our belief that such approaches are valuable and provide a more robust understanding of law, it can be challenging to deal with the complexities of law at the same time as contextualizing, critiquing, and connecting it with another discipline, usually one that brings its own intricate conceptual framework and methodological finery. At the undergraduate level there is a tendency to treat the study of law and legal doctrines as a subject that is the exclusive preserve of law schools. As a result, despite a growing interest in legal studies at the undergraduate level, the teaching of law itself remains underdeveloped. Concepts of law are often taught as part of a broader course (public policy and administration, criminology, etc.) but not given the full treatment they deserve. Some programs do have introductory law courses, but these are often narrowly focused, examining the institutional and "black letter" aspects of "what the law is" without highlighting the policy implications of those legal doctrines and their relationship to the state and self-government. Alternatively, some programs offer a "sociology of law"-type course, which emphasizes power dynamics and social impacts of law, but doesn't develop a robust understanding of either the institutional aspects of law or the importance of the internal logic of law and legal reasoning.

This book provides a more balanced path for undergraduate legal study. Our objective is to ensure that students understand the operation of law and legal institutions but are also equipped with the tools to conduct their own legal research. In this way, students will be able to integrate a pragmatic and critical understanding of law into other social science research perspectives. We also seek to draw out the public dimension and public policy concerns that inform, and are informed by, legal doctrines. While this approach will be especially useful for undergraduates in political science, public administration, or public policy programs, we think an awareness of these aspects of law and legal reasoning will also benefit a broad array of social science students.

The genesis of this book was a result of our teaching at the University of Guelph, where our popular Criminal Justice & Public Policy (CJPP) program continues to thrive. We noticed that our students craved more law-related courses and needed a stronger legal foundation to pursue advanced topics in criminology and public policy subjects related to law. We were frustrated, for example, when students studying the impact of a specific offence on marginalized populations did not know how that crime was defined in the *Criminal Code* or the importance of whether the offence was a summary conviction, indictable, or hybrid offence. For our non-criminology students, we regretted not being able to fully explore with our students the public policy dimensions of a variety of non-criminal legal phenomena, like the role of administrative tribunals, the role contracts and torts play in solving or exacerbating societal problems or how labour law affects our public services. As an increasing number of students have been interested in protecting the environment, we realized those students needed to better understand the very complicated nexus of federalism, multiple areas of law, and political behaviour. With all of these students in mind, we introduced a large second-year political science course in 2016 to introduce, expand, and enrich those topics. This textbook is a distillation of that course, and it is our hope that other instructors will find its approach useful for similar courses at other institutions.

Writing a book is a challenging process. Writing about law is particularly challenging, given the law's complexity and nuances. While we have endeavoured to be as accurate as possible, the law is ever-changing and usually dependent on specific facts. Nothing in this text should be construed as legal advice. If you are facing a legal problem in your own life, the best advice is to consult a lawyer as soon as possible.

For us, this project has consumed a great deal of our time and attention and has taken far longer to bring to fruition than we imagined at the outset. While writing this book, we both had very time-consuming and intensive administrative posts. Moreover, the demands of those positions only intensified during the global pandemic. Time set aside for research and writing quickly gave way to endless virtual meetings and contingency planning. This meant there was little time or energy left to devote to the project. Having said that, we are proud of the final product. We also have to thank many people, particularly the editorial team at University of Toronto Press, who showed us endless patience and tolerance. We frequently felt somewhat embarrassed when responding to their polite inquiries about the status of the project. In particular, we would like to thank UTP editors Rebecca Duce and Mary Lui, as well as our copyeditor, Melissa MacAulay, for all their hard work on our behalf. A special thanks to the helpful research assistance we received from Ana Nizharadze, Tallis Dalrymple, Charli Shapiro, Megan

McMeekin, Nathaniel Meakins, and Susannah Webster – you all worked at a pace we struggled to keep up with. We also need to thank all of our friends and colleagues in the Department of Political Science at the University of Guelph. The Department of Political Science has, over the past decade, become a centre for debates and discussions about law and politics. There is no other political science department in Canada with such a dedicated cohort of gifted faculty studying the intersection of law and politics. We owe much to this group of faculty, as well as to our graduate students and staff. They all contribute to making the University of Guelph a rich intellectual environment in which to do this work. In particular, special thanks to Troy Riddell, Kate Puddister, Dave Snow, Mark Harding, Minh Do, Jordi Diez, Ian Spears, and Tamara Small. Finally, we would be remiss not to thank our families, friends, and colleagues beyond the university.

Dennis Baker
Byron Sheldrick
Guelph, 2024

# Introduction

This book is about the law. It is a book about what the law is, and is not, but more than that, it is a book about how we analyze and study the law. It is important to consider this question because there are many different approaches to studying law, beyond what we might associate with "law school" and the legal profession. This book takes the view that law is a crucial subject for the social sciences generally; political science, sociology, criminology, economics, and other social sciences all have obvious connections with the law. Students of those disciplines should be able understand those connections and approach legal controversies from various perspectives. Each perspective has advantages and disadvantages that help us to answer some questions but may be less suited to answering other questions. The study of law is complex precisely because the law itself is complex.

It is not our intention to weigh into disciplinary debates between the social sciences. Sociology, criminology, law and society, political science, and economics all have important contributions to make regarding the study of law. Rather, we intend to equip students with the tools to engage with the law directly as a subject of research or learning regardless of the social science approach. Our starting point is that law, articulated by courts, legislators, legal professionals, and those responsible for applying and enforcing it, is critically important. We can certainly debate the implications of implementing an assisted suicide policy, but it is also important to understand how the *Criminal Code* provisions regarding homicide might frame such a policy. In doing so, it is also important to understand the principles the courts employ when interpreting and applying the criminal law. It is not our intention to argue that the legal doctrines as they are taught in a law school are the only things that matter but rather that there is merit in all social scientists understanding the parameters of those doctrines, how they impact public debates and public policy choices, and what limitations they might impose on the development of public policy.

While law is a body of rules and regulations, it is also, at the same time, a subject of academic study and inquiry. We prefer to call this academic discipline "legal studies" to clearly differentiate between the object of the study and the disciplinary approach. We fully recognize that in professional contexts, this differentiation is rarely made. For our purposes, however, it is important to keep the two distinct, since this book is about the content of the law as an object of study, including how it is interpreted and applied, and how it impacts and relates to issues of public concern. We also recognize that the term "legal studies" is used by some in academia to mean studying law with a sociological lens and as a near synonym for the field of "law and society." Here we are using "legal studies" at its broadest as incorporating the study of the body of rules and regulations and treating those doctrines seriously. But it involves more than just studying those rules; it also involves the study of how those rules get made and, subsequently, how they are interpreted, implemented, and enforced. It also involves the study of their impact and consequences, both on those who are subject to them and on society at large.

Our intention is not to provide a broad overview of the various approaches to studying law. This would be a vast undertaking, and there are many works that provide this sort of analysis (textbooks on law and society include Calavita, 2016, and Vago & Barkan, 2021). Rather, we intend to provide students with a sufficient understanding of the content of key areas of Canadian law and the various dimensions of its implementation, interpretation, and application, such that they can then apply this knowledge with confidence to supplement and enhance whatever broader methodological approach they might choose to employ.

The law is part and parcel of our day-to-day lives, but it can also be elusive when we think about it systematically. It permeates so much of what we do, yet at the same time very few of us have real encounters with the institutions and processes of the law – and, when we do, those interactions are often mysterious and intimidating. As such, the law is concrete and present, yet amorphous, uncertain, and something we perceive rather than experience. For many, our most concrete experience of the law is through popular culture. Songs, movies, and television shows all inform us of the law. Whether it be police procedurals, courtroom dramas, or even soap operas like *Suits*, each is, in some way or another, about the law. When Bob Marley sang "I Shot the Sheriff," or the Clash sang "I fought the law and the law won," or even Taylor Swift's "no body, no crime," each artist was making powerful statements about the law and state authority but also statements about resistance and political dissent. While popular culture performs an important function in transmitting conceptual ideas about law, it is often misleading. Actual courtrooms seldom operate the way they are portrayed on television. The necessities of the medium require dramatization, as well as the abbreviation and simplification of process (for more on these questions, see Posner, 2009). Legal practice mostly takes place *outside* the courtroom and many legal matters are settled before a matter is taken to trial.

Our limited awareness of law only scratches the surface of how law pervades our lives in so many other ways. When we drive to work or school in the morning, we find ourselves immersed in a web of intricate legal rules and norms of behaviour. If we rent an apartment, write a will, or make a purchase at the store, our behaviour, and the behaviour of others, is governed by the law. The fact that in many of these instances we may not even be aware of the reach of the law speaks to its unique power to govern our actions. We accept the legitimacy of law and allow ourselves to be governed by it, knowing that the alternative would be chaos and anarchy.

Law, then, rests on authority and legitimacy for its effectiveness. We obey the law because we accept that laws are made and created according to a legitimate and accepted governance process – what influential German sociologist Max Weber called a rational-legal basis of authority. By this, Weber meant that the authority of the state rested on the fact that it was "legally" empowered to make decisions. In other words, the scope of the government's ability to act is defined by legal rules. As legal theorist Martin Loughlin (2000) notes, political power is "a form of decision-making power which can only be exercised through institutions and processes, and therefore, in part at least, through the medium of law" (p.16). Normally, we understand those rules to be found in some sort of constitutional document which asserts and defines the authority of the state (an aspect further explored in Chapter 3). The recognition of the importance of law as an aspect of authority speaks to the critical connection between the nature of law and our systems of government. On one hand, we accept the legitimacy of law because it is established through legitimate governmental authority, while at the same time, the authority of government, in turn, rests on the fact that it is established and governed by law. Law operates as a lynchpin for the democratic legitimacy of our governance structures. It is, in many ways, foundational to the operation of modern governance structures. For this reason, law and politics are intimately connected (as described further in Chapter 1), and it is almost impossible to seriously study politics without some knowledge of law.

To achieve its ends, law necessarily has an important coercive element. Indeed, this makes the legitimacy and authority of law so vitally important. Failure to comply with laws can lead to state action and intervention in an individual's private life. While, on a day-to-day basis, we may have very few encounters with the law, the encounters we do have may be particularly significant. A failure to pay taxes, for example, can lead to a seizure by the state of one's home and belongings. Failure to comply with the criminal law can lead to fines or imprisonment. Workers engaged in an illegal strike might find themselves detained by the police.

In short, the state can use coercive force to ensure compliance with the law. Weber (1919/1970) understood that the state possessed a "monopoly on the legitimate use of force," by which he meant that the state alone has the ability to deploy the police and (in rare cases) the military to ensure that the law is followed (for a discussion of the essentially coercive nature of law, see Schauer, 2015b). The coercive element of the law alone, however, is an insufficient basis for explaining the law's legitimacy and acceptance as a governing framework for society. If this was all there was to it, we would live in an extremely authoritarian and ultimately unstable political system. To understand this, we need to think about the state and how it operates within the context of law.

## THE IMPORTANCE OF THE STATE

The above discussion highlights the importance of thinking about the law in relation to the state. Law provides a key mechanism by which state power is legitimized and converted into authority. We obey the law because we feel deeply that it is legitimate, and compliance is the appropriate and right thing to do. Most of us feel there is something inherently "wrong" about breaking the law. In this sense, law also provides an ideological basis for state legitimacy. Law is tied up in our understanding of how society is organized, how political power is exercised, and how relations between individuals and groups are structured. This does not mean that every individual accepts the "legitimacy" of every single piece of legislation. We can have debates about the value and desirability of particular laws. This is, after all, the essence of politics and political debates. However, our acceptance of the fact that those who make the law are entitled to do so also channels how opposition and advocacy for change is manifested. Indigenous Peoples and the Quebecois have challenged the legitimacy of the Canadian state, but they have largely done so by legal means. At the end of the day, if that legitimacy is entirely depleted, the state is in crisis and cannot effectively govern, which, in extreme cases, might lead to acts of civil unrest, terrorism, civil war, or the possibility of revolution.

Public law defines the structure and constitution of the state and our governing relationships, while private law sets out expectations and rules for governing relationships between citizens with state-backed enforcement. Contract law structures our economic relationships, while tort law creates expectations about how individuals should treat each other in their day-to-day interactions and what level of care is owed to others in society. Property law, by contrast, sets out expectations about what we own and possess and what we can do with those possessions. It also enables us to restrict the activities of others with respect to our property. It should be clear, then, that significantly important elements of our day-to-day lives are defined, mediated, and experienced through the law and the state, even if we are unaware of its presence as we go about our daily activities. If we fail to live up to a promise to a friend, there may be social consequences, but usually a contrite apology may be sufficient to set the matter right. The signing of a contract, on the other hand, signifies a level of formality that goes beyond a mere promise. In this context, breaching the contract may have more serious implications, even though there may have been very good reasons for deciding to abandon the agreement. We understand that it is "the law" that elevates the contract to something different and more serious than a mere promise. Moreover, it implicates the state in what would otherwise be a purely personal relationship, since the expectation is that the state will enforce the contract.

The strong connection between law and the state may seem odd to some readers since it is common to suppose there is a sharp divide between law and politics. In this view, the state is the realm of policy development and implementation, where outcomes are politically determined. This realm is highly dynamic: When one party is in power, the ideological direction of the state may lean one way, but when another party takes control, it may lean a different way. Policy outcomes, in this sense, are highly dependent on political values – not only those in society, but also those of political actors within the state.

However, many assume that the basic underpinnings of our laws will not vary with ideological or political shifts. Law, as a system of rules and regulations, prioritizes consistency and predictability. While the laws that are produced by a particular government may be ideologically informed, the expectation is that the approach of the courts to interpreting and applying those laws should not be. Criminal law, for example, should not be politically informed by how offences are interpreted and enforced by the police. Direct political interference in criminal law is rightly considered highly inappropriate. Similarly, we expect judges to approach their job with neutrality and impartiality.

There is much merit to this broad conceptualization. But already there are cracks that might be apparent to you: The selection of those impartial judges is carried out by governments, sometimes with political ends in mind; and judicial decisions are not self-enforcing since they rely on public authorities who are willing to carry out their intentions and may do so in a politically sensitive manner. Moreover, an entirely apolitical law would be an affront to democracy and would call into question the very notion of self-government. Statutes, so long as they are consistent with the constitution, allow our democratically elected representatives to radically change any area of law instantly upon enactment. We may want to *minimize* the political influence over law, but the connection between law and politics is essential and unavoidable.

The intersection of law and politics is clearly seen in the state's structure. The state is "constituted" by law – after all, we need legal rules to have elections, to bestow representatives with responsibilities, and to recognize Parliament's law-making power. At the same time, our political institutions clearly "make" law. Every first-year political science student will have learned that most modern "states" in the liberal democratic tradition are composed of three branches: the legislative branch, which makes laws; the executive, which both plays an important role in initiating laws passed by the legislature and is responsible for implementing those laws after enactment; and a judicial branch, which settles controversies arising from the laws. All three branches have an important role to play with respect to law. As political scientist James B. Kelly (2005) notes, it is now common to recognize the Department of Justice as a central agency at the heart of government, confirming the pervasiveness of legal considerations throughout the government. A hallmark of a "good state," however, is a functional separation between the judicial branch and the other two. As one British judge put it, the legislative and executive branches tell us what the law *is to be*, and the judicial branch, on a case-by-case basis, says what the law *is* (Sedley, 2015, p. 173).

This attitude is encapsulated in the notion of the "rule of law," discussed in greater detail in Chapter 1. One of its components is the primacy of legal instruments, which means that legal norms trump political, moral, or ethical norms. The whims of the prime minister have no relevance whatsoever to Canadians unless and until they are enacted into law by the proper legislative process. Then and only then are Canadians obliged to obey them. Moreover, the rule of law requires the law be applied equally to all individuals, regardless of their station, and regardless of whether they hold governmental office. State officials, according to this doctrine, hold only the authority they are given by the law and are constrained and governed by that same grant of authority. Outside of that context, the law applies to them the same way it applies to ordinary citizens. The rule of law helps establish the law as separate from the politicians and state actors involved in its creation. To this end, judges, while appointed by the state, are generally guaranteed very long tenures in office and can be removed only in extreme circumstances with an address from the House of Commons and the Senate. In Canada, the discipline and oversight of judges is given to the Canadian Judicial Council (CJC), an organization of judges themselves, who are responsible for determining whether a judicial officer's behaviour has warranted discipline or a recommendation to Parliament for removal (see Dick, 2024, for recent developments involving the CJC).

The structure of the legal profession itself also helps insulate law from politics. Lawyers and legal professionals are generally organized into self-governing professional associations. In each Canadian province, a law society (or bar association) regulates entry into the profession, determining who is able to practise law and call themselves a lawyer. These associations set the required qualifications, accredit law schools, and oversee and set bar admission processes. They also regulate fees that lawyers can charge and oversee professional codes of conduct. They are responsible for enforcing those codes of conduct and investigate complaints from members of the public; they can impose discipline on members and even remove the right of a member to practise law. Disbarment from the profession is the most serious sanction that the profession can impose. The existence of a self-regulating profession ensures that the practice of law is independent and apart from the state. The state doesn't license lawyers to practise law, but rather lawyers license themselves, albeit through a complex and rigorous regulatory process. Typically, these associations have an internal governance structure that often involves an elected leadership and decision-making body and a professional staff. Indeed, the legitimacy of the legal profession rests largely on these regulatory bodies, which ensure not only a separation from the state – a state official cannot remove a lawyer's right to practise because they take on cases challenging its political priorities – but also the assurance of quality in training, accreditation, and oversight for the standards of legal practice.

This is not to say that the legal profession is unified or homogenous in nature. Rather, it is divided and fragmented. Concerns of judges are different from the concerns of practicing lawyers, with the latter having clients and the former concerned solely with what they see as the public interest. Within the legal profession itself there are some obvious divisions. Crown prosecutors and defence lawyers, for example, may share a common concern for the integrity of the criminal justice system but have very different concerns regarding the day-to-day dimensions of their legal practice (see Hennigar, 2002, 2010, for the different incentives Crown attorneys and executive actors might have). These concerns, however, will be completely different from those of a real estate or corporate securities lawyer, who face a completely different set of ethical and practical issues. Law societies and bar associations mediate these complex divisions and provide lawyers with both representation and a common structure of governance and oversight, but it remains a complex and fragmented structure of interest.

Similarly, the state is also fragmented in terms of its connection with law. Different legal regimes apply to different sectors of the state, for example. The legal and regulatory framework that governs environmental regulation (Chapter 10) is different than the legal framework that governs the organization and delivery of social services. Health departments are governed by a complex regulatory framework that bears little resemblance to the concerns and imperatives of a department of transportation. Simply put, the issues involved in regulating air travel, railways, and highways is completely different than the issues of regulating pharmaceutical approvals and the management of public health. Administrative law, discussed in Chapter 5, attempts to define and delineate a set of overarching accountability and oversight frameworks between the courts and the various elements of the state, but the sheer complexity and variation raises tensions that are difficult to overcome.

There are, of course, a variety of different theories of the state and approaches to understanding how the state operates and how it interacts with members of the public.

This is not a book about state theory, but our approach to understanding both the state and law rests heavily on theories of neo-institutionalism. Neo-institutionalism emphasizes the importance of institutions in shaping political behaviour (Hall & Taylor, 1996; March & Olsen, 1983; Smith, 1988). It emphasizes both the formal structures of institutions – how they are created, the legal constraints on office holders, etc. – as well as the more subtle cultural norms and practices that emerge and develop over time as office holders engage with each other, perform their roles as they perceive them, and respond to demands placed on them. One could, for example, draw out an elaborate organizational chart of any state bureaucracy, but it would not tell you very much about how that organization functions. One also needs to understand a host of cultural and normative practices, such as the merit principle, ministerial accountability, responsible government, and how discretion is exercised, as well how these practices are both observed, and sometimes not observed. If we think about the criminal justice system, it would be self-evident that a full understanding of criminal law needs to be supplemented by an examination of how police officers do their job, when they decide to lay charges, and when they decide to overlook what, on the face of it, might be a violation of the law.

The neo-institutional approach to understanding the law employed in this text appreciates the content of legal doctrines – the "law on the books" – but also recognizes that those doctrines are applied and developed in an institutional context by state (and sometimes non-state) actors. It reminds us of the need to understand legal principles, how courts understand their role, and how lawyers and judges act and discharge their duties, in addition to the actual content of the law itself. This more robust understanding of law can be challenging because it cannot ignore the often-complex doctrines of law even as it seeks to place them in a broader institutional context.

The initial task of understanding the content of the law is often described as a formalistic exercise – referred to in law schools as "black-letter law" – although we prefer the term "doctrinal legal research" (Bhat, 2020), which highlights that there is a distinct methodological approach to this sort of study. The primary focus of this approach is determining and identifying what constitutes the legal rules of a jurisdiction. A particular emphasis, then, is on the sources of law – legislation, regulation, judicial cases – and their interpretation. Attention is focused on a close reading of legal texts to determine how the law should be correctly interpreted. One can understand where the term "black-letter" comes from, in that this approach seeks to look to the actual printed word, the letters on the page, to understand what constitutes law.

One feature of doctrinal legal research is that it understands law as largely self-contained. In this view, the law is both autonomous and its reasoning is "immanent." By this, we mean that the law is something that exists independently, and it unfolds and develops through its own processes. For the empirical social scientist, this can seem like almost supernatural hokum – even famous US Supreme Court Justice Oliver Wendell Holmes warned against thinking of the law as a "brooding omnipresence in the sky." Still, this view is often held as a background assumption by lawyers and judges as they perform their duties. The common law, which we will talk more about in later chapters, is a prime example. The common law, which is the predominant legal system throughout those countries that were once part of the British Empire, is a system of law where legal rules emerge from the decisions made by judges to resolve the concrete disputes that come before them. The law unfolds, not in an instant case decided by a single judge but over time and through following precedent (when appropriate) and arriving at a remarkably stable and predictable system of law. It is an axiom of the common law that judges do not "actually make" the law, but rather they "find it." Of course, such a statement is a fiction, and serves to justify and legitimate the practice of judge-made law, but it also reflects the view that the law is in an important sense independent of any single judge and the result of immanent reasoning and juridical processes (this account of "legal reasoning" is further explored in Chapter 2).

Traditionally, law schools have adopted a more black-letter approach to the study of law. Their goal has been the creation of a professional group of lawyers who are skilled in the art and technique of legal reasoning, legal interpretation, and legal argumentation. This means an emphasis on the study of legal topics – criminal law, contract law, property law – through the reading of judicial decisions and statutes relevant to that area of the discipline. While much has changed at law schools, and there is a greater emphasis on understanding the social, economic, and political context of the law, the curriculum is still overwhelmingly organized in this fashion, with most courses continuing to emphasize "learning the law." A typical law school exam, for example, often involves the presentation of a hypothetical fact situation, for which the student must analyze the facts to identify the legal issues and how they might be resolved. In essence, this sort of exam replicates the mode of decision-making that epitomizes the common law and trains students to "think like lawyers," imprinting this analytical approach on the minds of those pursuing legal careers.

For our purposes, however, we want to emphasize that understanding the doctrinal approach is also critical for understanding the broader implications of law and its implications for public issues. This is precisely because lawyers and judges do feel obligations or fidelity to "the letter of law." Even though there is much scope for discretion when applying the law, the norms and traditions of legal interpretation, as well as formal understanding of the limits on courts and judges, do impact outcomes and results. When a judge reads a piece of legislation or interprets a past judicial decision, their training and approach to legal reasoning, and their understanding of the legislative process, will impact the outcome of their decisions. It might be tempting to reduce these questions to simply "political choice" or "judicial preference" ("attitudinalist" political scientists like Segal & Spaeth, 2002, take this view). But this, in our view, is almost always an oversimplification. Decisions are not usually simply random, dependent on the judge's idiosyncratic views and beliefs or their "feelings" on a particular day. As political scientist Emmett Macfarlane (2012) argues, "role formation" – the very idea of being a judge and having an awareness of the appropriate limits of the position – plays an important factor in how judges make their decisions. As part of this role, judges – like other legal actors – are deeply informed by the internal logic of legal institutions. One needs to understand the law, its structure, and the agency of those who work within the legal system to understand how the law operates and what it means. Within the language of the social sciences, these institutional cultural norms and practices can themselves be considered variables that need to be assessed and understood.

Neo-institutionalism recognizes that the complexity of law means that the "law" can operate as both a dependent and independent variable (Baker & Sheldrick, in press). Law may have profound impacts on social structures and processes, while being affected and shaped by those same social structures. It is precisely for this reason that social science approaches, which emphasize mapping out complex relationships of interaction, are so well-suited to the analysis of law. Methodologically, we rely on principles of doctrinal legal research (Arthurs & Bunting, 2014; Bhat, 2020; Hutchinson & Duncan, 2012) in order to explicate and illuminate how legal normative principles shape both the law and the outcomes of political and public issues. Doctrinal research can be criticized for ignoring or downplaying the political and social context within which the doctrines operate. This can be a valid criticism. However, it is important to always recognize that the development of legal doctrine itself typically incorporates elements from a background of social facts and political context (Bhat, 2020, p. 147; Sherry, 2011). At the other extreme, to focus on context, without understanding legal doctrine, risks missing an important component of the dynamic by which outcomes are generated.

## ORGANIZATION OF THE BOOK

To help you achieve the goal of understanding the neo-institutional contours of law, we have organized this volume into two parts. The first part looks at foundational elements of law and legal reasoning. These are the core principles and practices that shape law into a more-or-less coherent body of thought. Chapter 1 examines the sources of law. Where do we look when we wish to determine what the law is (or might be) at any point in time? This chapter also sets out two different approaches to law, the legal positivist and natural law approaches, and suggests how these might be reconciled. It also looks at core concepts such as the rule of law and different systems of law. Chapter 2 examines legal reasoning and principles of statutory interpretation. These are the primary analytical tools that judges and lawyers employ as they engage in legal decision-making. This chapter also provides an overview of the how courts are organized in Canada. Finally, Chapter 3 examines the Canadian Constitution and describes its core features, including its interpretation and application.

The second part of the book examines various fields of legal doctrine and practice. In each field, we explain the core legal doctrines, including key terms, concepts, and principles. This is critical knowledge that students studying law, including those in the social sciences, need to understand why courts and judges make the decisions they do, and the real limitations these decisions have on public outcomes. The chosen fields are drawn from both public and private law fields, and in each case our neo-institutional approach highlights the role of the state and identifies some of the implications for public policy. Chapter 4 looks at criminal law, where the coercive power of the state is most starkly revealed. Criminal law tries to balance defining the limits of both acceptable and unacceptable behaviour (what is criminal?) but also tries to limit the capacity and ability of the state to impinge upon the freedom and liberty of citizens. Chapter 5 examines an area of public law that is less publicly visible: administrative law. In this chapter we explore how courts have dealt with the state integrating judicial-like functions into policy and regulation. The next three chapters explore traditional areas of private law: contracts (Chapter 6), torts (Chapter 7), and property law (Chapter 8). Each of these private law fields has traditionally been neglected by political scientists and scholars of public policy, but we demonstrate that each has significant public dimensions that lend themselves to further study. By better understanding the doctrines they advance, the role of the state and the impact on public policy can be more easily discerned. Finally, in Chapters 9 and 10, we provide introductions to labour law and environmental law. Both areas of law lie clearly at the intersection of law and politics, with complex legal doctrines blending private action, public concerns, and state power in a fashion that make them a compelling conclusion to the ideas threaded throughout the book, and which we hope will inspire student engagement in future research.

Each chapter begins with specific learning objectives related to our aim of both explaining core doctrinal concepts and highlighting neo-institutional public policy features. Throughout the text, we highlight key terms and, while we explain their usage in text and in the Glossary, we encourage students to consult an online law dictionary for elaboration and usage in other legal contexts. (*Barron's Canadian Law Dictionary*, available through LexisNexis's QuickLaw service, is an exceptional resource; the American and openly accessible dictionary.law.com is also useful for better understanding general legal terms.) Finally, each chapter ends with a series of Review Questions intended to guide students as they reflect on the material and begin their own in-depth research and study. For some chapters, we have included "Moot Court Topics" at the end. While we recognize that full simulations might be impractical in large classes, we hope that the controversies can serve as the inspiration for classroom activities and spark further discussion.

# PART ONE

# Foundations of Law

# CHAPTER ONE

# Sources of Law

## LEARNING OBJECTIVES

- Begin to understand the relationship between law and authority.
- Be able to distinguish the concepts of positive and natural law.
- Understand the importance and relevance of the rule of law.
- Understand the difference between civil law and common law systems and why Canada is considered bi-jural.

Law can be productively situated within social science. There are many potential approaches to law – there are economic accounts, feminist accounts, Marxist accounts, critical race theory accounts, and many more – all of which have something potentially useful to add to our understanding of law. While valuable, those approaches tend to see legal doctrines as primarily the outcome of larger societal forces (class, race, gender) instead of focusing on the doctrines themselves. In this chapter, we focus on two approaches that are more doctrinal – legal positivism and natural justice – not because they are superior to those other approaches but because they allow us to better understand how judges and lawyers themselves understand legal doctrines (and how they evolve) and because they directly connect with self-government and the state in the neo-institutional manner described in the Introduction. By doing so, this chapter presents an opportunity to examine the nature and origins of law and asks what law is and where it comes from. Some answers are easy and obvious: Canadians accept that our primary political institution, Parliament, has a clear process by which it enacts statutes that are routinely accepted as law. This direct connection between law and politics leads to harder questions: Do these statutes need to conform to a higher order of "justice," whether embodied in a constitution or not? Are there laws that exist independently of formal statutes and constitutions? Do judges simply follow the laws as they find them or do they, in some important sense, "make law"? All of these questions flow from an understanding of what law is and where it comes from.

## LAW AND AUTHORITY

What is law? This question is one of the richest veins in Western culture and philosophy but one where the answers are still ultimately unsatisfying for many. The question was puzzling enough for one of the greatest legal minds of the twentieth century, H.L.A. Hart (1961), to remark that "nothing concise enough to be recognized as a definition could provide a satisfactory answer" (p.16). This might seem strange given the relative ease we have in identifying things that compose at least part of what we mean by law: statutes passed by Parliament; written decisions delivered by judges; speed limit signs that we see on the roads we travel; the rules we respect when getting married or divorced; and the will we write that gives our property away according to our wishes as our last earthly act. But that all-pervasiveness of law is part of the problem: No simple or singular part captures what we mean by the whole of "law" and finding the connective tissue is harder than it seems.

Most dictionaries offer a primary definition of "law" that refers to a "body of rules" or "a code or system of rules" (Oxford English Dictionary, n.d.). Your family probably has a form of "law" that governs your household: "No snacks before dinner" or "one hour of screen-time per day" are rules that together might constitute a "law" of your family home. The fact that these rules were not always obeyed or enforced did not disqualify them as recognized rules (although routine non-enforcement or non-compliance could diminish their status as "house law"). Here the jurisdiction – the territory where the rules apply – is small and restricted to your house and your family members; the authority is likely your parents but perhaps with some democratic input from some or all family members. When we speak of "law" we are usually speaking of the rules of a more general association of people: cities, provinces, and countries. In these cases – where the jurisdiction is larger and affecting people whose bonds are not familial but civic – laws are enforced by state authority.

With a larger number of people who are expected to be governed by a set of rules, two complications will inevitably result: (1) people will disagree with the rules, and (2) people will disregard or disobey rules they disagree with. Having rules and seeing them respected is a public good – it is in everyone's interest to have a system of rules. In this way, law may present a solution to what are called "collective action problems," situations where we would all be better off working together but where there are obstacles (such as self-interest, lack of trust, and predictability) that might prevent us from doing so. Think about some of the alternatives to a legally ordered society: anarchy, where everyone does as they please and consequently no one is secure, or, relatedly, a "rule" that depends entirely on who has physical power and is willing to use violence to achieve their ends. The collective good of an ordered society can be undermined by non-compliance by both individual acts and widespread disobedience. When non-compliance occurs on a small scale (consisting of only individuals or small groups), concerns about "free riders" are raised. If taxes are to be used to pay for roads, for example, your best position is to *not* pay the tax and still enjoy the use of the roads. Needless to say, this is going to anger the many who *do* pay the tax and, unless the non-compliance is addressed, they will be enticed to evade taxation too. The solution to this problem is a system of enforcement (police, inspectors, auditors, etc.), but more widespread disobedience is better addressed pre-emptively by ensuring that laws are fashioned legitimately. By this, we mean that those who make the laws are viewed by people as having the authority to make those rules.

In the liberal democratic states we are most familiar with, the legitimacy of state authority hinges on the notion of self-government. We expect law to reflect the idea that laws operate with the consent of the governed. The consent of the governed is routinely invoked in legal thinking and modern political theory, often portrayed as a "social contract," but an empirical social scientist might consider it as a bit of "folk wisdom" or a "fairy tale." The "social contract" concept cannot be taken literally; do you remember signing a contract agreeing to obey the laws of Canada? Moreover, the idea of a social contract between citizens is strikingly individualistic and assumes that one's identity is solely an individual matter, not as part of a group, and is thus somewhat out-of-step with modern notions of group identity and intersectionality. That said, the metaphor of the social contract is a deeply ingrained conception that reflects the idea that, at some basic level, we agree to the laws that govern us. To settle disagreements, even provisionally and tentatively, we need institutions that represent, deliberate, and ultimately enact the authoritative rules. In Canada, we generally expect Parliament to play this role. Other liberal democracies have similar legislative bodies.

## POSITIVIST APPROACHES TO LAW

The enactments of Parliament are part of what is called "positive law." Positivism – in this narrow, legal sense – accepts only what is "factually" law, namely, that which has been the product of a socially agreed-upon process and can thus be demonstrably identified as law. A very simplified positivist account of law thus provides a definition of law: It is the body of rules enacted and applied by public officials through procedurally recognized means and ultimately backed by state force. ("Positivism" can also refer to a different but related concept in the social sciences, where only empirically verified phenomena are accepted and metaphysical explanations are to be rejected; the legal variant is typically more limited to the definition above; Priel, 2012, p. 274). The basis for legal positivism can be traced back to philosophers such as Jeremy Bentham (1748–1832) and John Austin (1790–1859), but its most well-known modern articulation is associated with the work of legal theorist H.L.A. Hart (1907–92).

In his influential book, *The Concept of Law* (1961), Hart described the "rule of recognition." The basic idea behind this "meta-rule" is that societies need a way of determining what is law and what is not. The easiest case – what all Canadians would surely recognize as a "law" – are those enactments of Parliament that have properly proceeded through the legislative process. The heart of positivism is the separation of the identification of law from any evaluation of it. For the positivist, the question of what law is must not be influenced by questions about whether the law is wise, just, ethical, or moral – the "rightness" of the law is entirely beside the point. The status of "law" is strictly a matter of whether the enactment has been passed in accordance with an agreed-upon process (in Canada, passed by both the House of Commons, the Senate, and, finally, granted Royal Assent; see the section on "Statutes," below). The question of whether other declarations – judicial decisions, administrative actions, executive orders – count as "law" are matters that positivists can disagree upon. The identification question for positivists is a strictly a *factual* question: If there is a process that confirms societal acceptance of a rule, then anything that undergoes that process may be identified as "law."

The difficulty with positivism is two-fold: Sometimes it goes too far and sometimes it doesn't go far enough. The focus on positive law tends to lead towards thinking of law in terms of prohibitions (such as criminal law: thou shall not murder, etc.) and downplays the notion that law can be enabling (giving you the power to write a will, adopt a child, or form a company). From this perspective, some simplistic positivist accounts might appear cramped and describe only some aspects of how law truly operates. On the other hand, the positivist might be too accepting of what counts as law, permitting the dignified label of "law" to be applied in a way that might make us uncomfortable. It connects law squarely to political power and political will and attempts to separate it from broader notions of justice and morality. Consider the existence of what are sometimes referred to as "wicked legal systems": Did the Nazi's have rules we are comfortable labelling as "law"? Should the racially discriminatory apartheid laws of South Africa be properly considered law? The positivist is committed to answering both questions in the affirmative, but others view this disconnection between law and justice deeply problematic (Dyzenhaus, 2010). For non-positivists, law should mean something more than the simple fact of obedience to the current dictates of the state. By reducing law to a "bare minimum" of state enactments and by accepting even "wicked" laws, positivism arguably fails to capture what we value most in the concept of law.

## NATURAL LAW APPROACHES

Another view of law – one much older than "positivism" – connects law very intimately with justice. In the view of "natural law" theorists, laws enacted through the political process must conform to a higher law. If it does not reflect the current democratic will, where does this higher law come from? Contemporary Canadians would likely point to the constitution as just such a "higher law," but natural law predates our notion of constitutionalism. The earliest forms of natural law are rooted in divine law and thus one answer to the question of where the "higher law" standard comes from is easy: God. The relationship of religion to law is a very complicated one, but they are undeniably entwined historically (indeed, the dictates of many ancient religions are called "laws"). Obviously, a faith-based account of law would not have much currency in modern, secular Canada. However, the connection between natural law and its religious origins should not blind us to natural law's lasting impact on law and politics. This is because, in at least three important ways, natural law continues to inform contemporary Canadian law: it emphasizes "reason" in law; it is the root of procedural fairness in law; and it provides a rationale for justly resisting positive law.

Whereas positivism relied heavily on political will, natural law stresses reason as the foundation of law. Here the works of thirteenth-century Catholic theologian Thomas Aquinas are instructive. Although Aquinas readily accepted the notion of divine law, he understood humans as having reason and free will. These gifts from God required that they be used to determine the laws that would be best for our nature. Thomistic philosophy thus puts reason – and not religious revelation – at the centre of what we should consider law. This introduces a strain of thinking that opposes the positivist account: What if a law is properly passed but obviously unreasonable? A legal principle barring "impossibility" is a good example: If the Canadian Parliament passed two statutes, the first saying that you must sing the anthem every Wednesday morning, and a second saying you may never sing the anthem, both cannot be considered law, even if they had been passed according to the correct procedures. (A legal rule, reflecting reason, would actually determine the outcome here: The *latest* law passed would rule and the earlier contradictory one would be considered repealed.)

Natural law's commitment to reason extends itself into a notion of fundamental "fairness," sometimes referred to as "natural justice." A reasonable law is one that, regardless of its content, is administered fairly. This is the primary and most direct way we can see natural law continue in modern Canadian law. For example, natural justice insists upon giving citizens the opportunity to speak to state officials who make decisions that seriously affect their interests. In addition to being elements of Canadian administrative law (see Chapter 5), these procedural rights are now reflected in section 7 of the *Canadian Charter of Rights and Freedoms* (see Chapter 3), but their influence can be seen throughout Canadian law.

The existence of natural law – even when contested and uncertain – can also serve as an inspiration for civil disobedience. Faced with truly unjust laws backed by state power, Martin Luther King Jr. and Mahatma Gandhi based their resistance on the call of a "higher law" (in both cases, relying on religious doctrines and ideas). To the extent that these natural law principles are shared by the citizens, they can be a powerful resource for political change. Here the space between positivism and natural law shrinks, since, in a democratic society, obviously unjust laws are likely to be unpopular. There is certainly no guarantee citizens will not favour unjust laws in all cases – if security is at risk, unjust measures can be very popular, for example – but this is the gamble democratic societies rely upon. In the final analysis, the calculation may simply reflect Joseph de Maistre's adage that "every nation gets the government it deserves." In other words, if we don't care about the civil liberties of our fellow citizens, we can hardly expect good government, and we will surely watch our own liberties erode.

## RECONCILING POSITIVISM AND NATURAL LAW

The popularity of just measures is not the only possible reconciliation between positivism and natural justice. Legal scholars, particularly those that see the logic of positivism but think that it does not capture the full content of law, have attempted to bridge the gap with a number of theoretical innovations. One of the most influential accounts comes from Lon Fuller's classic book *The Morality of Law* (1965), which presents Fuller's side of one of the most well-known exchanges in legal theory between him and positivist H.L.A. Hart (known as the "Hart-Fuller Debate").

Fuller expressed a view at odds with both Hart's strict positivism and any full-blown morality that conflated law with substantive justice. Fuller's middle ground was to identify the "morality that makes law possible." By this he means that a number of underlying moral judgments have to be made and adhered to in order for law to make sense *as law*. Through the extended allegory of King Rex (a frustrated ruler who tries and fails to make law, using the sole powers granted to him by legal positivism), Fuller demonstrates that our intuition of "what law is" includes more than simply an enactment passed in a procedurally proper way. Fuller argues that, *at a bare minimum*, law must have a background morality that allows for it to operate in the way we expect. Any legal system worthy of the name, Fuller argues, must observe eight "directions," which we have condensed to six: (1) there must be general rules, not simply ad hoc decisions made up on-the-spot; (2) the rules must be understandable and be publicized, so that people know what they are expected to do; (3) the rules must be prospective, not retrospective (i.e., they cannot be made after the alleged violation has occurred); (4) rules must not be impossible to obey, either because there are directly contradictory rules or because they require something beyond what a person is capable of performing; (5) the rules cannot change too frequently (a new set of rules enacted every day at 9:00 a.m., for example, should not be considered law); and (6) there must be some congruence between the rules and their actual enforcement.

Fuller's "morality" is attractive, since it meets most of what we hope from law while also giving considerable freedom for different sets of laws to differ in terms of substantive outcomes. The United States and Canada's legal systems differ in all sorts of substantive ways, but they would both meet Fuller's standard, with only a few potential quibbles. "Wicked" legal systems may be less likely to meet the standard, since some of the most well-known vices of such systems (the use of secret laws and the differential and often arbitrary enforcement of the rules) would disqualify them as "law" in this view. Fuller's position may go too far, though, as it might surprise Canadians to learn that some "retroactive" laws are permissible (see the *Imperial Tobacco* case described below). Even though it does not adhere precisely to Fuller's specifications, it would be rather silly to deny that Canada has a legal system. Moreover, Fuller's directions say little about the application of law to King Rex himself – is he bound by the law as much as his citizens? Indeed, Canadians and others generally speak of having a "rule of law," which might fall short of Fuller's morality in some respect but may go even further in other dimensions.

## THE RULE OF LAW

By suggesting that law must, to some degree, be general, knowable, and certain, Fuller points us towards one of the most central concepts in law for Canada and other Western, liberal democracies: the rule of law. Nineteenth-century English legal theorist A.V. Dicey (1885/1982) is credited with perhaps the most well-known articulation of the concept:

> No man is above the law [and] every man, whatever be his rank or condition, is subject to the ordinary law of the realm and amenable to the jurisdiction of the ordinary tribunals. (p. 114)

There cannot be, in Dicey's formulation, one set of laws for the rich and another for the poor, or one for the noble born and another for the commoner, or one for those who support the government and another for those who oppose it. For this principle to function, political power must be expressed in the form of rules, instead of simply the commands of some people – whether they be kings, emperors, or tyrants. Thomas Paine (1776/1994) once celebrated that "in America, the law is king." (The recent decision of the Supreme Court of the United States in *Trump v United States* (2024), establishing sweeping immunity for the "official acts" of the president, might cast Paine's claim in doubt.)

As we shall see below, political power expressed through law has a special, superior authority ("the primacy of legal instruments") over the discretion and whims of political actors, but for now it is sufficient to note the conceptual importance of there being rules at all. One should not underestimate the importance of "rules" simply being articulated in a way accessible to citizens. "Laws provide tools with which rulers can order and control their societies," legal historian Fernanda Pirie (2021) notes, "but they also offer resources to which people can turn as they seek justice and resist the arbitrary exercise of power" (p. 18). It would at least be theoretically possible for people to hold their governments to account if the rules were recorded and made public; as Pirie suggests, "the determined dictator might tear up the rule book, but he could not do it unnoticed" (p. 20).

In order to perform this function, laws must be impersonal. One of the foremost English jurists of the eighteenth century, Sir William Blackstone, stressed that law "is a rule; not a transient sudden order from a superior to or concerning a particular person; but something *permanent, uniform and universal* [emphasis added]" (1893, p. 44). Legal theorist Brian Tamanaha (2004) traces this aspect of the rule of law back to Aristotle, who argued that "it is better for the law to rule than one of the citizens ... so even the guardians of the laws are obeying the laws" – a sentiment echoed by Dicey centuries later. It is a deep connection between law being "knowable" and "impersonal" and they are both necessary if we hope law will allow us to hold power to account.

While everyone attests to the importance of the rule of law, there is much disagreement about the content and scope of the principle beyond the more platitudinous account above. The ambiguity about what is truly meant by the rule of law led political theorist Judith Shklar (1986) to argue that the term had become meaningless: "just another one of those self-congratulatory rhetorical devices that grace the utterances of Anglo-American politicians" (p. 21). Judges, no less than politicians, have been generous with their overuse and ambiguous use of the phrase. The Supreme Court of Canada (SCC) refers to it as a "highly textured expression," and at the time of the *Patriation Reference* (1981), it conveyed "a sense of orderliness, of subjection to known legal rules and of executive accountability to legal authority" (pp. 805–6). Later in 1999, the Court said it "provides a shield for individuals from arbitrary state action" and "at its most basic level, the rule of law vouchsafes to the citizens and residents of the country a stable, predictable and ordered society in which to conduct their affairs" (*Secession Reference*, para. 70). So, does the Supreme Court endorse the "morality of law" that Fuller proposed? Not quite, since in the 2005 *British Columbia v Imperial Tobacco* case, the Court upheld a retroactive law that was not general in character (British Columbia legislated to be able to recover health care costs from tobacco companies that resulted from their knowing distribution of an unhealthy product over decades). The Court in that case cautioned that the rule of law is not "a tool by which to avoid legislative initiatives of which one is not in favour" (para. 67). It is "difficult to conceive of how the rule of law could be used as a basis for invalidating legislation ... based on its content" (para. 59). This is sometimes referred to as the "thin version" of the rule of law because its scope is limited more to the procedural implementation of laws, rather than a standard of judging the law itself.

In Canada, "rule of law" questions are often resolved under the rubric of "arbitrariness." The classic case of *Roncarelli v Duplessis* (1959) stands, at least in part, for the proposition that governments cannot exercise their power "arbitrarily," meaning the power wielded must be channelled through law. In that case, Frank Roncarelli, a tavern owner in Quebec, angered the provincial government, headed by Premier Maurice Duplessis, by providing bail to Jehovah's Witnesses who had fallen afoul of Quebec's increasingly restrictive laws on religious proselytizing. Roncarelli, a Jehovah's Witness himself, had not violated any law and simply (and legally) aided his co-religionists, but his actions attracted the wrath of the premier. Duplessis spoke to the chairman of the Quebec Liquor Commission and had Roncarelli's liquor licence revoked, effectively shutting down his business. Roncarelli fought the revocation all the way to the Supreme Court of Canada and won. (The damage was permanent, however, since the suspension of his licence during this period resulted in Roncarelli having to sell the tavern.)

The lessons drawn from *Roncarelli* are plentiful (and we will return to the case in Chapter 5, "Administrative Law"). Canadian scholars have rightly claimed that the case provides the following content for the rule of law: (1) no person or agency has "unlimited discretionary power" (no power is "untrammeled"); (2) decision-makers must not act in "bad faith"; (3) decision-makers cannot rely on irrelevant factors in making their decision, nor can they disregard the factors in the statute they are administering; and (4) a decision cannot be dictated by a person who is not authorized to make the decision (Liston, 2011, pp. 87–8). In general, *Roncarelli* is taken to stand against "arbitrary actions" by government. Note, however, that the actions of Duplessis's government were anything but "arbitrary" in the sense of being "random"; rather, they were fully intentional and ill-motivated actions prompted by Roncarelli's provision of bail to those the government disapproved of. The rule of law's limits on arbitrariness relate to the chairman's decision to revoke the liquor licence for reasons that were unrelated to the nature and purpose of the statute governing such licences; it would be one thing, for example, to revoke a licence for keeping unclean premises or serving alcohol to minors, but revoking it for legal activity outside the restaurant context is clearly beyond what is contemplated by the statute. This aspect of administrative decision-making will be discussed further in Chapter 5.

It is, of course, comforting to perceive law as an objective system of rules that prevents the abuse of power by unprincipled rulers. And while it is a narrative that fuels our aspirations for a truly just society, we should not complacently assume that law can do the work required of a vigilant, freedom-loving citizenry. "As a slogan, the phrase 'a government of laws and not of men' is appealing, but like most political slogans, it makes better sound than sense," economist Scott Gordon (2002) warns, since "the plain fact is that all government is, unavoidably, the exercise of coercive power by some people over others" (p. 6). Every law that attempts to limit power must be interpreted by someone and implemented by someone, which means *they* hold power even as it is limited for others. More players – and more "veto points" – can result in a system of checks and balances that offers the best environment for the rule of law to flourish in, but it will never be perfect and inevitably relies on good people exercising their power responsibly.

Even though the practice of the "rule of law" might not match our loftiest ambitions for it, we should still recognize it as the lodestar that always points us to better governance. It is perhaps best appreciated in the comparative perspective. Lord Bingham (2010) provides just such a helpful perspective:

> Belief in the rule of law does not import unqualified admiration of the law, or the legal profession…. It does, however, call on us to accept that we would very much like to live in a country that complies, or at least seeks to comply, with the principle…. The hallmarks of a regime which flouts the rule of law are, alas, all too familiar: the midnight knock on the door, the sudden disappearance, the show trial, the subjection of prisoners to genetic experiment, the confession extracted by torture, the gulag and the concentration camp, the gas chamber, the practice of genocide or ethnic cleansing, the waging of aggressive war. The list is endless. Better to put up with some choleric judges and greedy lawyers. (p. 9)

Lord Bingham is right that we should appreciate the rule of law, even if there are sometimes attendant costs to be borne and even if we cannot meet its highest ambitions. While an overly aggressive commitment to the rule of law might impede democratic choices, limit our sense of self-government, and aggrandize legal actors at the expense of elected representatives, the alternative where legal norms are presumptively dismissed is a far more troubling prospect.

## "AUTHORITIES" IN LAW

The "rules" in law are often referred to as "authorities." To better ensure that the "rule of law" trumps the "rule of persons," Canadians abide by the **primacy of legal instruments**. Legal instruments – constitutions, statutes, and regulations – carry authority that always has priority over other considerations (politics, convenience, customs, or traditions). Legal instruments themselves are prioritized in a clear hierarchy: Constitutions are "supreme," and while statutes must conform to the constitution, they themselves are superior to regulations and common law judgments of judges. The interplay of these forms of authorities is the basis of virtually all Canadian law. It is worthwhile to introduce them separately, as below, but the real operation of Canadian law consists in their relation to each other.

**Constitutions** are enactments which are considered the highest form of law. One can even say it is at the root of the state – it "constitutes" the state. The constitution can be a written enactment (as in the United States) or an unwritten set of understandings (as in the United Kingdom), or, as in Canada, a combination of written documents and unwritten **conventions**. (Constitutionalism and the Canadian Constitution are explored in greater detail in Chapter 3.) Anything that is considered part of the Canadian Constitution has the character of "supreme law" and, importantly, "any law that is inconsistent with the provisions of the Constitution is, to the extent of the inconsistency, of no force or effect" (s. 52 of the *Constitution Act, 1982*). In other words, if it violates what the constitution says, it is not really law.

This includes statutes, so that if these "ordinary" enactments of Parliament do not conform to the constitution they are denied any legal force or effect. This is what we mean when we say a law is "struck down" by the courts when it is adjudged to have violated the constitution. It is important to note, however, that this is a relatively rare outcome and, for the most part, statutes provide the legal "rules" settling most legal controversies. **Statutes** are simply the laws passed by Parliament and, for this reason, are sometimes referred to as "Acts of Parliament" or simply "Acts" of some sort (*An Act for the Establishment of a National DNA Database*, for example). The most recent statute on any given matter is considered authoritative, and statutes may *repeal* earlier statutes (essentially deleting them from the legal order) or *amend* them (revise or change them). As a result of Canadian federalism, we have statutes at two levels of government: federal statutes that apply nationwide and statutes in each of the provinces that are legally binding only within that province.

Statutes are often drafted in general terms and leave "operational" details to be elaborated in **regulations**. "Regulation" has a general meaning that could include virtually all government actions, but in law it has a more specific meaning. Here, it refers to an order made pursuant to a statute by a competent officer or agency. These regulations are more specific and detailed than the statutory provisions and may allow for some flexibility since they can be changed more quickly (through a new order) rather than the more cumbersome process of passing a new statute. These regulations have the force of law – meaning they are just as legally binding on citizens as the statute itself – because the statute "empowers" the regulations explicitly. Regulations are "delegated" authority; the statute is where legal power is expressly located and legitimated, but a common feature of statutes is that they include a section, typically towards the end, that permits additional decisions to be made by an executive actor (for example, the Governor General of Canada or the Lieutenant Governor of a province, acting under the advice of the government through what is known as an "Order in Council"). Since it is delegated authority, nothing in the regulation can contradict the statute.

Ontario's *Smoke-Free Ontario Act, 2017* provides a good example of how statutes work and how regulations complement them. Despite its name, this act does not abolish smoking everywhere in Ontario – in fact, it allows for the sale, advertising, and consumption of tobacco products under the certain circumstances described in the statute. Section 12(1) of the act says that no person may smoke tobacco, cannabis, or an electronic cigarette in a prohibited place ("subject to any exceptions that may be provided for in the regulations"). Section 12(2) lists those prohibited places and includes "an enclosed public place." Does this include a shopping mall? A taxi cab? Section 1 of the act ("Definitions") makes these questions easy: "Enclosed public place" means "any place, building, or structure or vehicle" that "is covered by a roof" and "to which the public is ordinarily invited or permitted access." So, both the shopping mall and the cab would be places where smoking was prohibited. The act also prohibits smoking in "a prescribed place or area," which is left undefined by the statute. Section 24 (1)(b) of the act permits the Lieutenant Governor in Council to make regulations "prescribing and governing … anything that is referred to in this Act as being prescribed." This allows the Ontario Government to make regulations that fill out the details of the statute. What about restaurant patios? They don't have roofs, so perhaps smoking is allowed there. Ontario regulation 268/18 forbids that by telling us that one of those "prescribed areas" are "restaurant and bar patios, and public areas within a nine metre radius." If the government decided that a twelve-metre radius would serve the public interest better, they need not amend the statute but instead simply pass a new regulation.

Finally, **judicial decisions** are another important source of law. If you were fined under the *Smoke-Free Ontario Act* – up to $1,000 for a first offence, $5,000 for further offences – you can challenge your fine in court. In some cases, smokers have done just that: An owner of a cleaning service had his fine overturned because it was issued for smoking in his SUV, which was registered in the name of the cleaning company and thus considered by the enforcement officer to be a workplace vehicle where smoking was prohibited under the act (Sims, 2017). The Justice of the Peace in that case accepted that the vehicle was not a workplace vehicle – despite the registration – because, among other things, it did not have the company's logo (as it did on other vehicles), there was no evidence the vehicle was used for any cleaning or administrative function, and the owner portrayed himself not as an employee but rather a shareholder of the company (Sims, 2017). In this case, the Justice of the Peace was *interpreting* the law on what is a "workplace vehicle," since the statute and regulations did not give definitive guidance. It should be emphasized that these decisions are interpretive, which means that (at least in theory) the legislature could change the law by defining "workplace vehicle" to include "any vehicle that is registered to a corporate entity," but they have chosen not to do so. In this respect, the interpretive decisions of the judiciary can themselves be considered a source of law. This is particularly important when the courts are interpreting the constitution, since those decisions are less susceptible to being altered by political actors unless the constitution itself is amended.

The discussion here has focused exclusively on formal sources of law. If we construe "sources" more generally, it is readily apparent that laws can emerge from practices and traditions. Indeed, many early laws simply codified behaviour and expectations that were already well established. Moreover, texts and scholarship like Blackstone's *Commentaries on the Laws of England* (1893) have been treated by judges as an authoritative account of what the common law requires. Today, Indigenous law provides another potential source of law, with Indigenous rules and practices being adopted into Canadian law, or in agreements between Indigenous Peoples and the Canadian state, or between Indigenous Peoples themselves. There is room with Canada's legal pluralism for a variety of informal, customary, and Indigenous laws, each contributing to the rich complexity of Canada's legal landscape. A full account of that complexity is beyond the scope of this introductory text, but students should be aware that the account here is simplified and some subtleties regarding potential sources of law are underexplored (for more information about legal pluralism as a theoretical approach, see Merry, 1988).

## SYSTEMS OF LAW

There are as many different legal systems in the world as there are countries, but there is a central division that essentially divides the world in two: civil law systems and common law systems. These two forms cover virtually all of Europe, the Americas, Australia, and parts of Africa. Another important system is *Fiqh*, Islamic jurisprudence, which is the human understanding of *Sharia* (Islamic divine law); this legal system, found primarily in the Middle East and Africa, differs radically from the other two and deserves an extensive separate treatment that we cannot provide here (see Emon & Ahmed, 2018, for a general introduction). Finally, Canadians should be aware of the

Indigenous legal systems that operate in self-governing Indigenous lands (see Borrows, 2010, 2016, for a general introduction).

Most students reading this text are likely to be more familiar with the common law system, and Chapter 2, "Legal Reasoning & Statutory Interpretation," will further develop an understanding of what we mean by "common law." Canada is, however, at least a **bi-jural nation**, meaning that it contains at least two general legal systems: A general common law system that applies nationwide but with a "carve-out" exception for Quebec, where the civil code system applies for some provincial matters. This means that most issues of law are determined by common law rules, but an important exception is private law matters that fall under provincial jurisdiction in the province of Quebec. Rules about contract, negligence, and wills and estates all are determined by an entirely different system of law in Quebec than they are in the other nine provinces and the territories. While its bi-jural nature adds to Canada's legal complexity, it is not uncommon for nations to combine legal systems; Scotland is a civil law jurisdiction in the common law United Kingdom, and South Africa, Zimbabwe, Sri Lanka, Guyana, Puerto Rico, the Philippines, and Louisiana all incorporate more than one legal system within their geographic jurisdiction. Moreover, the reality of Indigenous self-governing communities further complicates even the bi-jural understanding of Canadian law; overall, Canada is best described as embracing a form of "legal pluralism" that accommodates several overlapping systems of law.

That said, in Canada, the distinction between public law and private law is crucial because it tells us whether the common law or civil code system will be used when a legal matter occurs in Quebec. **Public law** refers to legal controversies in which the state is one of the parties to the case. Public law includes criminal law, constitutional law, tax law, and administrative law. **Private law,** on the other hand, refers to legal controversies that are citizen-versus-citizen or between citizens (and, by contrast, where the state is not a party to the case). This includes tort law, contract law, estate law, and family law. Confusingly, in provinces other than Quebec we often refer to private law as "civil law" – meaning law between citizens – but not according to a civil code. In this text, we try to use "private law" for this meaning, but students should be aware that it is quite common for commentators to use the terms "private law" and "civil law" synonymously. (You may hear terms like "civil litigation," "civil justice," and, of course, "civil rights," all of which usually refer to matters between citizens, not that they are resolved in the civil code system.) In truth, the usefulness of the distinction between public and private law can be questioned. Family law, for example, is usually considered an area of private law; however, the state is deeply implicated in family law through the provision of detailed statutory frameworks and the enforcement of resolutions. We argue throughout this text that private law always has important public dimensions, but the distinction remains relevant, not just because it sends a signal about the role of the state in such cases, but also because, in bi-jural nations like Canada, the distinction can have the important *operational* aspect of deciding which system of law governs.

Say a dispute arises about a mistake of fact in a contract dispute – you thought you were buying an iPhone but the seller was actually offering a Kindle. In Quebec, this would be resolved in the civil code system. In theory at least, this would mean turning to the Quebec's civil code – literally a codification that includes the rules of contract – and finding the rule that governed such mistakes. In the other nine provinces, to understand whether this mistake of fact meant the contract could not be enforced, you would look to cases that had been decided by judges in the past (precedents) and try to understand a common rule that arose from them. (This somewhat mysterious practice will be discussed at length in the next chapter). It is sometimes useful to think of civil code jurisdictions as "top-down" (or deductive) ways of thinking about law, and common law jurisdictions as "ground-up" (or inductive). This "philosophical" difference is somewhat overstated, especially given the important role statutes play in the common law universe and the reality that civil law judges have a healthy respect for precedent too (some claim that the two systems are "converging" for these reasons), but it remains a useful, if overly simplified, way of distinguishing the two systems.

Civil law systems are also distinguished by a different approach to judging and different procedures. With respect to judges, civil code judges are traditionally more "inquisitorial," meaning they are more likely to take the initiative and ask questions of witnesses, as opposed to common law judges, who are generally content to watch the adversarial lawyering that plays out before them. Anyone who has observed a common law judge knows this generalization is overstated too; they are hardly passive, silent observers.

So, much can depend upon whether the dispute is the domain of private or public law and whether the law is one of provincial or federal jurisdiction. If the law is within federal jurisdiction, then it is always within the common law system – this is the simplest formulation. If the law is public, then it is always common law too. If the law is private, things get tricky: If it is within provincial jurisdiction, you need to consider *where* the legal controversy comes from. If it comes from Quebec, it will be decided under the civil code system. In every other province, it would be decided under the common law. In Figure 1.1, only matters in Quadrant 4 are complicated; the other three quadrants are common law matters. The matters listed in Quadrant 4 are civil code matters in Quebec, but they are common law matters in all the other provinces.

With the exception of those private law matters in the province of Quebec, legal issues in Canada are resolved within the common law frame. For this reason, this text focuses on common law legal reasoning in the next chapter, but we will continue to explore some of the differences when they arise.

<table>
<tr><td>

<u>Quadrant 1: Federal Public Law</u>

- Criminal law
- Constitutional law
- Tax law
- Administrative law

</td><td>

<u>Quadrant 2: Federal Private Law</u>

- Copyright law/intellectual property
- Labour law (federal employers)
- Family law (marriage and divorce)

</td></tr>
<tr><td>

<u>Quadrant 3: Provincial Public Law</u>

- Provincial tax law
- Provincial administrative law
- Provincial offences (*Highway Traffic Act*, etc.)

</td><td>

<u>Quadrant 4: Provincial Private Law</u>

- Family law (unmarried relationships)
- Labour law
- Contract law
- Torts (including negligence)
- Estate law

</td></tr>
</table>

**Figure 1.1. Public and Private Law in Canada**

## CONCLUSION

As discussed in the Introduction, law is intimately connected to notions of authority and legitimacy. This chapter has provided more concrete answers as to what law is and where it comes from, even though we might also recognize Hart's conclusion that any short definition is likely to miss important elements. The "positivist" approach does point to some relatively uncontroversial sources of law – few Canadians would doubt that an enactment of the Parliament of Canada is a "law" – but positivist approaches can be critiqued for both accepting too much as law (in the case of "wicked" laws) and perhaps not being inclusive enough by excluding loftier, more aspirational elements of law. While the most robust versions of natural law would likely be inappropriate for pluralistic Canada, some limited aspects of the constitutional rights to fair treatment clearly draw on this tradition, and middle-ground approaches like Fuller's morality of law are attractive to many Canadians. Indeed, some of Fuller's requirements of law track what we mean when claim that the "rule of law" governs Canada. Certainly, the idea that the law must be public and not arbitrary are well accepted in Canadian legal and political discourse, while "thicker" accounts of what the rule of law requires are often contested.

In considering "what is law," we turned – on a more practical level – to systems of law. Canada is a "bi-jural" nation in that it uses both the common law and civil law system. It is important to keep the civil law system in mind, since it governs some legal controversies in Quebec (relying on another key distinction – that between public and private law) and is used by more countries in the world than the common law system.

Given our English Canadian readership, this textbook concentrates on the common law system, but we should always remember that it is not the only system of law possible. The next chapter focuses squarely on common law legal reasoning itself, and the important elements regarding the sources of authority discussed in this chapter should be kept in mind. The "judge-made" rules of the common law may be subordinate to constitutional and statutory enactments, but the common law legal mind integrates these sources into what is argued to be a unique and special form of reasoning.

## REVIEW QUESTIONS

1  In what way can law help address collective action problems?
2  To what extent is the Canadian legal system rooted in the "consent of the governed"?
3  What are the strengths and weaknesses of the positivist and natural law conceptions of law?
4  How can the law be considered as having its own moral content?
5  What is the rule of law and why is it important?
6  Rank the following in terms of legal authority: constitutions, statutes, and regulations. Where do judgments of common law courts fit in?
7  In what circumstances can you find yourself governed by civil law in Canada?

# CHAPTER TWO

# Legal Reasoning and Statutory Interpretation

## LEARNING OBJECTIVES

- Understand what is meant by legal reasoning and evaluate to what extent it differs from ordinary reasoning.
- Learn the importance of precedents to common law reasoning.
- Appreciate the importance of being sensitive to procedural concerns as a part of legal reasoning.
- Become acquainted with the elements and importance of statutory interpretation.

Law is a discipline. Like political science, sociology and criminology, it has both a body of knowledge to be mastered and, perhaps more importantly, a methodology of generating such knowledge. While the scientific method is often the source of social science methodologies, legal methodology hinges primarily upon "legal reasoning." This chapter will introduce the underlying assumptions and describe the core tenets of legal reasoning, particularly the crucial common law notion of *stare decisis*, as well as the importance of precise language (especially as it relates to legislative drafting). Why is this level of detail necessary? As discussed in the Introduction, this book adopts a neo-institutional approach to law and politics that recognizes legal norms as influential – or at least treated seriously by all of the key institutional actors involved – while also acknowledging the limits of those legal norms. Sceptical social scientists are right to assume that legal reasoning is not *determinative* of the outcome – other factors, including the preferences of the legal actors, likely come into play – but it is also dangerous to assume that the primary methodology in law plays *no* role in shaping outcomes. A better approach is to understand the features of legal reasoning, even if one remains sceptical of its normative force.

## A DISTINCT FORM OF REASONING?

Distinguishing legal reasoning from "ordinary" reasoning might sound a little abstract or precious, but the notion is central to the legitimacy of law. Consider this dramatic encounter in the early days of the English common law where the question of expertise in legal matters was put to the test: In 1607, Chief Justice Edward Coke found himself in the precarious position of rebutting King James's assertion that, since judges are simply delegates of the King, the King himself must be personally competent to rule on any legal matter. Since "the law was founded upon reason," King James is reported to have remarked, "he and others had reason as well as the judges" (*Prohibitions del Roy*, 1607). James was basically claiming that there's nothing special about the way lawyers and judges think and, as King, his personal reason should be preferred over that of his judges or, indeed, any of his subjects. This put Chief Justice Coke in a very difficult position: Defending a distinct form of legal reasoning – and privileging judicial outcomes – meant openly defying the King at a time when one could literally lose one's head for such disobedience. Aware of the potential dangers, Coke first buttered up King James by noting that "God had endowed his Majesty with excellent science and great endowments of nature," but then explained that the King was still not capable of *legal* reasoning. According to Coke, the King was "not learned in the laws of his realm," which we subject not to "natural reason" but to a specialized "*artificial reason and judgment of law*" that "requires long study and experience before that a man can attain cognizance of it." It was, essentially, a declaration that the King did not have the learned skill necessary to resolve legal controversies. Coke didn't lose his head and won the argument that day. Coke's successful defence of distinctive legal reasoning continues to resonate with today's lawyers and judges.

The claim of an "artificial reason" – a special kind of reason learned by lawyers – remains controversial. While "the forms of logic and reasoning in law are entirely familiar" to us, legal scholar Cass Sunstein (1997) notes, "much of what lawyers know is a set of practices, conventions, and outcomes that is hard to reduce to rules, that sometimes operate without being so reduced, and that is often taken for granted" (p. 13). This is what law professor Stephen Waddams (1992) means when he says, "the study of law is not the learning of rules" (p. 3). If Waddams were wrong, and legal education was simply the learning of substantive rules, the value of that education would be quite limited since substantive laws frequently change and are highly dependent on what jurisdiction you are currently in. The way in which lawyers understand the logic of the law and its application is what is truly taught by our law schools. In the words of the imposing law school professor Kingsfield in *The Paper Chase*, "you come in here with a skull full of mush … and you leave thinking like a lawyer." It is this learned understanding of law – a *fluency* in law – that defines artificial reasoning. It is one of the tasks of this text to provide students with an introduction to this mode of reasoning so that they may have some fluency, or at least an understanding of how it might impact their social science research.

Legal scholar Martin Loughlin (2000) draws attention to the legal "world-view." World-views are sensitive to "particular frames of reference," that help us to better understand the world, even if they appear wrong or inadequate from a different perspective (p. 19). Loughlin argues that world-views can be evaluated on three criteria: credibility, coherence, and utility. On all three, the "law" scores very highly: For the most part, law creates a fully realized, internally consistent version of reality that is extremely useful for a society that wants to govern itself and manage relations among citizens. This is true even when "legal fictions" are involved.

Legal reasoning incorporates and accepts "legal fictions," things that are true only or primarily in law. A good example is the notion of **legal identity** (sometimes called "legal personality"), according to which something can be considered a "person" in legal terms, even if it might not be true in other frames. You are both a corporeal entity – you have a body and a physical existence – and also an identity in law; with respect to the latter, you can make contracts, you may be a citizen of Canada, and you hold constitutional rights (these are just some of the ways in which your legal personality exists). In your case, as an individual, your physical existence and your legal identity are consistent and obviously aligned. But it does not need to be so. Corporations, for example, have a legal identity, but their physical existence is more tenuous. The creation of a corporation is an act of law (you have to legally "incorporate" a business) and, once it exists, it may enter into contracts, pay fines for its bad behaviour, and even exercise some constitutional rights (like the freedom of expression). Corporations have some physical manifestations: They have shareholders, offices, and sometimes retail locations. But none of those physical elements define it: If you magically removed all the Apple Stores, and all of its products disappeared, there would still be an Apple Corporation. Similarly, Apple's CEO Tim Cook and all its shareholders are not synonymous with the corporation itself (otherwise Apple would not have been able to continue existing after Steve Jobs passed away). The existence of a corporation is *entirely* legal – it is created by law, operates by law, and can only be dissolved by law. It exists in a legal frame, even if it might be inaccurate to say it "exists" in other frames. (Some of that tension is exposed when a corporation's criminal behaviour needs to be addressed, since one of the primary forms of criminal punishment, imprisonment, is impossible to apply). In Chapter 10's discussion of environmental protection, we will consider new claims of legal personality – do rivers and animals have legal identities? The question of whether such legal identities should be recognized, as they are routinely granted to corporations, is currently the subject of several novel legal cases and controversies.

The idea that law has its own frame is a crucial insight that helps shield the autonomy of law from the legal realist claim that it is nothing more than an expression of some other form of power or ideology. German legal theorist Carl Schmitt, no friend of parliamentary government or common law reasoning, critiqued the reliance on legal forms and suggested that, in an actual emergency, cherished legal protections would quickly evaporate. With respect to legal certainty, he suggests that any such certainty is the product of a shared assessment by judges of what the law requires: "A judicial decision is correct today when it can be assumed that another judge would have decided in the same way," (Scheuerman, 2020, p. 26; see also Loughlin, 2000, p. 92). Without some impersonal quality of law, we cannot have the rule of law and we cannot speak of the "judiciary" as a coherent political institution. For Loughlin (2000), this "consistency" is "achieved not because of a scientific application of the letter of the law but because of a cultural absorption of the spirit of the law" (p. 92). Matters have therefore already become quite messy: We are told not to expect "scientific law" but rather a "spirit" that has been culturally absorbed. Yet, this is the terrain upon which legal reasoning must be grounded.

One of the key purposes of legal reasoning, as Cass Sunstein explains, is to achieve some level of agreement in a pluralistic society, where citizens may disagree on just about everything. To bridge disagreement, legal reasoning employs *deductive* and *inductive* reasoning to move from one level of abstraction to another. This expands the scope of potential agreement: Maybe we disagree on broad principles, but we might agree on a specific, factual case; more likely, we may disagree on an individual case but agree on broad principles. In either of those cases, a chain of legal reasoning may allow citizens to find common ground and resolve controversies peacefully and rationally. Citizens might disagree, for example, on whether a witness at trial should be able to wear a niqab while testifying, but we might move inductively from that discrete controversy to more general principles that can be reconciled agreeably. Trial norms around concepts of witness credibility and the expectation that the accused should be able to "face their accuser" may be tailored to not excessively infringe the agreed-upon constitutional principle of freedom of religion. These chains of logic may not convince or create agreement in all cases. Some might choose to privilege religious freedom over criminal law protections, while others might come to the opposite conclusion. Nevertheless, the belief that both sets of principles are important and deserving of protection may create the basis for generating a reasoned consensus. For the most part, Canadian passions and prejudices have been cooled by the application of legal reasoning in just such a manner.

Finally, we should recall that legal reasoning will base itself upon the sources of authority discussed in Chapter 1. This alone can make legal reasoning distinct from other forms of reasoning. Legal scholar Frederick Schauer (2009) notes that in non-legal decision-making, "authority may play some role, but first-order substantive considerations typically dominate" (p. 67), which means that the best decision in the circumstance should prevail. In law, Schauer writes, "authority is dominant, and only rarely do judges engage in the kind of all-things-considered decision-making that is so pervasive outside the legal system.... Legal argument relies on sources [that remain] the touchstone of legal reasoning" (p. 67). Other political actors might base their decision-making on what the best public policy is or what is in the "public interest." Judges and lawyers, by contrast, are usually less concerned with what would be ideal or optimal policy and more concerned with what is *legal*. Frequently in judicial decisions you will see the claim that judges are not evaluating the "wisdom" of the policy being challenged but only its legality or constitutionality. Since they are human beings, judges may find it hard to meet this lofty standard and judges may be tempted to find a "legal" defect when the policy under consideration seems poorly conceived. When this approach is genuinely concerned with legality, however, we get close to Loughlin's spirit-that-is-culturally-absorbed.

## STARE DECISIS

While legal reasoning does have a *deductive* element (applying a higher-level rule to a discrete case), the common law approach emphasizes the *inductive* element: "It is the merit of the common law," Oliver Wendell Holmes noted, "that it decides the cases first and determines the principle afterwards" (Novick, 1995, p. 212). In its most elementary and perhaps overly romantic vision, the common law sees judges making discrete decisions in individual, concrete cases and, over time, a "common" approach should emerge. This "commonality" is encouraged by a respect for *precedent*. Thus, at the root of the common law system is a deceptively simple principle: *stare decisis et non quieta movere*, which is Latin for "to stand by decisions and not disturb the undisturbed." In practical terms, this means that a judge trying to resolve the case before her (the *instant case*) should consider whether her case is similar to a case that has been decided before; if she can find such a *precedent*, she should resolve the case in a similar way, regardless of how she feels about the precedent. The core instruction we give to common law judges sounds straight out of Sesame Street: "Treat like cases alike."

Despite its simple formulation, "treating like cases alike" can be tricky to apply. As Schauer and Spellman (2017) note, while analogical reasoning is "at the heart ... of the very idea of distinctively *legal* reasoning," it also "rest[s] on shaky foundations, often serving to mask the lawmaking dimensions of legal argument and legal decision-making" (p. 249). Schauer (2018) points out that for *stare decisis* to operate effectively, you need to have "some substantive criterion of likeness" (pp. 437–8). No two cases will be exactly the same. Each will have a factual context, a matrix of facts if you will. Some of those will be similar, while others will differ. The difficulty is in determining which elements of that matrix need to be similar in order for a precedent to be applicable. As Schauer (2018) notes, "given that any two items in the world share some but not all of the properties of the respective items, any two items can be deemed alike in some respects and unlike in others, thus making the mere idea of likeness or unlikeness singularly unhelpful" (p. 438). It might not matter, for example, that the instant case involved an illegal act that happened on a Tuesday, while in the precedent case it happened on a Thursday. In fact, we might expect the factual circumstances of the two cases to be quite different. It might, on the other hand, be very important that the crime was planned in a premeditated way, or that in both cases the accused was suffering from a mental illness that impaired their ability to understand what they were doing. Judges look for *legally relevant* similarities and differences. To discern them requires an appreciation of the reasoning in the precedent case and how that reasoning was applied to the facts before the court. This is also why *reading* cases is essential for those seeking to understand the law.

In the common law system, we speak of judicial decisions as having a "holding," which is the court's determination of the legal issue presented in the case. That holding is the result of the *ratio decidendi* (or *ratio*, as it sometimes shortened), which is Latin for "reason for the decision." These are the legally relevant factors the court has identified as justifying the outcome in the case. Everything else in the decision is *obiter dicta*, Latin for "things said along the way." *Obiter dicta* (or *obiter*, as it is sometimes shortened) is not legally binding and can sometimes be considered as judicial "editorializations" or "commentary." That said, we ignore *obiter* at our peril: Every word in a decision, especially those of the Supreme Court of Canada, can signal future decisions and important legal nuances even if they don't directly lead to the outcome in one particular instant case. For the most part, however, it is the *ratio* that is crucial for common law judges and lawyers to understand. Unfortunately, this is not as easy as it sounds, as judges do not typically use explicit labels to identify these elements of the decision.

Assuming the *ratio* and holding can be identified, the next task of the common law judge is to decide if the instant case is similar to the precedent in the legally relevant ways (see, e.g., Box 2.1). If so, the common law judge should *follow* the

---

**BOX 2.1. FOLLOWING PRECEDENT: *PIERSON V POST* AND THE NEWEST PHONE TECHNOLOGY**

The challenge of applying a precedent can be illustrated by this example of a real, well-known common law case from the early nineteenth century and a hypothetical instant case we can imagine today. The precedent is *Pierson v Post*, a milestone case in the development of property law. In December of 1802, fox hunter Lodowick Post was pursuing a particular fox along a remote piece of unowned beach property. Despite the fact that Post and his hounds were in "pursuit" of the fox, Jessie Pierson was able to kill the fox and take it before Post could reach it. The question for the New York court was to decide who owned the dead fox: Was it Post, who had put in efforts to obtain it, or Pierson, who ultimately possessed it? The court ruled that "mere pursuit" gave no property right to Post and to do otherwise would create more conflicts ("if the first seeing, starting, or pursuing such animals ... should afford the basis of actions against other for intercepting and killing them, it would prove a fertile course of quarrels and litigation"). It may have been "uncourteous or unkind" for Pierson to seize the fox in this manner, but his fatal blow and subsequent possession was enough to establish his property right against Post.

Imagine the following hypothetical: A tech company is on the verge of creating the first fully holographic cell phone display – it looks just like R2-D2's display of Princess Leia's message in the first *Star Wars* movie! It will be a revolution in phone technology, but it requires a very powerful computer chip that is made by one of its competitors and the tech company has contracted with them to provide the first ten million chips. The competitor hears rumours about the new display and promptly cancels the contract (paying agreed-upon damages) and then proceeds to rush development on its holographic phone. Does the original company have a "property right" to the holographic phone display?

A strict application of *Pierson v Post* would suggest they do not. The fact that they were in "mere pursuit" of the idea would not give rise to a right in property. Did the competitor's cancellation of the contract for the chips make a difference? It might simply have been as "unkind" as Pierson's conduct, but perhaps it could also be legally relevant? What about the difference between a fox, a tangible creature, and the *idea* of a phone display? Should *Pierson v Post* even be applied at all in such circumstances?

Those are the types of questions that are often raised when trying to apply precedents. They are often so tricky that they are ultimately resolved by statutes. In this case, the notion that an *idea* is a distinct form of property – requiring special rules and government procedures – has resulted in the development of *intellectual property* and the need for a patent system (where, essentially, ideas are registered with the government to preserve the legal right to its use; see Chapter 8). The rules for intellectual property are complex and vary according to jurisdiction, but one could easily imagine the original tech company applying for rights to their idea for a holographic phone, provided they had made enough progress in seeing it realized. In this way, we would be spared any difficult application of *Pierson v Post*.

precedent – this means the outcome of the instant case should follow the legal rule and outcome established in the precedent. If the cases are sufficiently dissimilar in legally relevant ways, the judge should *distinguish* it from the precedent – this means the outcome in the instant case can be different from the outcome in the precedent and the legal rule in the precedent is inapplicable. The instant case can be distinguished from multiple precedents, just as it might follow multiple others. A truly novel case – for which there is no sufficiently similar precedent – invites a judge to make new legal rules, but even then, they will be looking for the "best fit" with the universe of existing legal decisions.

There is reason to be sceptical that this ideal is achieved in practice. Schauer (2018) argues that justices of the US Supreme Court "have been, for generations, far better at announcing the importance of precedent than they have been in actually being constrained by it" (pp. 440–1). And the Supreme Court of Canada has been charged with being too willing to abandon their own precedents in cases like the 2013 *Bedford* ruling (invalidating the very same prostitution provisions the Court upheld in 1990) and the 2015 *Carter* decision (invalidating the assisted suicide provisions the Court upheld in 1993). More recently, in the 2022 case of *R v Kirkpatrick*, the Court sharply split 5 to 4 on whether an earlier precedent could be confined to its particular facts and with no general application, as the five-judge majority preferred, or whether *stare decisis* demanded respect for the precedent, as the four dissenting judges argued, even if the current majority would have decided the precedent differently. (Students interested in learning more about *stare decisis* should read the detailed discussion of the doctrine and its merits in paragraphs 171–269 of the dissenting opinion in *Kirkpatrick*.) While those high-profile cases cast doubt on *stare decisis*, it should be recognized that the vast majority of legal decisions in the common law system do follow well-established precedents.

And yet even the remote possibility of *not* following precedents puts the very idea of *stare decisis* in doubt, leaving us unsure whether it is faithfully adhered to in any given case as opposed to simply being a gloss on a pre-existing judicial preference. To put it bluntly, *stare decisis* is superfluous unless it has the following effect: A judge thinks the precedent was wrongly decided but follows it anyway. If the judge thinks the earlier decision is correct, then simply using her own judgment in the instant case would be sufficient and result in the same outcome. To be useful, *stare decisis* requires judges to respect even what they might think is a "wrong" decision.

This probably sounds odd to ears that have not been legally trained: Why follow something that is erroneous? Are judges required to perpetuate wrongly decided cases? The partial answer to this oddity is the high value law places on stability and certainty. As US Supreme Court Justice Louis Brandeis put it, "in most matters it is more important that the questions be settled than that it be decided right" (*Burnet v Coronado Oil*

*& Gas*, 1932, p. 406; Kozel, 2017). (The reference to "most matters" gives the needed wiggle-room to avoid being trapped forever by truly bad precedents).

Why is certainty so important and prized by the legal mind? It is essential to law's function as an "ordering mechanism" for citizens to plan their affairs and to know the legal consequences for any choice or action they make. There is no sense in signing a contract if its enforcement is uncertain and the other party can escape their obligations without penalty. Why make a will if it is uncertain how your property will be distributed upon death? It is unjust to hold someone criminally accountable for behaviour they had no way of knowing constituted an offence. Anytime we disrupt legal expectations, rational decisions people have made are undermined, and a law that cannot be relied upon is one that may become dangerously disregarded.

A second but important reason for adhering to *stare decisis* is the need for judicial impersonality. Even if we want justice-minded judges to prefer a correct decision over a settled one, it raises the question of whose assessment of correctness should be controlling in law. Recall that, as discussed in Chapter 1, the "rule of law" is not the "rule of men," and one of the ways we protect law from individual preferences is to insist that law have a continuity beyond any particular judge or case. The Supreme Court of Canada recognizes this when they suggest that *stare decisis* is "fundamental for guaranteeing certainty in the law.... Without this foundation, the law would be ever in flux – subjecting to shifting judicial whims or the introduction of new esoteric evidence by litigants dissatisfied by the status quo" (*R v Comeau*, 2018, para. 26). A healthy respect for judicial precedent can be a restraining force on judges, who might otherwise indulge in imposing their own values and preferences.

There is reason to be sceptical of this impersonal aspect of judicial decision-making. Generations of political scientists have done commendable work in demonstrating that precedent cannot be the sole factor controlling the outcome of a decision and that extra-legal factors, including judicial preference, are often more predictive (Hausegger & Riddell, 2020; Macfarlane, 2023). In some sense, this reflects the legal realist critique that "precedents march in pairs" (meaning that the adversarial process will almost always supply judges with opposing precedents to choose from) and we should be alive to the ample discretionary power of judges to resolve cases as they prefer. That said, the legal demand of impersonality is more than simply a story judges and lawyers tell themselves; in a very real way, the widespread acceptance that legal legitimacy hinges on *stare decisis* means that, at the very least, the exercise of judicial power must be justified in terms of prior decisions and in the context of legal choices made by other judges. This channelling of judicial thinking and reasoning likely inhibits some choices and encourages other in a manner that is beyond the conscious control of any one judge. However, proving and measuring such influence continues to be a challenge for rigorous social scientists.

The doctrine of *stare decisis* has also been criticized for being overly conservative. It surely privileges the status quo as the centre of legal reasoning. "Perhaps surprisingly to many people," Fredrick Schauer (2009) notes, "a legal argument is a better legal argument just because someone has made it before, and a legal conclusion is a better legal conclusion just because another court reached the same conclusion on an earlier occasion" (p. 73). Indeed, today's students may be surprised to learn that, throughout North American and English legal history, progressive reformers have often found their ideas thwarted by a judiciary that was resistant to change and often out-of-step with popular opinion. For example, courts across the common law world were resistant to the social safety net, labour laws, and often democracy itself. The idea that Supreme Court judges could be considered the leaders of social change is a relatively new one.

Any ideological commitments from *stare decisis* are usually quite weak, especially in comparison to demographic explanations of judicial conservatism (judges are typically older and drawn from a socio-economic elite that is unlikely to be representative). And while *stare decisis* does privilege the past, it does not demand blind obedience to it. As Charles J. Cooper (1988) notes, "the truth, of course, is that *stare decisis* has always been a doctrine of convenience, to both conservatives and liberals" (p. 402). Still, the "backwards" view of law remains an important element of its character. "Unlike most forms of policy-making, which are concerned with a proposed policy's future consequences," Schauer (2009) notes, "legal decision-making is preoccupied with looking over its shoulder" (p. 36). Social scientists should always keep in mind that law is generally reactive, historically grounded, and incrementally advanced.

## THE ORGANIZATION OF CANADIAN COURTS

*Stare decisis* is also a crucial mechanism of control within the organization of the judiciary itself. Most of what was discussed above constitutes **horizontal** *stare decisis*, where courts follow the precedents established by their own earlier incarnations. **Vertical** *stare decisis* refers to the requirement that courts lower in the judicial hierarchy are obligated to follow decisions made by courts above them. To understand the operation of vertical *stare decisis*, it is first necessary to understand how Canada's courts are arranged.

Canadian courts are organized in a hierarchical and unified fashion. To hear a case, a court must have **jurisdiction**, which can be territorial or related to subject matter. Territorial jurisdiction is perhaps the easiest to understand – you live in Canada, so you are under the authority of Canadian courts and Canadian laws – but it can be more complicated. A citizen of Toronto, for example, might be under three overlapping jurisdictions: Some matters might be resolved by bylaws passed by the City of Toronto, others by Ontario provincial law, and still others by Canadian federal legislation. Moreover, the courts do not easily map onto this territorial jurisdiction: It is common, for example, for the Ontario Court of Appeal to rule on municipal bylaws, Ontario laws, and national federal laws. Importantly, though, the Ontario Court of Appeal has only provincial territorial jurisdiction, so that its rulings are binding only on Ontarians. The Alberta Court of Appeal does not need to follow the rulings of the Ontario Court of Appeal, even though it will often consider its judgments carefully in their own rulings.

Some courts have **original jurisdiction** over cases – meaning they can be the first to hear the case – whereas others are higher in the hierarchy and mostly exercise **appellate jurisdiction** – meaning they can hear appeals of cases from the courts below them when requested to do so by at least one of the parties to the case (typically the losing party). The Supreme Court of Canada sits atop this judicial hierarchy and decides any legal matter put before it – for this reason, the Canadian system can be described as "unified." This makes it starkly different from the US system of courts, where some matters receive their final resolution at the state court level with no possibility of an appeal to the US Supreme Court. The US model is sometimes described as a "dual-track" model where issues proceed on a federal track or a state track. In Canada, there is also limited **subject-matter jurisdiction** where issues related directly to federal laws are (as declared in the legislation itself) litigated in the federal court system. These matters include federal tax law, federal administrative law, intellectual property law, and some elements of family law (significantly, it does not include the bulk of the federal *Criminal Code*, except for some offences like terrorism and a few others). Importantly, though, regardless of what court has subject-matter jurisdiction, the Supreme Court holds jurisdiction over every subject and, should it choose to do so, can hear any appeal brought to it. Indeed, the Supreme Court of Canada can also hear **reference cases**, which are not "live" cases brought by litigants on appeal but instead abstract legal questions submitted by governments. The Court's decisions in those cases are "advisory" and not legally binding, but the Court's political influence is considerable and most governments accept their opinions in reference cases as authoritative (see Puddister, 2019, for more detail about strategies governments employ with respect to the Court's reference power).

Courts below the Supreme Court of Canada, including courts of appeal (one for each province) and various "superior" and trial courts below them, are obligated to follow the decisions made by the Supreme Court of Canada (see Figure 2.1). Note, however, that the provincial courts of appeal – the highest court in any given province – need not agree with each other; indeed, one of the reasons the Supreme Court might hear a case is to settle an issue of law where the provinces might disagree. Within a given jurisdiction, however, vertical *stare decisis* is usually quite strong. Only in special cases can lower courts pre-emptively overturn Supreme Court precedents and defy vertical *stare decisis* (and even then, the Supreme Court can reverse that decision). Like horizontal *stare decisis*, much depends on how the judge in the instant case understands the alleged precedent: Is it sufficiently similar in legally relevant ways to warrant following it in the

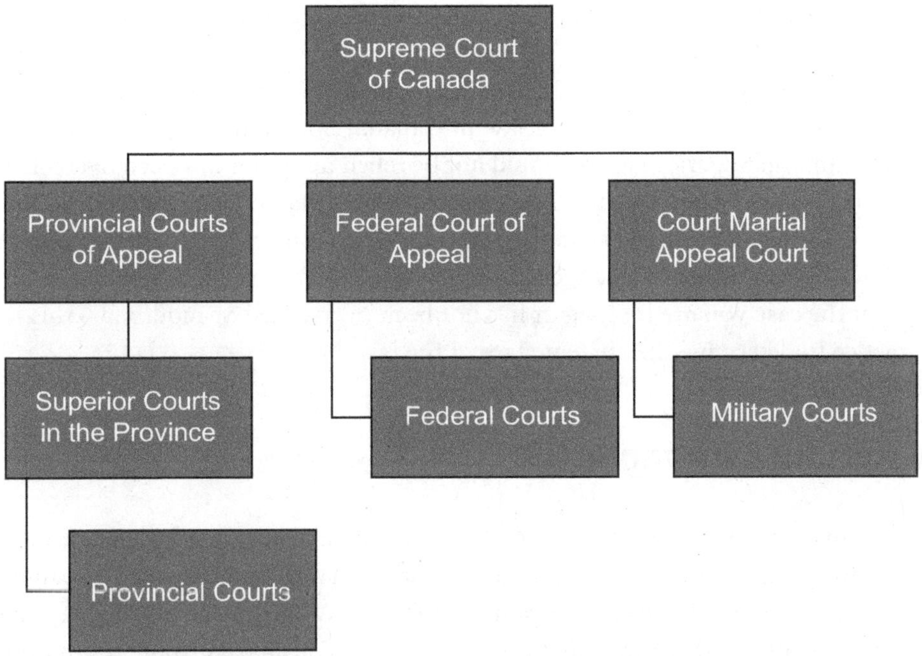


**Figure 2.1. The Hierarchy of Canadian Courts**

instant case, or is it sufficiently different to "distinguish" it from the precedent? That process has always been an accepted part of vertical *stare decisis* and grants every judge in Canada a degree of freedom to arrive at a just result in any given case.

While there are other significant parts of the Canadian judicial hierarchy (in addition to the federal courts, there is a separate set of courts martial for the Canadian Forces), the bulk of the judiciary's work in Canada takes place in what might be called "provincial courts." Even this nomenclature is confusing, since it could refer to the lowest courts in the hierarchy, where the provincial government is responsible for appointing the judges or the "superior courts in the province." The former – the lowest courts in each province – are entirely a provincial matter, with the provinces appointing the judges and responsible for administering the courts; this is the level where you would challenge your speeding ticket issued under the province's *Highway Traffic Act*, but it also hears some criminal law matters too. The more serious criminal offences, however, are heard in the "Superior Courts" – while the provinces are also responsible for their administration, the judges in these courts are appointed by the federal government. In each province there is a superior court trial level and a provincial court of appeal ("The Alberta Court of Appeal," etc.), but there is wide variation in the names used for the trial level: In Ontario we refer to the "Superior Court of Justice," but in Alberta it is the "Court of King's Bench."

The full details of the Canadian judicial process and arrangement of courts is beyond the scope of this text (Hausegger et al., 2025 is the best resource on the subject; a classic and still relevant text is Russell, 1987), but some awareness of the judicial hierarchy is necessary to understand the operation of law in Canada. For example, a judicial decision from the Ontario Superior Court should not be relied upon if it has been overruled by the Ontario Court of Appeal or the Supreme Court of Canada. Lawyers refer to this checking of the status of the law as "noting up" the case. In most legal search engines (CanLII, QuickLaw, and LexisNexis WestLaw), you can look at the "Citing Cases" tool to ensure that the case you are looking at has not been overturned or modified – this is a good practice to determine the current state of the law.

## THE IMPORTANCE OF PROCESS

Courts are institutions that resolve disputes through a judicial process. **Adjudication** is what courts do and is the method of dispute resolution that often comes most readily to mind, but it is not the only means of dispute resolution. Adjudication can be usefully compared to mediation and arbitration, two other common means of dispute resolution that employ different approaches and processes. To distinguish them, one can ask two questions: (1) who decides who decides? and (2) are the parties bound by the outcome? With respect to adjudication, it is the "harshest" point at one end of a continuum: Absent any clear objection for bias or a conflict of interest, the parties have no say in the identity of the judge who will decide their case; and, once the judge rules, the outcome is legally binding on the parties. At the other end of the continuum is **mediation**, which is a dispute resolution method entirely reliant on mutual agreement: The parties must agree on who the decision-maker will be ("let's ask our professor to help sort out our conflict") and anything the decision-maker decides or, really, proposes, must be agreed to by both parties. While mediation is useful for arriving at mutually beneficial outcomes that the parties might not have initially considered, it is less useful for actually resolving the dispute, particularly if there are significant and insurmountable differences between the parties. In between mediation and adjudication is a method that will be familiar to fans of professional sports: arbitration. **Arbitration** allows for the parties to agree to a decision-maker (so, the parties have the benefit of "picking" their judge) but with the understanding that the parties will be bound by the decision the arbitrator makes. This approach allows for specialization and a decision-maker who is familiar with the particular norms and practices of a given profession or industry but also allows for the final resolution of a dispute. In the labour union context – including many sports contracts – arbitration avoids going to court (where the decision-maker may know nothing about the sport) and the often cumbersome legal process but still allows for a definitive outcome to be made. (There are many forms of arbitration, including "non-binding arbitration," but capturing that full complexity is beyond the scope of this book.) Other forms of dispute resolution – including methods related to restorative justice – often rely on some combination of mediation, arbitration, and adjudication.

While those other methods of dispute resolution may be more informal with relaxed procedures, adjudication typically adheres to rather rigid processes and emphasizes legal reasoning. While it is true that all reasoning is dependent on the assumptions and "rules" that guide it, legal reasoning is inordinately channelled by accepted rules about "what counts" and what doesn't. These choices play a critical role in the manner that legal scholars and practitioners construct knowledge. Social scientists have their own methods for constructing knowledge too, ones that rely on survey data, qualitative observations, or historical records (to name just a few well-known methods in the social sciences). But a social scientist would never exclude sources of knowledge if they were thought to be relevant to their research question. That is because truth-seeking is really the only goal for social science. Law, on the other hand, is committed to both truth and fairness. This means that, in some cases, legal reasoning is prepared to forgo truth to serve other values (primarily fairness, but sometimes efficiency, stability, and certainty can be factors as well). This means that process concerns are much more central and contested than they are in the social sciences. A key element of legal reasoning that best illustrates this tendency is the privileged role given to the rules of evidence.

It is common for law schools to have full-year courses just on "evidence," and one can find a variety of legal textbooks that detail the rules of evidence in any given jurisdiction. The brief account here is limited and should serve mostly to alert social scientists to the existence of these rules – with the expectation that they will arise in many legal matters. A few examples should give the flavour of these important rules, even if we cannot account for them in a systematic and comprehensive way.

There are several key categories of "evidence." A trial might revolve around physical evidence (also sometimes known as "real evidence"; a murder weapon is the obvious example), but it must be introduced at trial by testimonial evidence (Who found the murder weapon? Who saw it being used?). This is generally known as direct evidence and can be contrasted with "expert evidence" (see Box 2.2) and "circumstantial evidence." The latter does not directly resolve the legal question at issue, but rather provides context about the circumstances surrounding that question. While the term "circumstantial evidence" is sometimes invoked to suggest the evidence is insufficient, it should be noted that strong circumstantial evidence can be compelling and result in a legal determination with little or no direct evidence. There are many crimes, for example, that are not directly observed and where there may be no physical evidence but still result in a conviction.

A good example of a well-known evidentiary rule is the exclusion of **hearsay**. At trial, witnesses can testify only to their direct knowledge; they cannot testify to things they heard from others in order to establish the truth of the statement. There are at least two potential problems with admitting hearsay evidence. First, the statement might be unreliable. Think about the campfire game of "telephone": Inaccuracies are introduced each time the "evidence" is communicated. The second related reason is that the person making the original statement is shielded from cross-examination. As the SCC notes, "without the maker of the statement in court, it may be impossible to inquire into that person's perception, memory, narration or sincerity" (*R v Khelawon*, 2006, para. 2).

While hearsay evidence is usually inadmissible, common law courts have generated many exceptions to the rule. Where a conspiracy is being charged, for example, the "co-conspirator's exception" allows for statements to be admitted (*R v Mapara*, 2005). "Dying declarations" are also allowed – "he killed me!" – since even though "a dying man does not lose his ability to lie," the Supreme Court accepted that "a motive to lie in such circumstances is at best remote" (*R v Baldree*, 2013, para. 115). The 1990 case of *R v Khan* shows the importance of allowing hearsay in some instances: A four-year old victim of sexual assault could not be a witness under the then-existing rules regarding oath-taking, so the evidence of what she told her mother (an unprompted statement by the child that the doctor she had just visited had assaulted her) was crucial. The Court found the statement reliable, given that the child had no reason to lie and it was supported by physical evidence, and allowed it to be admitted.

The hearsay rules reveal a dynamic that is seen in other areas of evidence and law generally. While there may be a broad principle at the outset, the common law is almost certain to produce exceptions. Over time, those exceptions accumulate and often develop into a thicket of complicated rules. Hearsay was once notorious for its "pigeonholes" of exceptions, a messy situation that the Supreme Court of Canada has mostly cleaned up by resorting to a more general meta-rule of evidence: Where the evidence is "probative" (offers proof that helps resolve the legal question at stake) and it outweighs the "prejudicial effect" (the disadvantage it might introduce because it is inaccurate or because it is inflammatory and irrelevant) it will likely be admitted. This balance is struck because we want trials to be fair, but we also want to find the truth. There is also an element of expediency at play in many of these exceptions in that without them, important evidence would never get before the court as the person who made the original statement may not be able to testify. This is surely part of the rationale behind permitting dying declarations.

While many of the rules of evidence have common law roots, legislation now plays an important role. The *Canada Evidence Act* is a crucial statute where political value judgments are clearly made. Consider section 4 of the act, which governs the rules of "spousal privilege." These rules have developed as the nature and character of marriage

---

**BOX 2.2. EXPERT EVIDENCE**

A form of evidence that might be especially important for social scientists is "expert evidence," especially since researchers may find themselves providing this testimony during a legal proceeding. Since judges themselves are the "experts" on the law, scholars cannot testify to their competing interpretations of the law, but almost any other area of research, including policy impacts, historical context, statistical analysis, survey data, etc., can be brought before the court. The 1994 Supreme Court case of *R v Mohan* explained that expert evidence must be relevant and reliable, necessary for the judge to understand the facts of the case, and given by an expert who is properly qualified, having been "shown to have acquired special or peculiar knowledge through study or experience" (p. 25). The Court was clearly concerned with the dangers that might come with evidence that was largely based on opinion but dressed up in scientific language. This is particularly problematic for the social sciences, where the empirical and normative divide is often fuzzy. (See Paciocco, 2009, on potential biases of expert witnesses, and Yowell, 2018, on the challenges courts face when dealing with empirical studies).

---

in our society has changed. The common law rule treated husbands and wives as "one," which meant that their legal interests should be treated as inseparable. In a criminal trial, where one spouse was the accused, the other spouse was deemed "incompetent" (meaning they could not be a witness at the trial) in most cases. Section 4 of the *Canada Evidence Act* changed the common law rule so that spouses are competent witnesses for the defence but not the prosecution. It also allowed for spouses to be "compellable" (forced to testify) for the prosecution for a few select charges, mostly related to domestic violence and assaults against children.

These statutory changes to the common law recognized that the spouse's interests were not identical in law to those of the accused. This was the existing state of Canadian evidence law prior to 2015, when Stephen Harper's Conservative government eliminated the rule of spousal incompetency altogether. At the time, the government argued that in serious cases (murder, terrorism, high-level fraud), it would be unjust if a spouse were unable to provide important evidence. The government maintained the spousal communication privilege, however, which allows the spouse of the accused to refuse to testify about anything the accused said during their marriage. This reflects the notion that we still see marital communications as private (nobody's business but the couple's) but that each party is autonomous and can decide for themselves whether to reveal that information. The rules of evidence, in other words, have evolved from treating the marital unit as singular to understanding it as a private commitment between two independent people.

In addition to what does and does not count as "evidence," legal reasoning also emphasizes the *standard* for evidentiary proof. A hint or small amount of evidence is generally not taken as having any legal significance. To *prove* something in law means that there is sufficient evidence to support the legal claim. Here there are two general standards in law: **beyond a reasonable doubt (BARD)** and the **balance of probabilities (BOP)**. BARD is the standard generally used for most criminal matters and, although the standard is very high, it does not require "absolute" certainty. You can have far-fetched doubts – it is always possible, of course, that space aliens intervened at a critical moment – but if you have any doubt that is based on reason or logic, then the standard is not met. In the 1997 *Lifchus* case, the Supreme Court of Canada rejected many short-hand rewordings of "reasonable doubt," such as a "serious" or "substantial" or "haunting" doubt, as well as simply saying you have to be "sure," and arrived at the following definition: "A reasonable doubt is not an imaginary or frivolous doubt. It must not be based upon sympathy or prejudice. Rather it is based on reason and common sense. It is logically derived from the evidence or absence of evidence" (para. 39).

This high standard can be contrasted with the much lower BOP standard that is widely used in private law matters. BOP simply requires proof that is "more likely than not," so essentially a 50 per cent +1 standard. This is a lower level of proof and prone to mistakes (reasonable doubts here can be safely ignored if they don't affect what is "likely"), but it isn't the lowest level of proof in law. We allow police to intervene when they have "reasonable suspicion," for example, when it may not even be "likely" that a crime is committed. With all of these standards, each piece of evidence need not meet any probabilistic standard, but rather the evidence can be viewed holistically to arrive at the overall understanding of whether the standard was met. It is important that social scientists be aware of these standards when dealing with legal phenomena, since the impact of evidence on the outcome is almost entirely dependent on whether the standard is reached. Focusing on the evidence and ignoring the standard can lead to errors in understanding the legal process and the meaning of legal outcomes. Indeed, it is the interplay between standards of proof and the probative value of evidence that explains many rules of evidence. Evidence of a person's bad character, for example, may be probative in the sense that bad people might be considered more likely to have committed a crime. However, that evidence may fall well below the BARD standard and have tremendous prejudicial impact. A jury might be inclined to convict not because the accused is guilty of the charge before the court but simply because they are perceived to be a bad person. As a result, this sort of evidence is usually excluded because its high prejudicial impact outweighs its limited probative value.

# THE IMPORTANCE OF LANGUAGE

Perhaps the primary distinctive feature of legal reasoning is its insistence on precision in language. As Waddams (1992) notes, "every task that a lawyer performs requires the use of language. Whether he is arguing in court or drawing documents or giving written or oral advice, the lawyer must have the ability to transform his meaning effectively into words" (p. 37). Waddams suggests that the best preparation for law school, and one that will give you "a very great advantage," is "to acquire the ability to write the English language quickly and effectively" (p. 37). Social scientists are taught to be precise with their language too, but, in law, the way something is phrased can change the legal effect and have immediate real-world consequences.

One might be wondering if this reduces lawyering to grammatical pedantry, but, in fairness, it is required if we are to expect the law to mediate relationships where shared understandings are critical but sometimes contested. In the "Oxford comma case" (see Box 2.3), the law clearly meant different things to the drivers and the dairy company,

---

**BOX 2.3. THE OXFORD COMMA: THE IMPORTANCE OF PRECISION IN THE USE OF LANGUAGE**

Grammatical controversies can translate to very real legal problems. You might be aware of the dispute over the "Oxford comma": When you are ending a list, do you write "a, b and c" or "a, b, and c" (the comma after the "b" in the second example is the Oxford comma)? For most people, the choice to use the extra comma is simply a stylistic preference; for lawyers, it can literally mean millions of dollars. The United States Court of Appeals for the First Circuit had to interpret a Maine law that denied overtime wages to workers engaged in the "canning, processing, preserving, freezing, drying, marketing, storing, packing for shipment or distribution of" perishable foods. A dairy company had denied its truck drivers four years of overtime pay on the basis that the law clearly included them since the drivers "distributed" the perishable foods. The drivers argued that the last part of the list needed to be read as a whole and thus only workers who "packed" the food "for shipment or distribution" were to be denied overtime pay. The court decided that the legislation was at least ambiguous and should be interpreted liberally, which meant that the argument of the drivers won in this case (*O'Connor v Oakhurst Dairy*, 2017). When millions of dollars hinge on the placement of a comma, lawyers and legislative drafters have strong incentives to be very careful with their writing.

and perhaps neither meaning was what the drafters of the law meant. Ruth Sullivan (2007) notes the centrality of this communicative function of law: "It is impossible to do anything in law without interpreting the words of others and anticipating how others will interpret (or misinterpret) one's own" (p. 1). This anticipation of how one's language will be received means that precision will be paramount and often jargon or "legalese" will be necessary. While it is sometimes fun to ridicule lawyers for their tendency to use ten words when one might do, and for invoking Latin phrases at every opportunity, specialized terminology is usually employed to attempt to communicate with reference to shared conceptions of legal principles and ideas (Schauer, 2015a). That said, we might still suspect that "legalese" is sometimes overused to allow for the legally trained to mystify their profession and exclude others from their privileged conversations. Professions, by their nature, try to control knowledge and limit those who have access to that knowledge.

## STATUTORY INTERPRETATION

As the debate over the Oxford comma would suggest, the lawyerly preoccupation with precise language reaches its apotheosis in the exercise of "statutory interpretation." Once a bill has been given Royal Assent, the legislative process is over and the judicial one begins; the product of the former must be given legal effect by the latter. To do so, primacy is given to the text of the statute itself. US Supreme Court Justice Felix Frankfurter's rule for interpreting statutes had three fundamental steps: "(1) Read the statute, (2) read the statute; (3) read the statute!" (Baude & Sachs, 2017, p. 1082).

While this approach – **textualism,** as it is sometimes called – is generally an appropriate starting point for statutory interpretation, it does not solve all matters of ambiguity in legislation. Since statutes are the product of political calculation and negotiation, we can expect there to be plenty of generalities and vague phrases. The generality is actually a feature – not a flaw – of statutes: Remember the rule of law points us towards laws of general application, not specific statutes for specific people or overly particular situations. Moreover, the ambiguity of statutes tends to reflect democratic functions and principles. As Jeremy Waldron (1999) writes in the *Dignity of Legislation*, the process of legislation can be characterized as allowing for decisive action in the context of disagreement: "The representatives of the community come together to settle solemnly and explicitly on common schemes and measures that can stand in the name of them all" and they do so in a fashion "that openly acknowledges and respects (rather than conceals) the inevitable differences of opinion and principle among them" (p. 2). If the statutory process is one by which citizens govern themselves in the context of widespread and persistent disagreement, one wouldn't expect the products of such a process to be uncontroversial when applied to the concrete cases that come before judges.

Judges, however, are tasked with the responsibility of applying general statutes to the particular cases before them. While simply reading the text (sometimes referred to as the "plain meaning") will resolve many issues, those uncontroversial applications are less likely to require adjudication. Judges are more likely to be faced with harder cases where the statute is ambiguous and open to multiple meanings. The judge will have to decide which meaning is legally binding. This is not simply a matter of language, nor should it be simply a matter of judicial preference; instead, we hope it is the legal context that determines the meaning.

This process requires there to be rules of construction and "canons of interpretation" that are generally accepted in the legal community. Some are found in legislation itself: In Canada, the federal government and all provincial governments each have "interpretation acts" to help clarify the legal effect of its statutory language. For example, section 33(1) of the federal *Interpretation Act* specifies that "words importing female persons include male persons and … words importing male persons include female persons." You don't escape the force of law simply because the law refers to a "she" or, more commonly, a "he." Similarly, the same section tells us that "words in the singular include the plural, and words in the plural include the singular." So if the law prohibits "dangerous vehicles," it prohibits a single dangerous vehicle too. The fact that we need such statutes itself points to the technicalities a lawyerly mind might seize upon. Amusingly, Canada's *Interpretation Act* contains a provision (s. 12) that undermines such "technicalities" by requiring statutes to be given a "fair, large and liberal construction and interpretation as best ensures the attainment of its objects." In other words, statutes should be interpreted so as to achieve the objective of Parliament in passing the law, although it is often the case that discerning Parliament's intention is far from certain.

Most of the rules about statutory interpretation come from the common law, however. In fact, the provision in the *Interpretation Act* is in part a response to common law rules that have been perceived as overly restrictive. Still, those rules provide the crucial link between those that draft legislation (bureaucrats in the executive branch of government) and the lawyers and judges that apply them. There are too many rules of statutory construction to list here – the curious can seek out Ruth Sullivan's (2007) authoritative text on the current Canadian approaches – but everyone dealing with legal instruments should be aware of some of the most important legislative drafting conventions. Tables 2.1 and 2.2 include some commonly used terms that have important, specific legal meanings. The common law is also replete with "canons" of interpretation, like those in Table 2.2.

**Table 2.1. Statutory/Legal Interpretation**

| Legal Term | General Meaning |
| --- | --- |
| Notwithstanding | Regardless of what the other listed parts of the act may say, the part following this list is the law and trumps those other parts. |
| Subject to | The other part is controlling. E.g., if the act says "Subject to s. 4," this means that, regardless of what follows, section 4 trumps what is said. |
| Includes | Whatever is listed is <u>not</u> exhaustive. What follows are examples, but there may be other examples that may fit within them. |
| Means | Generally understood to be exhaustive. Only those elements explicitly identified are to be used and others should not be included as part of an interpretation. |
| Shall | This is <u>mandatory</u> language and the action <u>must</u> be done (it is a duty that must be fulfilled). |
| May | Permissive language. The actor may or may not take the legal action identified. |
| And | Generally speaking, both conditions before and after "and" must be met. |
| Or | Only one part on either side of the "or" must be fulfilled to get the benefit/burden of the law. |

**Table 2.2. Canons of Interpretation**

| Legal Term | General Meaning |
| --- | --- |
| Sui genesis | Of its own kind |
| Nemo dat rule | One cannot give what one does not have |
| Expressio unius est exclusio alterius | The expression of one is the exclusion of the other |
| Ejusdem genris | Of the same kind |
| Noscitur a sociis | It is to be known by its association |

We do not dwell on these rules here, even though they are still routinely invoked by Canadian judges. For the most part, they have been incorporated by more general rules that suggest judges should interpret statutes reasonably. In *Rizzo & Rizzo Shoes Ltd* (1998), the Supreme Court of Canada declared that legislation should be given a logical interpretation consistent with what Parliament intended:

> It is a well established principle of statutory interpretation that the legislature does not intend to produce absurd consequences.… An interpretation can be considered absurd if it leads to ridiculous or frivolous consequences, if it is extremely unreasonable or inequitable, if it is illogical or incoherent, or if it is incompatible with other provisions or with the object of the legislative enactment. (para. 27)

This is consistent with what Elmer Driedger has summarized as the "modern rule" of statutory interpretation. The Supreme Court routinely cites this passage from Driedger as the starting point of any interpretation of legislation: "Today there is only one principle or approach, namely, the words of the Act are to be read in their entire context and in their grammatical and ordinary sense harmoniously with the scheme of the Act, the object of the Act, and the intention of Parliament" (quoted with approval by Justice Iacobucci in *Bell Express Vu v R*, 2002). The modern rule burdens judges with finding a sensible balance between the statute as enacted ("words read in their entire context and in their grammatical and ordinary sense") and their analysis of what Parliament meant the statute to do (thus the additional consideration of the "scheme of the Act," its "object," and Parliamentary intentions). Given that the judicial view of what Parliament intended can be very subjective, the modern rule allows for significant judicial discretion in how a statute will be interpreted, but if Parliament disagrees with the judicially constructed interpretation, it always retains the power to replace the statute with another that has clearer and more direct language that better captures its intentions.

Beaulac and Côté (2006) note that Driedger's modern principle has been referred to 724 times by Canadian superior courts and over 60 Supreme Court of Canada cases have invoked it from 1984 to 2005. Despite its widespread acceptance, Beaulac and Côté find that its usage is more "rhetorical" than actually providing "an outline of methods" to guide judges (para. 6). This is likely due to the unclear weighing of the different elements in the principle. In many cases, all of the components might point in one direction, but what if the "grammatical" context runs contrary to the clear intentions of Parliament? In the modern rule's statement, "harmoniously" does most of the work. It allows judges to resolve an interpretive controversy by finding some (and hopefully most) of the components that support their preferred interpretation. While this means that statutory interpretation is inherently political, it cannot be said to be a choice unguided by legal norms, since judges are committed to finding *something* in the modern rule to hang their decision on. In this respect, Canada's experience with statutory interpretation is consistent with the primary argument of this text: It is a phenomenon best understood as both legal and political.

## CONCLUSION

This chapter consists of several interrelated blocks that together form a robust picture of what constitutes legal reasoning in a common law system: a respect for both horizontal and vertical *stare decisis*; an emphasis on process, proof, and evidence; and a practice of using language precisely, often supplemented by complex rules of statutory interpretation. Does this amount to a form of reasoning distinct from ordinary reasoning? That debate continues to be contested, but it is undeniable that, at the very least, legal reasoning includes special elements that are obtained, as Chief Justice Coke explained, through "long study and experience." There is nothing inherent in ordinary reason or logic to respect precedent, for example, but it is essential to common law legal reasoning. Moreover, operationalizing the application of precedent – knowing which *parts* of the precedent will likely apply to a different fact situation – is something that is learned largely through the reading of many, many cases and the practice of being involved in them, and discussing them in a community of professionals. As Martin Loughlin suggests, this inculcates a shared legal "world-view" made by legal practitioners and scholars. Along with the shared respect for precedent, legal actors recognize "legal fictions," appreciate the importance of precise language and specialized terms, and recognize common grounds for interpretive arguments, even if they may disagree on the ultimate interpretation. These elements of legal reasoning are crucial for those practising law, but they are also extremely useful to all social scientists who are investigating law or dealing with legal topics. Any form of reasoning intrinsic to those disciplines will benefit from an appreciation of how legal actors themselves approach and think about law. For this reason, this chapter needed to be near the beginning of this book to provide a strong foundation for the chapters that follow.

## REVIEW QUESTIONS

1  What is "artificial reasoning"? Is legal reasoning truly distinguishable from ordinary reasoning? Why? Why not?
2  What does "legal identity" illustrate about the nature of legal reasoning?
3  How does *stare decisis* work and why is it important to the common law? What are some of the challenges in applying it?
4  Give an example of how a focus on process might differentiate legal reasoning from more ordinary forms of reasoning.
5  Is it enough to simply "read the statute" in order to apply it? Why or why not? What techniques can judges use to interpret a statute?

# CHAPTER THREE

# The Canadian Constitution

## LEARNING OBJECTIVES

- Understand what a constitution is, whether written or unwritten, and the function it is intended to perform.
- Be able to describe, in general terms, the content of the Canadian Constitution.
- Understand the importance of the limitations clause (s. 1) and the notwithstanding clause (s. 33) of the Canadian Constitution.

At some point in your life, you've probably claimed that your "rights have been violated." Sometimes this is done for dramatic effect – "I have a right to that last slice of pizza!" – but maybe you've experienced real injustice like a confrontation with the police that left you shaken, or you've been denied your right to speak out about something that is important to you. When we speak of rights, we are usually referring to *constitutional* rights, which are supposed to be given a higher status and greater protection in law. As discussed in Chapter 2, modern constitutions are the primary channel through which statutes and government actions can be challenged for their inconsistency with a "higher law." But that's not the only purpose of a constitution. As important as rights are, they are often conceived of as rights against government authority – and that system of government is usually established by the constitution too. Constitutions are essentially a framework for virtually everything related to government, and they therefore sit squarely at the intersection of law and politics.

## WHAT IS A CONSTITUTION?

In political and constitutional theory, there continues to be much debate over what is meant by a nation's "constitution." Americans tend to view it as a particular document, in their case one enacted in 1789, that forms the "contractual" basis of their government. In the United Kingdom, a much older nation-state, people are more likely to understand "constitution" less as a document or set of documents and more as a general sense of what "constitutes" their state. This meaning is less intuitive these days, but it may become clear if we compare it to the usage of "constitution" when applied to individuals, which generally means their health and well-being.

According to Oxford Professor of Jurisprudence John Gardner (2011), a constitution is "a conceptual necessity of any legal system" (p. 162). "In every legal system," Gardner explains,

> there are rules that specify the major institutions and officials of government, and determine which of them do what, and how they are to interact, and how their membership or succession is to be determined, and so forth. Without some such rules, as H.L.A. Hart explained …, there is no legal system. (p. 162)

As the invocation of Hart suggests, the political foundation of constitutionalism is positivist, in the most basic sense that the authority of the constitution is derived simply from the fact that it is recognized as such. (In other words, a constitution that wasn't accepted as such wouldn't be a constitution at all.) That said, it would be a mistake to assume that all constitutions are "designed" in a moment of national agreement; most elements of most constitutions reflect pre-existing institutional arrangements, customs, and practices, and reflect evolving norms and natural rights.

There is also considerable controversy about whether a constitution needs to be written down. To the extent that the constitution is considered a "contract" between citizens and the state, or between levels of government, it is attractive to have its provisions explicitly declared in writing. But, as the UK example suggests, this is not a requirement for a constitution. British scholar John Gardner (2011) cheekily addresses the assumption made by many Americans in the title of one of his articles: "Can There Be a Written Constitution?" His argument is that even the written American Constitution relies on some background assumptions about its legality – why is this document privileged over others? – that cannot be captured exclusively by the text itself. Just as contracts are meaningless without some pre-existing agreement about their significance and their enforcement, so too do constitutions rely on assumptions about the existence of some sort of national consensus. Some of those "background" assumptions and understandings are rightfully considered part of all constitutions.

That said, it is commonplace to identify a national moment where a constitution is deliberately enacted. The American Revolution led to a "constitutional convention" where the Articles of Confederation were first drafted and, when they were found wanting, another such convention arrived at the constitution that went into force in 1789 and governs the United States today. Their constitution was also ratified, meaning it was considered and voted upon by the colonial/state legislatures it was bringing together. While the constitution of the United Kingdom is the result of centuries-long evolution, not a deliberate moment of enactment, there were clear signpost moments in that development that can be identified: the Magna Carta in 1215, the Glorious Revolution in 1688, and the Act of Settlement in 1701 are some obvious "constitutional moments." For Commonwealth countries like Canada and Australia, the "constitutional moment" is typically associated with the passage of an act of the UK Parliament that established at least a degree of independence: the 1867 *British North America Act*, which federated Canada, and the 1900 *Commonwealth of Australia Constitution Act*, which did the same for Australia. While these enactments were treated as "constitutions" in their respective countries, they were simply statutes passed by the UK Parliament and could be modified through the ordinary statutory process in the United Kingdom (but, importantly, they did so only upon the request of the governments of those countries).

An important aim of any constitution is some degree of durability. Constitutions usually prescribe a process for their own amendment – see the discussion of the Canadian variant below – but the rules and processes are intended to last beyond the vicissitudes of ordinary, daily politics. Some see constitutions as framing rules in perpetuity, even though history is littered with discarded "eternal" constitutions, and others see constitutions as governing for only a single generation. US founder Thomas Jefferson, for example, argued that "the earth belongs always to the living generation," so he proposed that "every constitution ... naturally expires at the end of thirty-four years" (Koch & Peden, 2004, pp. 451–2). Jefferson's view is considered radical today and we now expect constitutions to last – and, in fact, their permanence is expected to be a source of their strength, with new deviations from the enduring constitution seen as political wrongs.

## CONSTITUTIONS AND COMMITMENT

As discussed in Chapter 1, a constitution is understood to be a "higher law." As such, it can be conceived of as a commitment made at one point in time that governs over the preferences and prejudices of the current moment. An oft-invoked image is that of Odysseus binding himself to the mast to prevent him from succumbing to the temptations of the sirens. The popularly elected officials might similarly be tempted by the worst majoritarian impulses and trample individual rights and liberties unless they are restrained by the constitutional promises made earlier. A more contemporary analogy is to think of Parliament as a partygoer that hands over its keys to the host to prevent drunk driving once alcohol starts to be imbibed. These depictions are deeply sceptical of Parliament's capacity to act appropriately and instead imply that Parliament may, at least from time to time, fall prey to its own bad impulses and enact fundamentally bad public policy.

Rainer Knopff critiques the idea of Parliament committing itself from its obviously bad future impulses by offering a competing metaphor that more closely matches the institutional questions of constitutionalism. Knopff (2003) introduces us to the "lay-about" Harry, who

> won't hold a job and neglects his children. One day Harry undergoes a personal change of heart and makes a solemn commitment to be a better father. He appoints his wife as "guardian of his conscience," asking her to help him live up to his commitment. Almost immediately, Harry faces a dilemma: should he take the better-paying job on offer despite its very long hours and travel commitments, thus enabling him to provide better for the children's education, or the lower-paying job, which will allow him to spend more quality with the children? He is torn, and when he turns to his wife, he finds her similarly ambivalent. (p. 204)

Knopff contends that this analogy more closely resembles the policy choices faced in the application of constitutional principles. Harry's commitment does not change, just that the commitment is made at a high level of abstraction and open to reasonable disagreement in its application. Similarly, one can find considerable agreement about abstract constitutional principles like "freedom of speech" and "freedom of religion," but then also have reasonable disagreements about whether campaign spending can be limited, the extent to which hate speech can be suppressed, or whether a religious belief can warrant refusing medical treatment for a child. Unlike the idea of drunk driving, which everyone should agree is obviously bad, the question of what Harry should choose is one for which there are competing reasonable alternatives. Real application of constitutional politics, Knopff (2003) warns, is more complicated than "the stark and facile distinction often drawn between reasonable/principled judges (keepers of the keys) and impassioned/interested legislatures (would-be drunk drivers)" (p. 205). "In matters of reasonable disagreement," Knopff concludes, "interest, passion, and reason are found on all sides, and in all participating institutions" (pp. 205–6). This complexity will be returned to in the discussion of constitutional interpretation at the end of this chapter.

# THE CANADIAN CONSTITUTION

Canadians are fortunate that their constitution avoids some of the messier, abstract questions of what a constitution *is* by the simple fact that there is a very specific, legal definition of the Canadian Constitution: It is "the supreme law of the land." As discussed in Chapter 1, any law that is inconsistent with this "supreme law" is "of no force or effect." In this very same section that makes the Canadian Constitution supreme, it also tells us that what is included in the constitution: It certainly includes the two key documents (originally statutes enacted by the UK Parliament), *The Constitution Act, 1867* (which created the Canadian state, formerly known as the *British North America Act, 1867*) and *The Constitution Act, 1982* (which includes the *Canadian Charter of Rights and Freedoms*) but also an assortment of other documents (some relating to the creation of new provinces after 1867, for example; see Box 3.1), and leaves space for unwritten elements to also be recognized as part of the constitution.

The content of the constitution can be changed through constitutional amendment. Prior to 1982, amendments to the Constitution of Canada would be made by an "ordinary statute" of the UK Parliament. In practice, this was done only upon request of the Canadian government and, since at least 1931, the British were more than willing for Canada to undertake this responsibility for itself. The difficulty was that Canadians themselves could not agree upon the rules for constitutional amendment, especially given some thorny issues related to provincial concerns and the status of Quebec. In 1982, with the assistance of a questionable Supreme Court decision and over the objections of the Quebec government, the constitution was "patriated" such that any future UK law would have no legal effect on Canada. The *Constitution Act, 1982* contained a complicated **amending formula** that prescribed different levels of agreement for different subjects. If the matter only affects the federal government, it may do so alone; if it affects one or two provinces, only those provinces and the federal government must agree. For most matters though, a "general amending formula" requires the agreement of the federal government and seven of the ten provinces as long as those seven constitute at least 50 per cent of the population (this provision is sometimes known as the 7/50 rule). Effectively, this means that either Ontario or Quebec must agree to any constitutional amendment. For a few important elements of the constitution, such as the composition of the Supreme Court of Canada and the Office of the Queen, there must be unanimous agreement (see Macfarlane, 2016 for a variety of scholarly views about the Canadian power of constitutional amendment).

Since 1982, there has been little success using the general amending formula. With the failure to obtain the agreement of the Quebec government in 1982, two "mega-constitutional" amendments attempted to rectify the situation: the Meech Lake Accord

(1987–90) and the Charlottetown Accord (1992). The first was a narrower agreement that primarily addressed Quebec's concerns and included a controversial provision recognizing the province as constituting a "distinct society" within Canada. The Meech Lake Accord failed for a number of reasons, but especially poignantly when Elijah Harper, a member of the Manitoba Legislative Assembly and former Chief of the Red Sucker Lake Band, voted against the Accord for failing to include Indigenous Peoples. With the Meech Lake Accord seen as elite-driven (with only the eleven first ministers negotiating), the subsequent Charlottetown Accord was the result of much broader consultation, including several cross-Canada committees and discussions with a variety of stakeholder groups, including Indigenous Peoples in Canada. The Charlottetown Accord was a lengthy and complex amendment – some described it as a "dog's breakfast" of provisions – that seemingly gave something to everyone but – fatally – also something for everyone to complain about. To ratify the Accord, two referendums were held in October of 1992 (one in Quebec and one in the rest of the provinces and territories) and both failed. Overall the vote was 55 per cent opposed and 45 per cent in favour: Quebec rejected the Accord by a 57-to-43 margin; Ontario approved of it by a razor-thin 51-to-49 margin; the West voted strongly against the Accord, with British Columbians the most opposed, with 68 per cent voting "no." The entire experience from 1987 to 1992 was as divisive as it was inconclusive, leading Canadians to turn away from "mega-constitutional" politics (see Russell, 2004, 2019). In the wake of a 1995 Quebec referendum on sovereignty, which failed by less that 60,000 votes out of almost five million, the strategy of using the general amending clause to address Canada's constitutional deficiencies was abandoned.

Given the practical unavailability of the general amending formula, constitutional change in Canada has been the product of either more discrete micro-amendments (affecting only one level of government or a small number of provinces and the federal government; see also Crandall, 2022) or shifts in the judicial interpretation of the constitution. With respect to the former, in addition to provincial amendments, a number of Indigenous Constitutions have been created as a result of comprehensive land-claims agreements between Indigenous tribes and the federal and provincial governments. These Indigenous Constitutions have many of the recognized elements of a constitution and "contain provisions expressing distinctive local political cultures framed against a backdrop of liberal democratic values and structures" (Alcantara and Whitfield, 2010, p. 6). With respect to "judicial amendment," a dramatic example is the change in the constitutionality of labour rights: In 1987, the right to freedom of association (s. 2[d]) in the *Charter* was read to have virtually no effect on collective bargaining; by 2015, the right was turned 180 degrees to constitutionalize many aspects of the collective bargaining regime, including unionization (see Chapter 9 for more discussion). If Canadians want to change their constitution, the most effective means appears to be persuading judges to do so.

**BOX 3.1. THE *CARON* DECISION – WHAT COUNTS AS THE CONSTITUTION?**

In 2015, the Supreme Court of Canada was presented with a particularly tricky "source of law" question regarding the Canadian Constitution. Section 52(2)(b) of the *Constitution Act, 1982* tells us that the Constitution of Canada includes "the Acts and Orders Included in the Schedule," which is essentially a list of 30 separate documents that are now treated as part of the constitution and superior to ordinary statutes. When provinces were added to Confederation, an order or act would be made to do so and those were recognized as constitutional. The *Caron* case delved into the origins of the province of Alberta to determine what language rights might be held over Alberta statutes.

Giles Caron challenged the constitutionality of a traffic ticket he received in Alberta that was written only in English (*Caron v Alberta*, 2015). The ticket complied with Alberta's *Languages Act* but was the failure to provide the ticket in French a violation of the constitution? The *Manitoba Act, 1870*, one of the documents specifically identified in section 52 of the *Constitution Act, 1982* as being part of the Constitution of Canada, did expressly require bilingualism for Manitoba, but the territory that would include Alberta was governed by an 1870 order passed contemporaneously. The 1870 order itself is also identified as part of the constitution in section 52, but it did not contain a bilingualism requirement like the *Manitoba Act*. So, no clause, no French requirement. End of story?

Not quite. While the 1870 order did not contain an express provision for bilingualism, the order had an "address" (essentially a speech made in Parliament) attached to it that contained statements made in 1867 saying that the order would respect the existing "legal rights of any corporation, company or individual" in these western territories. Consider how far we are as a source of constitutional law: an address appended to an order that is listed in a schedule attached to the *Constitution Act, 1867*! For a minority of the Court, this was enough to establish that Alberta was constitutionally required to publish laws in both official languages. The inferences were too much for a majority of the Court, however, which ruled that the reference to "legal rights" didn't include language rights and, in any event, the guarantee was not in the actual order itself. While Caron did not succeed, his case is illustrative of the challenges of finding the extent of the written elements of the Canadian Constitution – to say nothing of the even more ambiguous unwritten elements.

## INSTITUTIONS AND POLICY-MAKING

A key function of any constitution is to establish governing institutions, their powers, and their relationships with each other. For Canadians, to the extent it takes the form of written rules, most of these provisions are found in the *Constitution Act, 1867*. An important qualifier: The *Constitution Act, 1867* starts with a preamble that says Canada's constitution is "similar in principle to that of the United Kingdom," and a number of background assumptions in the UK "Westminster" Parliamentary system are adopted by nothing much stronger than this introductory statement. In 1997, Chief Justice Lamer called the preamble "the grand entrance hall to the castle of the Constitution" and described it as a "true source" for some of our commitments to foundational principles (*Reference Re Remuneration of Judges of the Provincial Court (PEI)*, para. 109). It is a sure sign that, especially when it concerns our governing institutions, the text is only going to provide part of the story.

The *Constitution Act, 1867* does describe three branches of power in Canadian governance: the executive power in Part III, the legislative power in Part IV, and the judicial power in Part VII. Executive power – the power to "execute" the law – is dealt with rather summarily in section 9, which holds that "the Executive Government and Authority of and over Canada is hereby declared to continue and be vested in the Queen" of Canada (the constitutional language also extends to "Kings" who are proclaimed in law and assented to by the Parliament of Canada). This is obviously not a personal power – no one expects King Charles III to come and prosecute someone for the theft of your iPad – but it set up an array of actors, like the Governor General, to administer the laws of Canada. The theft of your iPad can lead to a criminal charge that will be prosecuted by "the Crown," for example, which is bringing the charge in the name of His Majesty, which is really itself a proxy for the common good and public interest.

The legislative power – the power to "make law" for all of Canada – is granted to Parliament. Parliament is defined in section 17 as "consisting of the Queen, an Upper House styled the Senate, and the House of Commons." It is commonplace for Canadians to think of the House of Commons as Parliament – especially since newsclips often show elected politicians announcing and debating policies – but the unelected Senate, which requires its own three readings of any bill before it becomes law, and the King, who has to grant Royal Assent for every law (a power usually exercised by the Governor General in his name), remain important parts of the Canadian legislative process.

Students of Canadian constitutional law are sometimes surprised by how many of our institutional rules are *not* in the text of the constitution. The prime minister, probably the most visible elected politician in Canada and one with an immense say over the content of the laws of Canada, is barely mentioned in the text. Except for one minor reference in the *Constitution Act, 1982*, promising a constitutional conference now discharged, the prime minister goes entirely unmentioned in Canada's constitutional text. Compare that to Article II of the US Constitution that describes the president's role and powers in some detail. Even Canada's fundamental rule of governance – "responsible government" – which holds that the King must exercise his authority on the advice of a prime minister, who in turn must hold the confidence of the House of Commons, goes largely unremarked upon in the text (the financial powers in sections 53 and 54 of the *Constitution Act, 1867* strengthen and rely upon the notion of responsible government but do not explain it or codify it any further). The same can be said of other actors in Canadian politics – the attorney general of Canada, the minister of finance, the minister of defence – none of which can be found in the text of the *Constitution Act, 1867* or *1982*, even though they have considerable political power and constitutional responsibilities.

What explains this lack of textual authority for the most well-known parts of Canadian government? It is a testament to Canada's constitutional heritage and historical evolution from a dominion of the United Kingdom. As mentioned above, the United Kingdom's constitution is largely unwritten and many political rules are *conventional*. Political scientist Philippe Lagassé helpfully distinguishes between several types of potential "rules": **conventions**, practices, customs, and norms. Though there is considerable overlap and subtle distinctions, Lagassé (2019) contends that the distinctions help provide clarity about "what is required by the Constitution, what is currently considered politically prudent or democratically preferable, what is traditionally done, and what should be done in the interests of fairness, honour, and the spirit of the Constitution" (p. 4). All of the rules, therefore, may have some political purpose or content but only conventions are constitutional requirements. Conventions are not legally binding, but because they represent a shared understanding, reinforced by established precedents, they constitute effective rules for political behaviour. Violations of conventions do not result in legal sanctions – you cannot get a court to enforce a convention – but they can be enforced politically (a vote of no confidence in Parliament, for example, that might lead to an election where there the convention-violator can be punished at the ballot box). That said, Canadian courts have been active in *identifying* conventions and explaining how they operate. Given the esteem which Canadian courts are usually afforded the identification of a convention that may be broken by a political actor might be enough to deter them from action, especially if an attentive public is persuaded by the court's reasoning.

So, the prime minister is a *constitutional* actor, but he or she has very little authority in constitutional law. Prime ministerial authority is largely *informal*, but that should not be mistaken for being weak in a larger political-constitutional sense. By commanding the confidence of the House (especially where the majority of seats are held by members of the same political party), the prime minister is given the authority by convention to form a government, which can then propose legislation that is likely to be enacted into law. This is essentially the core of Canadian government; it goes relatively unnoticed in Canadian constitutional *law* but is fundamentally grounded in Canadian *constitutionalism*.

The prevalence of conventions in the Canadian political sphere has limited the need for a truly comprehensive constitutional text. Indeed, the *Constitution Act, 1867* might not even have been necessary as a legal text if it weren't for the need to establish the federation of the (then) four provinces. It was the adjoining of colonial jurisdictions and the creation of a multi-level state that made Canada's textual constitution a necessity.

## FEDERALISM AND THE CONSTITUTION

A written constitution was necessary for Canada in 1867 for at least that very important reason: Unlike the "unitary" United Kingdom, Canada was to be a "federation" with a national government (Canada) and more local, provincial governments. Without a document describing the powers of each level of government, a federation would be impossibly chaotic since every Canadian would be subject to two authorities. It would therefore be essential to know which government was responsible for any given subject.

The heart of Canada's *Constitution Act, 1867* is section 91, describing the powers of the federal (national) Parliament, and section 92, doing the same for the legislatures of each province (see Box 3.2). Any student of government – and perhaps every citizen – should be familiar with some of the powers listed in ss. 91 and 92.

What made sense in 1867 regarding the division of powers might not make sense today. Generally, the division of powers reflects what the 1867 framers thought should be matters of concern to Canada as a whole (national defence, the monetary system) and what might be best addressed locally (the licensing of retail establishments, the establishment of city governments). Some of these assignments may have been confusing even in 1867 ("marriage and divorce" is a federal power, but the "solemnization of marriage" is a provincial power), but an even more pressing question is what happens when the underlying assumptions of 1867 change? The powers of the federal Parliament are somewhat elastic, since they include the power to generally legislate for the "peace, order, and good government" of Canada and a residual power to legislate in areas not explicitly assigned to the provincial government. This has allowed the regulation of new subject areas unheard of in 1867 – like powers to govern radio and telecommunications – but the list of assigned powers can still be out-of-step with contemporary needs. Consider that the regulation of post-secondary education is assigned to the provinces, largely on the basis that all education is a local matter, despite the fact that universities and colleges might draw from outside the province and produce graduates that are highly mobile. In that case, provinces might have less incentive than the

**BOX 3.2. FEDERAL AND PROVINCIAL JURISDICTION**

Section 91 of the *Constitution Act, 1867* grants the federal Parliament the exclusive authority to legislate in the following subject areas (selected provisions):

- The regulation of trade and commerce (s. 91[2]) and the raising of money by any mode or system of taxation (s. 91[3])
- The postal service (s. 91[5])
- Militia, military and naval service, and defence (s. 91[7])
- Banking, incorporation of banks, and the issue of paper money (s. 91[15]), bankruptcy and insolvency (s. 91[21]), and currency and coinage (s. 91[14])
- Patents of invention and discovery (s. 91[22]) and copyrights (s. 91[23]).
- Indians, and lands reserved for the Indians (s. 91[24])
- Criminal law (s. 91[27])

In addition, the preamble for section 91 allows for the federal Parliament to make laws for the "peace, order, and good government of Canada" in relation to all matters not specifically assigned to the provinces.

Section 92 allows provincial legislatures the exclusive ability to make laws in relations to the following subjects (selected provisions):

- Municipal institutions in the province (s. 92[8])
- Property and civil rights in the province (s. 92[13])
- Shop, saloon, tavern, auctioneer, and other licences in order to the raising of a revenue for provincial, local, or municipal purposes (s. 92[9])
- The establishment, maintenance, and management of hospitals (s. 92[7])

In addition, section 91(16) assigns exclusive legislative authority to the province for "generally all Matters of a merely local or private Nature in the Province."

national government to invest in these institutions, and provincial decisions might not be in the best interests of Canada's post-secondary market as a whole.

Are Canadians stuck with the assignment of powers thought best in 1867? No; there is always the possibility of constitutional amendment (as discussed above), and such amendments to the division of power have occurred. A notable example is the addition of "Unemployment Insurance" as a matter of federal power in 1940, added in the wake of the dire economic circumstances created by the Great Depression. That amendment is instructive in that it occurred when one level of government – the provinces – was unable to meet the needs of citizens and were largely willing to cede responsibility to the federal government. In most cases and during ordinary times, both levels of government guard their power and jurisdiction jealously, which proves to be an enduring obstacle to any otherwise sensible changes to the division of powers. Given the unlikeliness of formal constitutional amendments, the more likely avenue to address broad problems with the division of federal powers is through judicial interpretation. The federal government's power to legislate for the "peace, order, and good government" of Canada was recently found by the Supreme Court of Canada to allow for a "carbon tax" to combat climate change (see Box 3.3). Such legal contestation is likely an inevitable

---

**BOX 3.3. THE CANADIAN CONSTITUTION, FEDERALISM, AND CLIMATE CHANGE**

On March 25, 2021, the Supreme Court of Canada announced their decision in *Reference Re Greenhouse Gas Pollution Pricing Act*. The Court was hearing a "reference" case, which means answering an abstract legal question put forward by the government (in this instance, several provincial governments). The Court was asked to rule on the constitutionality of the federal government's 2018 *Greenhouse Gas Pollution Pricing Act*, which set a minimum standard for carbon taxes across the country (the Court of Appeal of Alberta had found the act unconstitutional, but the Courts of Appeal for Saskatchewan and Ontario upheld the act; all of those decisions were appealed to the Supreme Court of Canada). Setting taxes for industries contained within a single province would normally fall to the provincial government, but the Court ruled that the federal Parliament has the jurisdiction to do so under the "well-established but rarely applied doctrine" of "national concern." In addition to the list of enumerate powers in section 91 of the *Constitution Act, 1867*, the preamble to the section grants legislative power to the federal Parliament to "make laws for the peace, order, and good government of Canada." Needless to say, if this provision were broadly construed, it could undermine the federal division of powers and centralize almost all policy-making at the national level. Given this concern, the majority decision was clear that the "strictly limited" doctrine supporting the legislation was warranted here because of the dramatic, nationwide (indeed, international) effects of climate change and the acknowledgement that any solution "requires collective national and international action" and "no one province, territory or country can address the issue ... on its own" (para. 12). By invoking the "Peace, Order, and Good Government" (referred to as POGG) clause, the Court was able to provide an answer to a division of power question – Who has the power to address climate change? – that could not have been contemplated by the framers in 1867 and is thus not obviously within the listed powers in sections 91 and 92.

element of any federation, but it takes on a heightened importance in Canada given the impracticality of constitutional amendment.

Given the difficulty in amending the constitution, Canadians have often looked to the courts to "effectively" change what is meant by the text. The federal Parliament, for example, was granted sweeping powers over "Trade and Commerce" (s. 91[2]), something that might justify broad interventions in all economic matters. Recognizing that such national powers would not fit Canada's more decentralized economy, first the Judicial Committee of the Privy Council, and later the Supreme Court of Canada, greatly limited the trade and commerce power – to the extent that, by 2011, the federal Parliament couldn't even use it to mandate nationwide rules regarding stocks and bonds. On the other hand, the provincial power over "property and civil rights" (s. 92[13]) was given an expansive interpretation that effectively made the provinces key players in virtually any economic matter. Interestingly, the opposite effect occurred in the United States: The national government there was originally bestowed with only limited power over "interstate commerce," but judicial expansion of this power has led to federal interventions in virtually all parts of the economy (and beyond). The lesson learned from both countries is that the constitutional text is only the starting point and its subsequent interpretation (see "The Politics of Constitutional Interpretation," below) must be accounted for.

## CANADIAN CHARTER OF RIGHTS AND FREEDOMS

The *Canadian Charter of Rights and Freedoms* was added to our constitution in 1982 to provide explicit constitutional rights protection. It says something about the Canadian *Charter* that it begins and ends not with the rights themselves but with express limitations placed upon rights. These bracketing provisions, in sections 1 and 33, serve explicit notice that rights in Canada are not absolute and that they are subject to limitations lawfully enacted by Parliament. The very first section of the *Charter* explains that the rights described are "guarantee[d]" and "subject only to such reasonable limits prescribed by law as can be demonstrably justified in a free and democratic society." As an *entrenched* statement of rights, this provision tells us exactly how certain those rights are in a number of significant ways. The "only ... by law" is significant, since it tells us that other means of curtailing rights – say, by the whim of a politician – are expressly prohibited. But rights can be "reasonably limited" by laws if they can be shown to be justified for some public purpose. The standard for this justification must be compatible with the express understanding that Canada is free and democratic. If a law infringes a right and falls short of that standard, it is, by virtue of section 52, "of no force or effect."

Accordingly, rights-claims undergo a two-stage process in Canada. First, you – the challenger – must establish that the law does infringe one of the specific rights in the *Charter*. Once that threshold has been met to the court's satisfaction, the government has the burden of demonstrating that its law is a reasonable limit on the right, effectively justifying the infringement. To make this determination, the Supreme Court introduced a test in a case called *R v Oakes*, something that is now routinely referred to as the *Oakes* test. Under this test, the government must prove its law is aimed at a "pressing and substantial" objective and that the means the law uses are proportional to that objective. In other words, is the law doing something important enough that it warrants the interference with the rights of citizens, and does the law do so in a way that balances the benefit of the law with the cost to the right? Since the legislative process itself requires some rationale to enact a law, it is relatively easy for the government to establish some "pressing and substantial" objective. That said, there is also considerable scope for the judiciary to shape the understanding of a law's purposes, an interpretive task for which the Supreme Court has provided some guidance (see the Court's discussion of legislative purpose in the context of section 7 "overbreadth" in *R v Safarzadeh-Markhali*, 2016, paras. 24–36). The challenge for the government more often comes in proving that their law is proportional to that objective. Here the *Oakes* test considers three important questions: (1) Are the means used by the law "rationally connected" to the objective (in other words, does the law plausibly achieve what the government says it does)? (2) Do the means "minimally impair" the right? and (3) Is there a general proportionality between the means and the objective?

In practice, virtually all of the action in the *Oakes* test occurs over the second question of "minimal impairment." This part of the test invites judges to imagine a different law that would still achieve the government's objective but would interfere with the right less. If a less-rights-infringing law can be identified, then the existing law is likely to be an unreasonable limit and therefore unconstitutional. It is worth asking whether judges are truly capable of engaging in this exercise of imagining legislative alternatives? Can they, in the context of a single case, have a command of all the factors that might be at play in the creation of a law? Able counsel will help judges with these multifaceted decisions, but they too may have incentives and interests that differ from the general public opinion that informs the legislature. This part of the test may amount to judges "second-guessing" the legislature, but it is also an opportunity for "second thoughts" about legislation that may have been passed rashly or without due regard for how it might impact the rights of citizens.

Section 33 of the *Charter* creates an "override clause" that permits legislators to declare that statutes operate "notwithstanding" certain *Charter* rights. This clause applies to the "fundamental freedoms" in section 2 of the *Charter*, the legal process rights in sections 7–14, and the section 15 equality clause. Such declarations last for five years (the maximum length of any Parliament, effectively ensuring that an election will occur at some point during the "notwithstanding" period) and may be renewed by the legislature at five-year intervals. While some politicians and scholars have suggested that the notwithstanding clause made *Charter* rights "not worth the paper it's written on," the clause has been used only infrequently since 1982. For the most part, governments have been cautious about being seen to be "anti-rights," such that even when a particular issue may have invited the use of the clause, the political risks of being seen to undermine the *Charter* itself have been a deterrent. The political calculation can, in some cases, favour its use: The Quebec government of the 1980s, fuelled by the *Constitution Act, 1982* being enacted without its consent, invoked a blanket use of the notwithstanding clause over all of its legislation. Similarly, recent controversies in Saskatchewan and Ontario have resulted in the usage of the clause to reverse the effect of judicial decisions contrary to the aims of provincial governments (see Box 3.4; see also Lawlor & Crandall, 2023; Sigalet, 2023; Snow, 2023).

---

**BOX 3.4. THE NOTWITHSTANDING CLAUSE AND CAMPAIGN FINANCE**

Ontario premier Doug Ford's usage of the notwithstanding clause to defend his campaign financing law in 2021 brought together a number of threads of Canadian constitutionalism: freedom of speech, electoral participation, the operation of the *Oakes* test, the role of social science evidence in judicial proceedings, and, of course, the legitimacy of the notwithstanding clause itself. Vexed by interventions in the previous election by "Working Families Ontario" (an umbrella organization of labour unions), Ford sought to further restrict Ontario's election financing rules as they apply to "third parties" (i.e., individuals and organizations with an interest in the election but not candidates or political parties themselves).

Legal limits on the spending of third parties in elections had been held as constitutional in the 2004 Supreme Court case of *Harper v Canada (Attorney General)*. Despite the clear infringement of free speech, the Supreme Court upheld limits on advertising expenditures in order to better ensure electoral fairness.

So, what was the problem with Ford's new law? The existing Ontario law applied only to the six months before the election and the Ford Government amended it to be in effect for an entire year preceding an election. This longer restriction was found by the Ontario Superior Court to be unconstitutional.

The Court relied on evidence, given by former chief election officer Jean-Pierre Kingsley and political scientist Harold Jansen, that both the original six-months and the amended one-year laws were "reasonable" means to ensure electoral fairness. Factored into the *Oakes* test, this social science evidence then led to an easy legal conclusion: The "minimal impairment" of a right would suggest that a shorter time of infringement should be preferred to a longer period. But this illustrates the problem of using that part of the *Oakes* test in the context of ambiguous social science evidence. No one, with any scientific exactitude, can determine the benefit in terms of electoral fairness for each day the limitation applies. Would we be better with a five-month limit? That too might achieve the end of electoral fairness but would impugn the original six-month Ontario law. There might be an expert consensus that *no* period of restraint would imperil election fairness and five years of application (an entire election cycle) would be overkill, but what about everything in between? That's where we are likely to see room for reasonable disagreement. In that context, the use of the "minimal impairment" test effectively substitutes the Court's determination for what is reasonable for that of the government. Whose assessment should prevail?

The Ontario Government responded to the invalidation of their law by quickly passing a new law, the *Protecting Elections and Defending Democracy Act, 2021*, which declared that it was to operate notwithstanding the *Charter*. While controversial, the exercise of section 33 might not be seen as "against constitutional rights," but rather a reassertion of legislative reasonableness over the judicial appraisal. This is a power explicitly assigned in the *Charter* itself and, as Sigalet and Woodfinden (2021) write, "reflects a [Canadian] political culture and history that has sought to correct the democratic dangers of having reasonable disagreements about rights settled exclusively in the courts."

Nevertheless, there is reason to be concerned with the exercise of the notwithstanding clause in this instance. Every citizen should be concerned with governments bending election laws to their own advantage. Just because the *Charter* invalidation was effectively reversed does not mean that there is no remedy for those who continue to see the limits as a rights violation. It is just that the remedy is political – at the ballot box – instead of flowing from a judge's pen. Nor does the invocation of the notwithstanding clause necessarily mean the end of constitutional litigation: While the freedom of expression challenge was overcome, the same litigants then challenged the new law successfully as a violation of the right to vote in section 3 of the *Charter* – one of the provisions that is outside the scope of the notwithstanding clause (*Ontario (Attorney General) v Working Families Coalition*, 2025).

## CONSTITUTIONAL EQUALITY

All of the above frames *Charter* claims as against the government and its legislation. You may be thinking of rights infringements that don't actually involve the government: What if your employer is treating you differently because you are a woman or a racialized person? What if the local restaurant won't install a ramp to allow wheelchair access? Aren't these rights violations too? You might be surprised to know that the *Charter* does not *directly* deal with these sorts of claims. Section 32 of the *Charter* restricts its application to government action only (see Bateman, 1998). When private (non-government) actors discriminate on prohibited grounds, they run afoul of statutory human rights codes. Such codes are found in every Canadian jurisdiction, but they vary in their wording and details. But aren't those codes themselves considered government action? That's how the constitutional right to equality – section 15 of the *Charter* – *indirectly* affects those sorts of cases.

Section 15(1) declares that "every individual is equal before and under the law and has the right to equal protection and equal benefit of the law without discrimination and, in particular, without discrimination based on race, national or ethnic origin, colour, religion, sex, age or mental or physical disability." The opening phrasing of section 15 is intentionally broad, attempting to give little room for any government discrimination related to law, even though section 15 itself remains subject to the "reasonable limits" of section 1. The *Charter* framers knew that section 15 could potentially undermine every law that drew some sort of eligibility line, so they also delayed the implementation of section 15 until 1985, three years after the rest of the *Charter* went into force. Moreover, section 15(2) sidesteps all of the American controversies over "affirmative action" programs that provide benefits to historically disadvantaged groups in an attempt to "level the playing field"; some Americans see such programs as infringing formal equality, but section 15(2) makes it clear that any "law, program or activity" that betters the conditions of disadvantaged individuals or group does not run afoul of section 15's guarantee of equality.

The 1998 case of *Vriend v Alberta* demonstrates the interaction of the constitutional guarantee of equality and provincial statutory schemes against discrimination. The Alberta *Individual's Rights Protection Act* (IRPA) prohibited discrimination on a number of grounds, including race, gender, and religion, but it did not include "sexual orientation" as a prohibited ground. This was no accident: The legislative record "makes it clear," the Supreme Court recognized, "that the omission of sexual orientation was deliberate and not the result of an oversight" (para. 4). When Delwin Vriend, a laboratory technician, was fired by King's College, a Christian university, for "non-compliance with the policy of the College on homosexual practice," he had no recourse to the complaint mechanism in the IRPA that would have been there if he had been fired on the discriminatory grounds explicitly identified in the legislation.

The *Vriend* Court distinguished between "private activity" and "laws that regulate private activity," ruling that "the former is not subject to the *Charter*, while the latter obviously is" (para. 66). In one sense, this is entirely unobjectionable: The IRPA is a statute, so it is hard to see that it is anything other than government action. On the other hand, when applied to sweeping human rights legislation like the IRPA, such an approach effectively undermines the limitation on the *Charter*'s scope as articulated in section 32. To some extent, this is simply a function of the increasingly broad scope of human activity that is touched by one statute or another. Even if the benefits of such expansive regulation warrant increasing impositions, the correlative loss of liberty should at least be recognized and, in some instances, might be regretted.

Once the IRPA is subject to the *Charter*, Vriend's case turns on the question of whether section 15 protects Canadians from discrimination on the grounds of "sexual orientation." Three years earlier in the *Egan v Canada* case, the Supreme Court upheld discrimination in the denial of Canadian Pension Plan survivor's benefits to a gay man but, in the course of their reasons, held that sexual orientation was a ground "analogous" to the protected grounds covered explicitly by the guarantee. The listed grounds of section 15 are "in particular," which leads logically to the conclusion that there are other prohibited grounds and, as a "deeply personal characteristic that is either unchangeable or changeable only at unacceptable personal costs," sexual orientation was found to be sufficiently similar to race, religion, sex, and the other listed grounds. "By its omission or underinclusiveness," the Court ruled, the IRPA "denies gays and lesbians the equal benefit and protection of the law on the basis of a personal characteristic, namely sexual orientation" (para. 88).

Delwin Vriend won his case: The words "sexual orientation" were read into Alberta's human rights code and discrimination on that ground would be prohibited just as it would be on the other listed grounds. In this fashion, the constitutional guarantee of equality modified the statutory protection and, in turn, checked private discrimination. Despite this jurisprudential victory, Vriend wasn't reinstated in his old job, nor did he receive a monetary award for a wrongful dismissal. The case only decided whether or not the Alberta Commission had to investigate the claim – they had rejected it outright when he originally brought it – and the high court victory meant they would have to allow such claims in the future. Investigations of complaints exactly like Vriend's would have to deal with thorny issues of religious freedom and conscience, but the principles established by Vriend's case meant that in more clear-cut cases (say, a retail worker fired for being gay) the discrimination would not be tolerated (for other cases relating to s. 15, see Box 3.5).

In addition to its expanded "analogous grounds," section 15's multiple guarantees of equality ("equal *before* and *under* the law," the "right to equal *protection* and equal *benefit* of the law without discrimination") suggest a very broad ambit for Canada's equality provision. Ironically, this breadth has made it very difficult to apply it

> **BOX 3.5.  OTHER NOTABLE S. 15 CASES**
>
> *Andrews v Law Society of British Columbia* (1989): The requirement to be a Canadian citizen to practise law in British Columbia was successfully challenged under section 15 and the requirement was not saved under section 1. This case gave rise to the "Andrews Test," which was dominant in the early years of section 15 jurisprudence, but discrimination on the basis of citizenship has been upheld as a reasonable limit in other subsequent cases decided under new iterations of the section 15 equality test (*Lavoie v Canada,* 2002, found civil service preferences for Canadian citizens constitutional).
>
> *M. v H.* (1999): Discrimination between same-sex couples and opposite-sex common law couples for some family law purposes was found to be unconstitutional. This case was a milestone in the sequence of cases which would lead to the *Reference Re Same-Sex Marriage* and, ultimately, the legislative decision to allow for same-sex marriage in Canada.
>
> *Fraser v Canada (Attorney General)*(2020): An RCMP pension policy that disadvantaged employees who "job shared" (in lieu of part-time status, and primarily undertaken by women employees) was found to be unconstitutional under section 15. This most recent articulation of the section 15 test attempts to clarify "adverse impact discrimination," which may be found unconstitutional even when a policy seemingly respects formal equality and when the discrimination is a result of a "choice" made by the affected party.
>
> *R v Sharma* (2022): The Supreme Court clarifies the test for "adverse effect" discrimination under section 15 and, in this case, declines to find that the unavailability of a conditional sentence for an Indigenous offender was unconstitutional.

consistently, since there is seldom widespread agreement on the Court, much less among Canadians generally, about the limits of formal and substantive equality, how much emphasis should be put on the intentions of the lawmakers versus the effect of the law, and whether "equal opportunity" or "equal outcomes" should prevail. A further wrinkle is the Court's use of "human dignity" as part of its section 15 jurisprudence, a concept that is rhetorically useful but highly subjective (Bateman, 2012). A testament to section 15's complexity is the now-regular restatement by the Supreme Court of Canada of its equality jurisprudence: In the 35 years the *Charter*'s equality provision has been in force, the Court has articulated four different tests for constitutional equality (see Watson Hamilton, 2021, pp. 3–4, for a review of these tests). That averages out to a substantially new test every nine years. The jurisprudence notoriously focuses on "context" as the most crucial element, which is understandable given the complexity of most claims, but it means also that the general principles are difficult to discern, leaving lower courts with little guidance on how to resolve cases before them. The convoluted section 15 jurisprudence has led, in recent years, to most of the "blockbuster" constitutional cases, which could have been decided as a matter of either equality (in s. 15) or liberty (in s. 7), being decided using the latter provision, to which we now turn.

## CONSTITUTIONAL DUE PROCESS

As mentioned in Chapter 1, the natural justice requirement on fairness and process finds its modern Canadian incarnation in section 7 of the *Charter*. Section 7 has two parts: The first guarantees everyone the right to "life, liberty and security of the person" but then a second part allows anyone to be deprived of that right as long as the deprivation is done "in accordance with the principles of fundamental justice." The first part implicates a significant amount of government activity since many laws can be construed as restricting *someone's* liberty in *some* sense. The second part provides a massive caveat to counterbalance the broad first part: The state can "restrict liberty" as long as it does so in a proper fashion. It can do so, section 7 says, so long as the manner of the deprivation is consistent with the "principles of fundamental justice." As political scientist Matthew Hennigar (2022) notes, while section 7 is fertile grounds for a variety of *claims*, many of those attempts to challenge laws fail.

The format of section 7 puts a great deal of stress on what is meant by the "principles of fundamental justice." There is ample evidence that the drafters of the 1982 *Constitution Act* used the term as a simple proxy for "due process" (meaning "done by the correct procedures"). In other words, legislation restricting section 7 rights simply had to be passed and applied in a procedurally correct way. This meant that section 7 was not really intended to introduce any new "substantive" rights. It would not mean judges could evaluate the "wisdom" of a law or decide whether it was "good" or "bad" law, but rather task them with reviewing whether the government had followed proper procedure. This construction of section 7 would resemble the "natural justice" requirements discussed in Chapter 1. Clearer constitutional language like "due process" and "natural justice" was considered in 1982 but ultimately rejected because the usage of similar terms in the United States Constitution had, perversely, led to American courts finding substantive rights. The phrase "principles of fundamental justice" was considered an adequate substitute because it had previously been used in this procedural/natural justice sense in Canada's 1960 statutory *Bill of Rights* and in existing case law.

In the key early section 7 case, *Re B.C. Motor Vehicle Act*, the Supreme Court of Canada decided that the "principles of fundamental justice" should be interpreted anew and that it incorporated substantial principles as well as procedural ones. The

Court has never provided an exhaustive list of those principles, but they include the right of young people to be less blameworthy ("diminished moral culpability"; *R v DB*, 2008), a right against any punishment that would "shock the conscience" of Canadians (*Schmidt*, 1987), and a requirement that criminal offences that lead to prison must have a *mens rea* element (*Re B.C. Motor Vehicle Act*, 1987); more serious criminal offences even require subjective *mens rea* (*Vaillancourt*, 1987). Some of the principles of fundamental justice even repeat other "legal rights" found in sections 8–14 but allow the Court to apply them more generally than their specifications in those sections allow. For example, while the right to counsel in section 10(b) only applies to those arrested or detained, the section 7 principle applies against imposing duties on counsel – like money-laundering reporting requirements – that may undermine a lawyer's commitment to their client's causes (*Canada (Attorney General) v Federation of Law Societies of Canada*, 2015, para. 84). In recent years, the Supreme Court has articulated principles of fundamental justice that relate to the drafting and ambit of laws. In cases like *Carter*, where the criminal prohibition against assisted suicide was invalidated, and *Bedford*, which decriminalized elements of the existing laws surrounding prostitution, the Court developed a jurisprudence that required laws to not be "arbitrary," "vague," "overbroad," or "grossly disproportionate" (see Box 3.6).

The distinction between process and substance has been notoriously hard to maintain in any event. The famous 1988 *Morgentaler* decision, which decriminalized abortion in Canada, is a good example of how the demands of procedural fairness can blend into substantive outcomes. The *Charter* was enacted in 1982 while the political fight over abortion in the United States was at a fever pitch, in the wake of their *Roe v Wade* decision in 1973. With pressure to include a "right to an abortion" and a "right to fetal life" coming from opposite sides, the drafters chose to simply leave the *Charter* silent on the issue. At the time of the case, Canada's abortion law had been liberalized to permit abortions but only in cases where a therapeutic abortion committee (TAC) at an accredited hospital approved of the procedure. The TAC was a considerable burden for women seeking an abortion: A committee of four doctors would have to agree that an "exception" to the criminal prohibition was necessary when the continuation of the pregnancy "would or would be likely to endanger her life or health." Any abortion outside of this procedure was prohibited by criminal law, placing both the doctor who performed it and the patient in legal jeopardy.

The *Morgentaler* Court split into four factions: an opinion by Chief Justice Dickson (joined by Justice Lamer), an opinion by Justice Beetz (joined by Justice Estey), an opinion by Justice McIntyre (joined by Justice La Forest), and an opinion by Justice Wilson. The seven justices broke down 2-2-2-1, with only Justice McIntyre's dissent upholding the existing criminal law provision. The other five justices in the plurality – the opinions that would settle the case in favour of invalidating the criminal regulation of abortion – could

**BOX 3.6.  OTHER NOTABLE S. 7 CASES**

*Singh v Minister of Employment and Immigration* (1985): An early application of section 7 that ensured refugee claimants would get an oral hearing, instead of a mere written application. This is a good example of a core procedural right of fairness (akin to the "natural law" approach described in Chapter 1) being incorporated into a constitutional right.

*Re B.C. Motor Vehicle Act* (1985): A key early Supreme Court case interpreting the meaning of "principles of fundamental justice" and allowing for substantive – not merely procedural – rights under section 7. In the case itself, B.C.'s mandatory prison sentence for driving without a licence was deemed unconstitutional because it allowed for imprisonment even in situations where someone might not have known their licence had lapsed and was unable to find this out despite their due diligence to do so.

*Canada (Attorney General) v Bedford* (2013): A successful challenge to the then-current criminal laws surrounding the practice of prostitution. The act of prostitution was not itself criminal, but communication and "living off the avails" were making sex work an unsafe activity and jeopardizing the right to life and security of person guaranteed by section 7. The Harper government responded to the *Bedford* ruling by criminalizing – for the first time in Canada – the "commodification of sex" and making the purchasers of sex work the focus of the criminality (and shielding sex workers themselves from prosecution).

*Carter v Canada (Attorney General)* (2015): Reconsidering its earlier decision in *Rodriguez v British Columbia (Attorney General)* (1993), the Supreme Court found the *Criminal Code* offence of aiding someone to commit suicide to be an unconstitutional violation of section 7. The *Charter*'s "right to life" did not mean a "duty to live" even though section 7 is "rooted in a profound respect for the value of human life" (para. 63). The criminal provisions interfered with medical decisions and bodily integrity, especially when such interference might cause someone to endure intolerable suffering, so the liberty and security-of-person elements of the section were engaged. The criminal provisions could not be saved under section 1 because it was a blanket prohibition on all medical assistance in dying (MAID). The Trudeau government continues to struggle with balancing the constitutional right to MAID with the protection of populations who might be vulnerable to its abuse.

not agree upon how the constitution applied to the law. Only Justice Wilson, the sole woman on the Court at the time, found a substantive right in section 7 that included the right to personal autonomy and conscience underlying a right to not "be compelled by law to carry the foetus to term" (p. 161). The other justices found procedural problems with the existing law that warranted invalidation, such as the vagueness of what "health" meant, or the prohibition of some doctors from serving on TACs. For a majority of the Court, it was not the regulation of abortion itself that was unconstitutional, but rather the improper procedure for accessing it. That meant, of course, that the government could respond to the decision with procedurally improved legislation that might pass constitutional muster. In fact, the Mulroney government tried twice to enact such legislation but was defeated by a coalition of pro-life and pro-choice forces that found the regulation either too permissive or too restrictive (Morton & Knopff, 2000, p. 163; for more fallout from the abortion decision, see Johnstone, 2017). In any event, we cannot be sure that the Court's procedural approach in *Morgentaler* was anything other than a mask for a substantial right; Justice Lamer later justified his decision in *Morgentaler* in terms of popular opinion, saying that he "should not impose upon others my personal beliefs" and "you should not make a crime out of something that does not have the large support of the community.... Who am I to tell 50 percent of the population that they are criminals?" (Morton & Knopff, 2000, p. 51). We will never know whether the Court would have accepted or rejected revised abortion regulation, but the entire saga suggests a very fine line between procedural rights and substantive ones. The Court's more recent return to more procedurally focused approaches that emphasize "vagueness" and "arbitrariness" are likely to continue generating substantive results. For this reason, section 7 cases are likely to remain the most fertile ground for legal-political contestation and controversy.

## FREEDOM OF EXPRESSION

Freedom of expression is crucial for our own human fulfillment and our never-ending search for the truth in all matters. Nothing is perhaps more human than wanting to express your own ideas, positions, opinions, and views. Legal protection for expression is often understood to be the foundation for all other liberal democratic rights for the simple reason that the ability to express dissent and to rally others to your cause is essential for democracy to function. It is the key to keeping governments accountable: Being able to criticize the government without repercussion allows other citizens to accurately assess and evaluate the government's performance. Moreover, without freedom of expression, it is possible we would not even know when other rights infringements are occurring. The primary protection of all your rights and interests is often dependent on your ability to make others aware of infringements. This explains why many see the freedom of expression as the first and most important of our civil liberties.

Canadian protection of free speech existed well before the enactment of the *Charter*. Parliament itself is a protected venue for expression, both in terms of parliamentary privilege (to the extent that members of parliament can even make defamatory comments in the House that would subject the other Canadians to civil penalties) and by the very existence of a parliamentary opposition that provides a contrary account of the government's positions. In terms of protections for individuals, the common law has long been protective of some degree of free speech, even while other common law doctrines restrain Canadians from expressing themselves (to prevent the spread of malicious falsehoods, for example). Prior to the enactment of the *Charter*, this balancing was achieved primarily through statute.

Section 2 of the *Charter* recognizes that "everyone has the following fundamental freedoms: (a) freedom of conscience and religion; (b) freedom of thought, belief, opinion and expression, including freedom of the press and other media of communication; (c) freedom of peaceful assembly; and (d) freedom of association." These "fundamental freedoms" are intertwined and together protect individual thoughts and beliefs, so that they may not only be held but also transmitted to others in society, potentially forming a path from those beliefs to peaceful political action. The use of "free expression," rather than "free speech," in section 2(b) sidesteps a number of controversies in the American jurisprudence about what counts as "speech." For example, in *Tinker v Des Moines School District* (1969), the US Supreme Court ruled that high-school students wearing black arm bands in protest of the Vietnam War constituted "symbolic speech" that is "akin to pure speech"; in Canada, there would be no question that such activity constituted protected expression. The Canadian Court has subsequently interpreted "expression" so broadly that the only substantial limit is that "violence" must be excluded, no matter how "expressive" that violence might be.

This broad protection for expression does not lead to an absolute right to free speech in Canada, however. Once again, the "reasonable limits" clause in section 1 allows governments to curtail even this "fundamental freedom" so long as it does so in a fashion that is "demonstrably justified in a free and democratic society." Fortunately, the "free and democratic society" invoked in that formulation is obviously one that cherishes and respects free expression, so the barrier for governmental limits to hurdle is substantial, even if it might not be as high as some would prefer. Pornography is protected expression, but "undue exploitation of sex" can be prohibited if it is "degrading or dehumanizing" (*Butler*, 1992). Hate speech is also protected expression, but the "wilful promotion of hatred" can be criminalized (*Keegstra*, 1990; see Box 3.7) and "hate-inspiring expression that adds little value to political discourse or to the quest for truth, self-fulfillment, and an embracing marketplace of ideas" can be prohibited by human rights codes (*Whatcott*,

**BOX 3.7. NOTABLE S. 2(B) CASES**

*Irwin Toy Ltd. v Quebec (Attorney General)* (1989): Quebec's restrictions on television advertisements aimed at children were found to be a violation of section 2(b) but justified as a reasonable limit under section 1. This early *Charter* decision articulated the Court's approach to the purposes of free expression, and adopted the wide, inclusive interpretation of expression to include almost anything other than violence.

*R v Keegstra* (1990): The *Criminal Code* provisions against "willfully promoting hatred against an identifiable group" (commonly known as "hate speech") were found to infringe section 2(b) but justified as a reasonable limit under section 1. Before she was Chief Justice, then-Justice McLachlin wrote a vigorous dissent stating that "if the guarantee of free expression is to be meaningful, it must protect expression which challenges even the very basic conceptions about our society" and "any questionable benefit of the legislation is outweighed by the significant infringement on the constitutional guarantee of free expression." In *Canada (Human Rights Commission) v Taylor* (1990) and *Saskatchewan ( Human Rights Commission) v Whatcott* (2013), the Supreme Court has repeatedly upheld human rights restrictions on expression in order to protect vulnerable groups.

*R v National Post* (2010) and *Globe and Mail v Canada (Attorney General* (2010) both protect journalistic sources, from criminal proceedings in the former and civil cases in the latter. Importantly, both decisions demonstrate that the right to free expression and the right to a free press complement each other and that confidential sources are essential to democratic governance by enhancing accountability.

2013, para. 171). With the broad ambit given to section 2(b)'s application, most free speech controversies are decided under section 1, and thus under the Court's *Oakes* test as described above. Generally, cases turn on the government's objective and on whether the limit they are proposing minimally impairs the right to free expression.

The Supreme Court of Canada has repeatedly claimed that political speech "lies at the core of the guarantee of free expression" (*Harper*, 2004, para. 11; *Thomson Newspapers*, 1998, para. 92) or at the "heart of freedom of expression" (*Guignard*, 2002, para. 20). But even supposedly core political speech is vulnerable to a "reasonable limit" under section 1. In the 2007 case of *R v Bryan*, the Court considered the constitutionality of a section of the *Canada Elections Act* that prohibited the reporting of election results from one part of the country to another on election night (a possibility created by Canada's multiple time zones). On the one hand, this seems a relatively innocuous restraint made necessary by the expansive Canadian geography. On the other hand, fining Canadians up to $25,000 for simply posting on the Internet the results of an election seems contrary to the most basic understanding of our civil liberties. When BC blogger Paul Bryan purposely violated the *Elections Act*, his case split the Supreme Court. A majority of the Court upheld the provision on the grounds that "informational equality is a fundamental principle of electoral democracy" (para. 35), noting that Canadians "feel very strongly about premature release of election results" (para. 36). In dissent, Justice Abella argued that "it is difficult to imagine a more important aspect of democratic expression than learning the results of their vote" and that the ban "impairs the right both to disseminate and receive election results at a crucial time in the electoral process" (paras. 128–9). Abella took further issue with the majority's assumption that this was just a minor, temporary infringement: "To suggest that this is only a delay, not the suppression of information, unduly minimizes the significance both of the information and of the delay.… News is news precisely because of its immediacy, especially during an election, where a great deal of information and analysis must be passed on to the public in a short period of time" (paras. 128–9). Once again, the protection of a right was to be balanced with government aims. The majority thought the law struck the right balance, but Abella was unconvinced and noted the actual restraint on speech to achieve only a relatively abstract objective of shielding West Coast voters from information that might sway their vote: "Any evidence of harm to the public's perception or conduct in knowing the election results from Atlantic Canada before they vote is speculative, inconclusive and largely unsubstantiated.… The harm of suppressing core political speech, on the other hand, is profound" (para. 107). The majority of the Court was unwilling to strike the section down, but the section was repealed in 2014, largely because it was difficult to enforce. The Court's permissive approach to curtailing political expression should convince Canadians to continue jealously guarding their expression rights and to be wary of any future encroachments by any governing institution (for more on the effects of the *Charter* on election laws, see Small, 2022).

## INDIGENOUS RIGHTS

For the most part, the *Charter of Rights* was not intended to impact the rights and freedoms of the Indigenous Peoples in Canada. Section 25 specifically notes that the *Charter* should not be construed "as to abrogate or derogate from any aboriginal, treaty or other rights or freedoms that pertain to the aboriginal peoples of Canada." While not technically part of the *Charter* portion of the *Constitution Act, 1982*, section 35 is arguably more important because it crucially affirms and recognizes the "existing aboriginal and treaty rights of the aboriginal people of Canada" (and specifically notes that "treaty rights" includes those that "now exist by way of land claims agreements or may be so acquired"). Section 35(2) defines the "aboriginal peoples of Canada" to include "the Indian, Inuit and Métis peoples of Canada." Sociologist Jeremy Patzer and political scientist Kiera Ladner (2022) argue that "neither the Courts nor Canadian government have heeded the transformative and decolonizing constitutional visions of Indigenous peoples … [and] instead they have insisted on maintaining the status quo" (p. 349). The Supreme Court first interpreted section 35 in the *Sparrow* case (1990) in the context of a Musqueam food fishing licence offence. The Court ruled that, while section 35 could not revive an Aboriginal right that had been extinguished prior to 1982, the phrase "existing aboriginal rights" must "be interpreted flexibly so as to permit their evolution over time." Moreover, it ruled that section 35 incorporates a **fiduciary relationship** between the Crown and the Indigenous Peoples. A fiduciary duty means that one has the legal responsibility to act in the best interest of the other party, so, in this case, the Canadian Crown is legally obligated to put the best interests of Indigenous Peoples ahead of any other interest it might hold or advantage it sought to advance. As the jurisprudence has evolved, the fiduciary relationship has provided the rationale for a legal "duty to consult," since deciding what is in the best interests of Indigenous Peoples without consulting them could be fraught with colonial assumptions (and even the consultative right "may already be perceived as an inadequate framework for upholding enduring engagement with Indigenous groups to protect Aboriginal rights"; Do, 2022, p. 384).

In the 2024 decision of *Dickson v Vuntut Gwitchin First Nation*, the Supreme Court struggled to reconcile its commitment to Indigenous self-government while upholding the *Canadian Charter of Rights and Freedoms*. The Vuntut Gwitchin First Nation (VGFN) is a self-governing community in the Yukon established by a lands claim agreement that was approved and given effect in federal and territorial legislation. The VGFN Constitution requires that Chiefs and Councillors reside on the settlement land, leading a Canadian citizen and citizen of the VGFN residing in Whitehorse to challenge this requirement as a violation of her section 15 *Charter* right to equality. The VGFN argued that the *Charter* did not apply to it because they are a self-governing First Nation. A majority of the Supreme Court found that the *Charter* did apply (and the VGFN is considered a "government" under section 32 of the *Charter*) but that the residency requirement, even if construed to violate section 15, was protected by section 25 since to do otherwise would mean that section 15 would abrogate or derogate from the VGFN's "right to govern themselves in accordance with their own particular values and traditions *and* in accordance with the 'self-government' arrangements entered into in 1993 with Canada and the Yukon" (para. 224). Justice Martin and Justice O'Bonsawin (the only Indigenous member of the Court) would have gone further, applied the *Charter*, and found the residency requirement of no force or effect. In a notable dissent, Justice Rowe argued

> **BOX 3.8. OTHER NOTABLE S. 35 CASES**
>
> *R v Marshall* (1999a) and *R v Marshall* (1999b): Donald Marshall, a Mi'kmaq member of the Membertou First Nation, was charged for eel fishing without a licence during the off-season. The Court ruled that Marshall had a treaty right to secure a "moderate livelihood" through fishing and dismissed the charge. The decision sparked uproar among non-Indigenous fishers and prompted a rare clarification from the Court, which reaffirmed that treaty rights could be subject to regulation if they can be justified on "conservation or other grounds of public importance."
>
> *Tsilhqot'in Nation v British Columbia* (2014): An important case clarifying some aspects of Aboriginal title and the connection with section 35. The Court found that when Aboriginal title was established, government action that intrudes upon it must be for a "compelling and substantial public purpose" and must be "consistent with the Crown's fiduciary duty to the Aboriginal group" (para. 2). For more discussion of land claims, see Chapter 8.
>
> *R v Desaultel* (2021): An American citizen, but member of the Lake Tribe of the Colville Confederated Tribes based in the State of Washington, was charged with shooting a cow-elk without a hunting licence in British Columbia. The Court found that the reference to "aboriginal peoples of Canada" in section 35 is to be interpreted purposively and can include "modern-day successors of Aboriginal societies that occupied Canadian territory at the time of European contact" even if those "members are neither citizens nor residents of Canada" (para. 23).

that the *Charter* should not apply, holding that "ultimately, this case is about whether, in crafting their own Constitution, the Vuntut Gwtichin can make their own choices about their affairs – including as to how they wish to protect fundamental rights and freedoms – or whether their choices are subject to judicial scrutiny under the *Charter*." The *Dickson* case challenges us to consider what is really meant by "self-government" and how it fits within our constitutional framework. With such sharp divisions on the Court, one can expect future decisions to further explore this difficult legal terrain (for other cases relating to section 35, see Box 3.8).

## THE POLITICS OF CONSTITUTIONAL INTERPRETATION

A recurrent theme in Canadian constitutionalism is the question of which institution has the "final say" over what the constitution means. The constitutional text does not settle this question definitively. Most assume that the Supreme Court holds this power, but that collapses Canada's constitutional supremacy into pure judicial supremacy. In a 1717 sermon before King George I, Bishop Benjamin Hoadly warned that "whoever has an absolute Authority to interpret any written or spoken laws; it is He, who is truly the Law-giver, to all Intents and Purposes; and not the Person who first wrote them or spoke them" (Baker, 2010, p. 91). If the Supreme Court has no limits on its supposed interpretive power, how can we be sure it is interpreting the text at all and not just substituting its preferences and views? Future US Chief Justice Charles Evan Hughes summed up this concern by declaring that "we live under a Constitution, but the Constitution is what the judges say it is" (Baker, 2010, p. 3; Huscroft, 2004, details the uses and misuses of this quotation by Canadian authorities at pp. 249–50).

In reality, constitutional interpretation in Canada is much more complex than that (Harding, 2021; Hiebert, 2002). Parliament can participate in the development of constitutional jurisprudence by offering "reasonable limits" as contemplated by section 1, by invoking the "notwithstanding clause," and sometimes even by using ordinary legislation to make the Court rethink its decisions. The relationship between the Court and Parliament has sometimes been conceived of as a "dialogue" – that is a clear overstatement, with the Court's decisions usually accepted as final by most political actors, but it recognizes that, when the politics merit it, constitutional interpretation is not a one-institution game. Since the Court itself can only hear a small number of constitutional controversies every year, Canadians should encourage all of their representatives to take an interest in constitutional matters and hold them accountable for the constitutional decisions that are implicit in every enactment of legislation and exercise of executive authority. For the Constitution of Canada to be truly supreme, it requires our governing institutions to take their responsibilities seriously and, when necessary, challenge the Court's perception of our enduring constitutional principles.

## CONCLUSION

In many ways, the notion of a "constitution" seemingly allows us to short-circuit some of the more difficult questions raised in Chapter 1, "Sources of Law." A constitution can be understood as the "higher law" that hems in the government's power over positive law and commits its leaders and citizens to values that might otherwise have been the domain of natural law. Constitutions are attractive to liberal, democratic nations at least in part for this reason. As described in this chapter, however, the content of any such commitment can sometimes be difficult to ascertain because constitutions have unwritten elements, and their written elements are often phrased in very general and sometimes aspirational terms (see Table 3.1). Bringing a constitution to legal life, therefore, requires interpretation, and interpretation can always be contested. While we should not diminish

**Table 3.1. Selected Provisions of the *Canadian Charter of Rights and Freedoms***

| Section | Name | Text |
| --- | --- | --- |
| 1 | Reasonable Limits clause | "The *Canadian Charter of Rights and Freedoms* guarantees the rights and freedoms set out in it subject only to such reasonable limits prescribed by law as can be demonstrably justified in a free and democratic society." |
| 2(b) | Freedom of Expression | "Everyone has the … freedom of thought, belief, opinion and expression, including the freedom of the press and other media of communication." |
| 7 | Fundamental Justice clause | "Everyone has the right to life, liberty and security of person and the right not to be deprived thereof except in accordance with the principles of fundamental justice." |
| 15(1) | Equality clause | "Every individual is equal before and under the law and has the right to the equal protection and equal benefit of the law without discrimination and, in particular, without discrimination based on race, national or ethnic origin, colour, religion, sex, age or mental or physical disability" |
| 33(1) | Notwithstanding clause | "Parliament or the legislature of a province may expressly declare in an Act of Parliament or of the legislature … that the Act or provision thereof shall operate notwithstanding a provision included in section 2 or sections 7 to 15 of the Charter." |
| 25 | Aboriginal and treaty rights | "The guarantee in this Charter of certain rights and freedoms shall not be construed so as to abrogate or derogate from any aboriginal, treaty or other rights and freedoms that pertain to the aboriginal peoples of Canada…." See also section 35 of the *Constitution Act, 1982*. |

the certainty and stability a constitution can provide, we also should not assume that this political document can definitively answer all questions of societal importance.

The Canadian Constitution is no different in this regard. It provides a clear framework for governance – the *Constitution Act, 1867* delineates the federal division of powers and establishes (or allows for the establishment of) Canada's key governing institutions – and guarantees the rights and freedoms of individuals against government infringements (mainly, but not exclusively, through the *Canadian Charter of Rights and Freedoms*, part of the *Constitution Act, 1982*). This framework has political contestation built into its structure: The institutions it establishes are designed to work against each other as much as they are to work in concert, and the *Charter*'s guarantees are subject to "reasonable limits demonstrably justified in a free and democratic society" and the notwithstanding clause in section 33. In our system of constitutional supremacy, we expect law to accommodate politics even as we expect politics to be conducted according to the rule of law. Here then, at the very heart of the "supreme law" of Canada, the interdependence of law and politics is visible, vibrant, and vital.

## REVIEW QUESTIONS

1  Should a constitution be frequently amended? Why and why not?
2  Is the Canadian Constitution a single document? To what extent is it unwritten?
3  What role does the constitution play in federalism disputes?
4  What is the *Oakes* test and why is it important for the Canadian system of constitutional rights?

## MOOT COURT TOPIC

Is a government mandate to be vaccinated a violation of the *Charter* or can it be considered a reasonable limit that is demonstrably justified in a free and democratic society?

# PART TWO

# Fields of Legal Doctrine and Practice

# CHAPTER FOUR

# The Criminal Law

LEARNING OBJECTIVES

- Understand the structure and operation of the criminal law.
- Be able to distinguish between the criminal law and other types of law.
- Understand criminal defences and how they operate.
- Be able to explain the significance of the presumption of innocence and its relationship to burdens of proof.

An attentive reader will have noticed that many examples used throughout this text are drawn from the criminal law. This illustrates the importance of the criminal law, both from a political/public policy and legal perspective. More than any other area of law, criminal law invites us to examine the relationship between state and citizen and it does so in the heightened context where the stakes might literally be life and death. Criminal law raises issues concerning the role of the state, the legitimacy of state power, and what is acceptable within a political community. While the state regulates the behaviour of private citizens in many ways, only criminal law invokes the coercive power of the state in such a stark fashion. If one fails to comply with most state regulations, the result might be a fine. If one commits a crime, the consequences could be imprisonment. In countries where capital punishment is still practised, committing a crime could mean losing one's life.

Max Weber, a German sociologist, famously defined the state as possessing a monopoly on the legitimate use of force within a given territory. In other words, no other group or institution within a country can mount an army or have its own police force. The growth of private security throughout much of the world might challenge this idea, but for the most part it remains the case that only the state can detain, arrest, and imprison people. An important restriction on this power is that it must be conducted in accordance with the law (see the discussion of the rule of law in Chapter 1) – hence the importance of clearly defined principles of criminal law. This includes the definition and articulation of what constitutes a crime (criminal codes and other statutes that define crimes), a system for investigation and enforcement of criminal law (police forces), and a system for adjudicating guilt (involving prosecutors and defence lawyers) and sentencing offenders (courts and judges). In addition, there must also be an organizational structure for the incarceration of criminals or for their supervision in the community (corrections).

All these systems must be structured according to the law and have limits placed on their authority. Systems of appeal, for example, attempt to ensure that those accused of crimes have the fullest opportunity to challenge their convictions should errors be made by the initial trial court. Police are subject to requirements to obtain warrants, limits on their ability to search individuals and premises, and guidelines as to how they should conduct interviews and interrogations. Failure to comply with those rules might, depending on the context, lead a court to acquit an accused. Despite these various requirements, it is certainly true that sometimes the system of control and accountability does not work. High-profile wrongful conviction cases, for example, such as those of Steven Truscott or David Milgaard, demonstrate the serious consequences of system-wide failures in the criminal justice system (see *Reference Re Milgaard*, 1992; *Reference Re Steven Murray Truscott*, 1967).

The very definition of what constitutes a crime raises important policy questions and often involves debates about morality and community standards. Should it be a crime to attempt to take one's own life? If not, should it be a crime to assist someone else to take their life? Are there conditions one might attach to assisted suicide, so that in some circumstances it might be a crime, while in other contexts it would not? In Canada, the state has answered this question, after much debate and several high-profile Supreme Court decisions, by introducing legislation governing medically assisted suicide. Other "community standards" and values might also be difficult to discern: While we might all agree that child pornography should be criminalized, what standards should govern pornography more broadly? Just when is something so obscene that it should be prohibited by law and subject to criminal sanction? Other issues such as abortion and sex work all raise the important question of when it is appropriate for the state to use the criminal law to regulate what otherwise might be considered private behaviour. The answers to these questions reflect the deeply and sincerely held beliefs of those involved in the debates, such that consensus around these issues is difficult to achieve. As well, views on these questions are prone to change over time, so that what was considered unacceptable in the past might now be considered perfectly reasonable, or at the very least, tolerated. If crimes are routinely prosecuted for matters which the public do not believe should be considered crimes, broader questions regarding the legitimacy of the state, as well as that of the courts and police, can become important political issues.

**BOX 4.1. THE PROSECUTION OF HENRY MORGENTALER**

In 1969, Henry Morgentaler opened an abortion clinic in Montreal. At the time, the performance of an abortion was clearly a violation of the *Criminal Code of Canada*. Between 1973 and 1975, Morgentaler was tried three times for preforming abortions. He was acquitted all three times, and each time the jury took less and less time to deliberate. Eventually the Quebec government determined that it would no longer prosecute Morgentaler, as they concluded that Quebecers found the criminal law prohibition on abortions unreasonable, and no jury would vote to convict. Juries effectively nullified the operation of the criminal code provisions in the province of Quebec.

Eventually, Morgentaler opened an abortion clinic in Ontario, where he was again prosecuted. This time he was convicted, and he ultimately appealed his conviction to the Supreme Court of Canada, which invalidated the abortion provisions of the *Criminal Code* (see Chapter 3). In 2008, Morgentaler was named to the Order of Canada for expanding health care options for women, demonstrating that public values as to what should be considered criminal can change over time.

## WHAT IS A CRIME?

Defining "crime" is a difficult task. It must be more than simply something that is contrary to law. Certainly, crimes are by definition illegal activities, but there are many illegal acts that we would not call a crime. Failing to stop at a stop sign or driving without functioning headlights are both clearly illegal, but few of us would consider these crimes. In Ontario, these "offences" would constitute violations under the *Highway Traffic Act* but not the federal *Criminal Code of Canada*. Another way to define "crime" is to suggest they are illegalities punishable by imprisonment or possibly by monetary fines. This is helpful, in the sense that there are many things which might be illegal, but for which there is no "punishment" as such. If I am found in breach of contract, the court might force me to honour my obligations or pay damages to the other party. This is not a punishment as such, but rather a mechanism for compensating those who have been injured by my actions (see Chapter 6). Moreover, even though an order to pay damages might be made in court, it is a stretch to say that this involves punishment "by" the government. This is an important distinction to remember; crimes are punished by the state and prosecutions are brought by the state. This is why criminal cases are styled as they are: The names of criminal cases in Canada are *Rex v Smith* (often shortened to *R v Smith*), reflecting that prosecutions are brought in the name of the King. (Rex is Latin for "King"; when Queen Elizabeth II was sovereign, cases were style *Regina v Smith*.) In the United States, where criminal law is a state responsibility, the prosecution is brought in the name of the state where the crime took place: *Massachusetts v Smith*. This is not merely nomenclature, since it reflects that crimes are committed against the public order and not merely the individual victim. While victims of crimes may seek a remedy in the civil courts for damages they have suffered, the criminal courts are principally engaged with the task of punishment, not restitution.

Crimes, then, have a public dimension. A crime, while potentially directed against one person, impacts all of us in a collective sense. If people are entitled to steal and rob with impunity, none of us are truly safe or secure. On the other hand, if there is a beach of a contract, there may be few implications that go beyond the parties to that deal. Crimes are understood to be sufficiently serious that the state believes a punishment of some sort, as opposed to simply civil liability, is warranted. This distinguishes crimes from other violations of the law, which might be considered "regulatory offences" in addition to being subject to civil liability. Simon Verdun-Jones (2020), referencing Justice Rand in the *Margarine Reference* case (*Reference Re Validity of Section 5 (a) Dairy Industry Act*, 1948), argues that this "serious" element of a crime involves a degree of "evil" that represents an injury to the public (see Chapter 1).

This gives us a sense of what a "crime" is, but it does not provide a complete or exhaustive definition. Some crimes are obvious: murder, sexual assault, assault, robbery, theft. Others may be less so. Should gambling be considered a crime? What about drinking, which during periods of prohibition during the twentieth century was criminalized in some jurisdictions? The possession and use of marijuana were considered crimes in Canada for a very long time but are now legal in Canada. The issue of whether abortion should be a criminal offence has been hotly debated in Canada and elsewhere. At one point, having or providing an abortion was criminalized in Canada but, once again, now it is not (see Box 4.1). Until quite recently, fraudulently practising witchcraft was actually a criminal offence in Canada, although very few of us believe in witchcraft (for more on "obsolete laws," see Baker & Janzen, 2013).

At one level, this discussion takes us back to the positivistic understanding of law discussed in Chapter 1. We know that crimes are illegal acts, punished by the state, and usually involve serious matters. At the end of the day, however, what exactly is "criminal" will depend on the laws of a particular jurisdiction and what specific acts have been prohibited. So, while we may be able to define what we mean by a "crime," we cannot define what actions will be considered criminal. This is particularly important when dealing with crimes that have a "moral character," like drinking, drug use, sexual conduct, and pornography. The degree to which criminal law attaches to these various activities will vary from country to country, and jurisdiction to jurisdiction. Over time, societal attitudes and values will change, and as a result so might our definitions as to what should be considered a crime. So, while marijuana might now be legal in Canada, it is still illegal in most of the United States. One could not cross the US border carrying marijuana as this would violate US federal drug laws. However, once in the United States, one would find that in some states marijuana remains illegal, while in others it has been decriminalized and is acceptable to possess and use. Once again, if we think back to our discussion of the rule of law, it becomes very clear why it is important that laws be published and discernible by the public. The old adage that "ignorance of the law is no excuse" (explicitly codified in s. 19 of the *Criminal Code of Canada*) is true only if it is possible for people to know what the law actually is.

If criminal law is ultimately determined by what is criminalized, it is very important to understand the sources of criminal law. How is the criminal law formulated, who has the jurisdictional authority to do so, and where can one look to find it? As with many legal questions, there is no single answer to these questions. Sources of criminal law will vary from country to country.

In Canada, the jurisdictional authority for dealing with the criminal law appears to be relatively clear. Section 91(27) of the *Constitution Act, 1867* states that the federal Parliament has jurisdiction over "The Criminal Law, except the Constitution of

---

**BOX 4.2. THE ASSASSINATION OF A PRESIDENT**

The aftermath of President Kennedy's assassination in 1963 provides an excellent illustration of the importance of the limits of US federal criminal jurisdiction. After the assassination, Congress passed legislation to make it a federal crime to kidnap, assault, or murder the president. In the absence of that legislation, the assassination of a president would be treated in the same way as any other murder, with investigative and jurisdictional authority falling to the state in which the crime took place. The investigation would be conducted by local or state police, rather than the FBI, and the prosecution would be conducted by state justice officials, rather than by the federal Department of Justice. The prosecution would also take place in a state court, rather than a federal court.

The legislation makes it a federal crime to assassinate, attempt to assassinate, or conspire to assassinate the president, the president-elect, or the vice-president. It also criminalizes kidnapping of any of these officials. Finally, the legislation also extends federal jurisdiction to all members of the president's office, including cabinet secretaries (see 18 USC, s. 1751).

Courts of Criminal Jurisdiction, but including the Procedure in Criminal Matters." This provides the federal Parliament with wide-ranging and comprehensive jurisdictional authority to create criminal law in Canada. The criminal law has furthermore been largely codified (brought together) in a single statute, the *Criminal Code of Canada*. This legislation is the starting point for determining the criminal law in Canada, and it details specific criminal offences, defences, procedures, and ranges of sentences for different types of offences. The first Canadian criminal code was enacted in 1892, one of the first such codes in the Commonwealth. Historically, in common law jurisdictions, criminal offences were simply developed through judicial decisions. Like other areas of the common law, criminal law was the product of judges (and juries) hearing cases and resolving disputes. While the criminal law was codified in 1892, that legislation was an attempt to bring together existing common law offences and processes. It wasn't until the 1955 amendments to the *Criminal Code* that the creation of new common law criminal offences was abolished in Canada. All new criminal offences must be created by statute. However, common law defences continue to exist and many of the most significant defences to a criminal law charge remain principally defined by the common law (this also allows new defences, like "battered woman syndrome," to emerge without a legislative change). Any attempt to understand the criminal law in Canada must pay careful attention to both the statutory provisions (and their interpretation) of the *Criminal Code*, as well as common law principles.

In addition to the *Criminal Code*, there are several other important federal statutes dealing with the criminal law. These include the *Youth Criminal Justice Act*, the *Controlled Drugs and Substances Act*, the *Firearms Act*, and the *Food and Drug Act*. Additionally, the *Canada Evidence Act* contains important provisions regarding the evidentiary rules to be followed in criminal trials.

Despite the apparent clarity of the Canadian Constitution, the provinces have significant jurisdictional authority to create provincial offences and regulatory offences. This primarily stems from two provisions in the Canadian Constitution. Section 92(14) of the *Constitution Act* gives provinces jurisdictional authority over the "administration of justice in the province, including the constitution, maintenance, and organization of provincial courts, both of civil and criminal jurisdiction...." This provision ensures that provinces are significant actors in the criminal justice system. It bestows the responsibility for organizing and administering the courts, but it also bestows the jurisdictional responsibility for policing and the prosecution of crimes (for more on the US context, see Box 4.2). As a result, Canada has a complex jurisdictional division over the criminal justice system (Baker, 2020). The federal government has primary jurisdiction over the creation of criminal law, while the provinces are the primary actor for policing and prosecuting offences. In most provinces, you will therefore find municipal police forces, established and regulated under provincial jurisdiction. In several provinces, there are also provincial police forces, such as the Ontario

Provincial Police, the Sûreté du Québec, or the Royal Newfoundland Constabulary, that have broad jurisdictional authority to enforce the criminal law. In other provinces, however, this responsibility is delegated to the Royal Canadian Mounted Police (RCMP). The RCMP is a federally constituted police force, with jurisdiction to investigate and enforce laws on Crown land and federal statutes. Its jurisdiction to operate as a provincial police force, however, comes from an agreement between the province and the RCMP, rather than an inherent federal jurisdiction. In other words, in provinces like Manitoba, Saskatchewan, and Alberta, the RCMP is contracted by the province to play a similar role as provincial police forces elsewhere. Despite all this complexity, it is simplified by the fact that all police officers, regardless of which force they belong to, are empowered as "peace officers" to enforce the *Criminal Code* and other laws.

The provinces in Canada also derive significant jurisdictional authority for imposing penalties and creating offences from section 92(15) of the constitution. This provision states that provinces have authority over the "imposition of punishment by fine, penalty, or imprisonment for enforcing any law of the province" made in relation to matters within their jurisdictional authority. This provision, in conjunction with section 92(13), which gives the provinces jurisdiction over "property and civil rights," a very expansive clause, effectively gives the provinces wide regulatory authority to enforce provincial laws through a variety of punishments, including imprisonment. If, however, we define crimes as serious offences, often involving imprisonment as a punishment, this would seem to blur the lines considerably between criminal and non-criminal matters. If, for example, the violation of anti-pollution measure can be punished by imprisonment, at what point is the province intruding into federal criminal law, even if the environment might be a valid area of provincial concern? These become important matters of both policy and federal jurisdictional authority. There have been several federal-provincial conflicts that have focused on exactly these questions. The federal government has, on occasion, attempted to extend its regulatory power into areas that might otherwise be considered provincial, and similarly, provinces have sometimes attempted to claim as "regulatory" matters which, from most points of view, would be considered criminal (Baker, 2020).

## CATEGORIZING CRIMINAL LAWS

It should be self-evident that not all criminal laws are of equal importance or significance. The *Criminal Code of Canada*, for example, contains a large range of criminal offences, which include the very serious – murder, sexual assault – to things such as mischief to property, which might not be considered as serious. It is important, therefore, to think about how we categorize criminal offences.

The first way to categorize criminal laws is, as the above suggests, by their seriousness. In the United States and many common law jurisdictions, this is often captured by distinguishing **felonies** (serious offences) from **misdemeanors** (less serious offences). In Canada, we do not employ this terminology but instead distinguish **indictable offences** from **summary conviction offences** to capture the seriousness of a crime. While categorizations like this do convey a sense of the seriousness of an offence, they also reference that a different set of judicial procedures are utilized. This makes sense, in that we would want rigorous and exacting procedural safeguards before the state should be entitled to deprive an individual of their freedom for a lengthy period of time. Accordingly, serious offences are associated with more fulsome and elaborate judicial processes, while less serious offences are often associated with more streamlined procedures.

Summary conviction offences are the least serious criminal offences. These include such things as causing a disturbance, trespassing, and public nudity. Summary conviction offences do not typically result in the accused being arrested. Rather, a notice to appear is issued, which stipulates the date and time the individual is required to attend court. Summary conviction offences are prosecuted by a judge alone, usually in a provincial court. As well, there is a one-year limitation period on these offences, meaning that charges must be laid within six months of the offence being committed. Unless the *Criminal Code* provides otherwise, the maximum penalty for a summary conviction offence is imprisonment for "not more than two years less a day," a fine of up to $5,000, or both.

Indictable offences, by contrast, involve much more serious matters. Murder, sexual assault, and assault are all indictable offences. These matters usually involve the accused being arrested, and an "indictment" being laid against them. The indictment sets out the offence with which the accused is charged, as well as the material elements of the offence as alleged by the Crown and the police. The laying of the indictment is the start of the criminal process. Indictable offences, however, cover a wide range of types of offences, and some may be more serious than others. This is reflected in the penalties for an indictable offence, which can range from an absolute discharge to life imprisonment. The wide range for many serious offences means that trial judges are given tremendous discretion in determining the appropriate penalty for an offender. Many offences are also "hybrid," which means the prosecution can choose whether to proceed by indictment or as a summary conviction offence; this gives prosecutors considerable discretion to shape the ultimate outcome even before the case arrives before a judge. That choice also means that there can be tremendous variation in how the case gets treated by judges. Unlike summary conviction offences, which have a one-year limitation on the laying of charges, there is no statute of limitations on indictable offences. The offence may be charged any time after the commission of the offence.

The variation in the seriousness of indictable offences is also reflected in the processes followed by their prosecution. Indictable offences may be tried by judge and jury or a judge without a jury. In most instances the accused may elect whether they wish to have a jury or not. There are some exceptions to this. Section 469 of the *Criminal Code* provides a list of the most serious crimes, which include murder, treason, and terrorism offences. These crimes must be tried with a jury. Similarly, section 553 of the *Criminal Code* contains a list of criminal offences over which provincial courts have exclusive jurisdiction. Generally, these are relatively minor offences, and the accused does not have a right to a jury trial in these matters (the *Canadian Charter of Rights and Freedoms* guarantees a jury trial only if the maximum penalty is five years imprisonment or more).

A final feature of indictable offences is the existence of a **preliminary inquiry** process. This is a hearing in which the evidence of the prosecution is tested. During a preliminary hearing, which is held before a provincial court judge, the crown presents the evidence they would intend to bring at trial. At the end of the hearing, the judge determines whether there exists sufficient evidence for a trial to proceed. This is an important step which does not exist for summary conviction offences or indictable offences where the offence is punishable by less than 14 years imprisonment. Even where they are available, the preliminary inquiry can be waived by the accused and is available only in cases that will be tried before a jury.

Offences can be characterized in ways other than trial process. Indeed, these other bases of characterization are probably more intuitive and understandable to most people. The most obvious differentiation is between **crimes against the person** (crimes of violence) and **crimes against property**. Popular culture largely focuses on the former, which includes such things as murder, manslaughter, assault, and sexual assault but also could include such things as criminal negligence, administering dangerous and/or poisonous substances, among others. Crimes against property constitute a broader and more diverse category of crimes, which include such things as trespassing, damage to property, theft, and breaking and entering. Crimes such as fraud, forgery, embezzlement, and obtaining goods or services under false pretences all fall within this category.

In addition to these broad categories, there are other ways offences interrelate to each other. Firearms and weapons offences often relate explicitly to other crimes. For example, committing a robbery with a firearm is a specific criminal offence. It carries greater penalties than robbery committed without a firearm. At the same time, there are offences that relate specifically to weapons in and of themselves. The *Criminal Code* contains a list of prohibited weapons. Mere possession of these weapons would constitute a criminal offence, regardless of whether the weapon was used.

A final area of criminal offences relates to questions of public order. Disturbing the peace, public mischief, making a false criminal complaint, uttering threats, and disorderly conduct fall within this category. These offences might not be directed at any particular person but relate to questions of overall social welfare. The question of social welfare also is raised when we consider offences that relate to moral issues. Often these offences also involve harm to individuals or categories of individuals. Pornography and obscenity offences, as well as offences dealing with hate speech, would fall within this category.

## ELEMENTS OF A CRIMINAL OFFENCE: *ACTUS REUS* AND *MENS REA*

All criminal offences can be understood as comprising two elements. These are commonly referred to by the Latin terms **actus reus** and **mens rea**. *Actus reus* refers to the "guilty act" – in other words, the behaviour that attracts criminal sanctions. In a case of murder, for example, the act of taking a person's life constitutes the *actus reus*. In most instances, the *actus reus* for a crime is relatively straightforward, although in some instances it may be more complicated, particularly if there are complex questions of causation. If a person participates in an armed robbery, and someone is shot and killed, did that person commit murder if they were not the person who pulled the trigger? Does it matter if the accused was in the room? What if they were the getaway driver and never entered the premises and had no control over the events that took place? What if a security guard or a police officer responding to the robbery is the person who shoots and kills an innocent bystander? The accused is certainly guilty of armed robbery, but can they also be held accountable for the death that resulted from the robbery? In many jurisdictions this situation is dealt with by statute, which extends the *actus reus* for murder to anyone who was involved in the broader criminal enterprise. By contrast, a conviction for murder in Canada has a very high, constitutionally mandated requirement of subjective foresight of death, meaning you have to know that killing someone was a likely outcome of your action (*R v Martineau*, 1990; *R v Vaillancourt*, 1987).

The above example brings us directly to the second element of a crime, namely the *mens rea*. Surely, in our example above, it matters what the accused person knew and intended. If the getaway driver did not know their partners-in-crime carried weapons, is it fair to hold them responsible for murder if their partner uses a gun? *Mens rea* translates as "guilty mind," and it is a fundamental principle of criminal law that an individual, to be liable for a crime, must display the required "intent" to justify being found guilty and punished. Intention is, however, very difficult to prove. It is impossible to "look into someone's mind" and know what they were thinking. Often, intent can be presumed or inferred from actions, so *actus reus* and *mens rea* come together in natural and logical ways. The burglar caught in someone's house must presumably have intended to break and enter, otherwise how would they have gotten there? Despite this, questions of intention may be thorny and difficult to prove. Many of the most important debates within criminal law focus on how we understand intention. It also needs to be kept in mind that there are different levels of intention. One can "know things" or be aware of them. In other instances, one might actually intend or plan things. The old term for this, in a criminal context, was "malice aforethought." One might also intend something, but in an immediate and reactive fashion, so that a planning element is absent from the equation. This is the difference between an impulsive "crime of passion" and a criminal act that is methodically planned and executed.

The nature of the *mens rea*, whether the commission of a crime is intended or not, can determine how we characterize the *actus reus*. In other words, it can actually determine the nature of the crime. Murder is an excellent example. The *actus reus* is the taking of a life; but the *mens rea* determines whether the crime is first degree murder, second degree murder, or manslaughter. Homicide that was deliberate and planned is first degree murder; in other words, there was a high degree of intentionality. As well, the *Criminal Code* determines that certain types of *actus reus* will always be considered first degree murder, even if it wasn't planned and deliberate. This includes the killing of an on-duty police officer or prison guard, as well as killings committed during a hijacking, sexual assault, kidnapping, hostage-taking, or any terrorist act. It also includes any offence committed on behalf of a criminal organization. Second degree murder, by contrast, involves killings that were deliberate but not planned in advance. Manslaughter charges are often laid where a person commits a crime but unintentionally kills a person during the commission of that crime. It can also be a charge that is applied in cases of criminal negligence, where the death was the result of the accused showing a reckless disregard for the lives of others. In both these cases, the intent was not to kill, but rather there was intent to commit some other criminal act. In both first and second degree murder charges, Canadian law provides for a sentence of life in prison. For first degree murder, the accused is not eligible for parole for 25 years, while in second degree murder cases the accused might be eligible for parole after a minimum of 10 years, depending on the sentence passed by the judge. In manslaughter cases, by contrast, there is no minimum period of incarceration. The only exception is where a firearm is involved, in which case the minimum sentence is four years in prison. This reflects the fact that manslaughter encompasses a broad range of criminal possibilities, with varying degrees of severity and culpability. Critical is the recognition that there was no intention to kill, unlike with first and second degree murder charges. As a result, greater discretion is given to the judge.

## THE PRESUMPTION OF INNOCENCE AND ELEMENTS OF AN OFFENCE

One of the most important principles of criminal law is the **presumption of innocence**. This means that the accused is to be thought of and treated as innocent until proven guilty through the judicial process. In terms of the operationalization of a criminal trial, it means that the prosecution must produce evidence that establishes, to the required

**standard of proof,** all the elements of the offence. To put it simply, the prosecution must establish that the accused "did it." The accused does not have to prove anything, and indeed, there is no obligation on the accused to even produce evidence at trial. What must be proved by the prosecution is, in turn, defined by the *actus reus* and *mens rea* of the offence, as established by statute and common law.

The requirement to prove something at law is referred to as the **onus of proof.** Quite simply, this answers the question of who is obligated to prove something in a trial. In criminal prosecutions, the presumption of innocence is operationalized by the requirement that the prosecution bears the onus of proof to establish all elements of the offence to the required standard of certainty. Other familiar criminal law protections, such as the privilege against self-incrimination, flow directly from these operational principles. The accused cannot be compelled to give evidence or to testify at their trial, precisely because there is no onus on them to prove they did not commit the crime.

The second operational principle associated with the presumption of innocence is the standard of proof. The prosecution must not only prove the elements of the offence but must do so beyond a reasonable doubt. As discussed in Chapter 2, this is considered a very high standard of proof in judicial terms, and essentially means that any doubts about guilt must be resolved in favour of the accused and lead to an acquittal. This differs from civil cases, where the standard of proof is on a balance of probabilities (see Chapter 2 and Chapter 7). A balance of probabilities requires that the court merely be satisfied that something is more likely than not true. If this were the case in criminal trials, the presumption of innocence would largely be meaningless if we were prepared to convict and incarcerate based on something being "likely" true.

Courts have used a variety of formulations to try and capture the notion of what constitutes a "reasonable doubt." While precision is likely not possible, in general courts agree that a doubt must be "real," that it cannot be fanciful, made up, or trivial, and that it must be based on the evidence presented at trial. For our purposes, it suffices to know that, in criminal trials, we have opted for a high degree of certainty before a court will convict a person, and that the onus on satisfying the judge or jury that it is safe to convict rests exclusively on the prosecution.

## DEFENCES

The notion that the defence in a criminal trial does not have to introduce any evidence to demonstrate their innocence is, of course, subject to some practical limits created by the nature of the trial process. It is certainly the case that the accused might opt to call no witnesses, testing the strength of the prosecution's case through the cross-examination of witnesses. Such an approach might be risky, so in most cases the defence introduces some evidence to counter the evidence of the prosecution. It is important to always remember that this is not to "prove innocence," but rather to raise doubts. To this end, the defence may wish to raise any number of "defences" to a criminal charge. Some defences are established and regulated by statute (in the *Criminal Code* and elsewhere), but most defences have evolved through the common law and remain available, regardless of whether they have been codified in criminal statutory law.

For a defence to be taken into consideration, either by the judge or the jury, there must be an "air of reality" to it. In other words, the plausibility of the defence must be supported by the evidence presented at trial. It is always *possible* that aliens intervened and committed the crime the defendant is accused of, but such an improbable defence would not have that "air of reality" and could not be seriously advanced at trial. The evidence presented against the accused by the Crown might itself give rise to the viability of certain defences; however, in many instances the defence will lead evidence in support of a particular defence.

Many criminal law defences will be familiar to readers. Self-defence, for example, is a well-known defence and frequently figures in crime dramas and mystery novels. Some defences are really nothing more than a failure on the part of the prosecution to establish all the elements of the offence. A defence that the accused has an **alibi**, if accepted by the jury, really is a statement that the prosecution hasn't proven beyond a reasonable doubt that the accused committed the crime. Other defences, though, may operate to excuse what is clearly criminal behaviour. Self-defence falls into this category. The defence concedes that the accused committed the offence (assault, murder, etc.) in both action and intention. The defence, however, asserts that the accused should be excused from criminal liability because they committed the action to protect themselves. Defences are not unlimited. So, for example, in the case of self-defence, it is usually required that the accused honestly and reasonably believed they were under threat of physical harm, and that the force they used in response was reasonable in the circumstances ("no more than is necessary to enable him to defend himself"; *Criminal Code*, s. 34).

Table 4.1 provides a list of the most common defences and the basic elements of each. It should be noted that the descriptions of these defences are generalized, and specific elements will vary from jurisdiction to jurisdiction.

## CRIMINAL LAW CONTROVERSY: THE EXTREME INTOXICATION DEFENCE

Criminal law is not without controversies. Many of these have to do with broader normative questions regarding when it is appropriate to punish individuals. Competing values over questions of what constitutes a fair trial, what the appropriate scope of

**Table 4.1. Defences in the Criminal Law**

| Defence | Key Elements |
| --- | --- |
| **Self-defence** | Offence committed to defend oneself or others from an assault. The use of force must be reasonable. |
| **Consent** | In limited circumstances an individual may consent to a criminal offence. This may be the case where two people agree to fight. |
| **Necessity** | Circumstances are such that the accused had no choice but to break the law. This is a rare and uncommon defence. Breaking into a building to save someone, for example, would not be considered breaking and entering. |
| **Duress** | The accused is compelled to commit a crime due to immediate threats of bodily harm. Duress can also be considered a form of necessity. Duress is unavailable for many serious offences, including murder, treason, piracy, sexual assault, attempted murder, arson, kidnapping, and robbery. See s. 17 of the *Criminal Code of Canada*. |
| **Intoxication** | In general, intoxication is not a defence to a criminal charge. There are a limited number of exceptions to this general rule. In some instances, extreme intoxication may lead to a state where the accused is completely unaware of their actions and unable to form the *mens rea* required for a conviction. In these situations, the accused may be in a state of automatism with no awareness or control of their actions. The issue of extreme intoxication as a defence has been the subject of considerable debate, as discussed in "Criminal Law Controversy: The Extreme Intoxication Defence," in this chapter. |
| **Automatism** | Automatism refers to a state where the accused has no control and/or awareness of their actions. This can occur due to mental illness or some other medical cause. A blow to the head, for example, may trigger a state of automatism. |
| **Mistake of Fact/ Mistake of Law** | Ignorance of the law is not generally considered an excuse, but there may be circumstances where being mistaken about the law can operate as a defence to a criminal charge. For example, if an accused relies in good faith on advice provided by an official of the state, which turns out to be incorrect, they may have a defence to any charge that results from their actions. A mistake of fact occurs where the accused believes the factual circumstances are such that their actions would not be criminal if true. For all mistakes, the defence can only operate if the accused honestly believes the mistake, and that there would be no offence if the mistaken circumstances were true. |
| **Mental Illness** | The *Criminal Code* (s. 16) provides a defence of "not criminally responsible" in the case of mental illness. The accused must demonstrate they were suffering from a mental illness that made them unable to "appreciate the nature and quality of their act" or "know that it was wrong." |

criminality is, and how victims of crime can/should be protected are often at the heart of these disagreements. The question of when intoxication should operate as defence to a crime is one such issue. These controversies have often led to legislative interventions to clarify the scope of criminal law.

As indicated above, the common law provided only a very narrow scope for a defence of intoxication. As a policy matter, it was considered inappropriate for an individual to escape criminal punishment because of a choice they made to consume alcohol or drugs. However, this policy preference needed to be squared with the doctrine of *mens rea*. In cases of intoxication, there may be instances where the accused committed a criminal act but where intoxication may have made it difficult for the accused to have formulated a clear intent, especially if that required intent was complex and specific. This often led judges to make inconsistent and inexplicable distinctions between offences of specific and general intent. Intoxication could never affect the accused's ability to form a generalized broad intention, but it might impact the ability to form a more specific and concrete course of action. So, for example, the intent to get in a car and drive while intoxicated might involve a generalized intention. By contrast, the act of killing someone in a premediated fashion requires a level of specific intent that an intoxicated person might not be able to form. Whether the accused possesses the required intent remains a question of fact to be determined at the trial. Someone might be intoxicated and still have the specific intent for an offence like first degree murder (premeditated). However, if they do not, they would likely still be guilty of second degree murder or manslaughter.

There has been general agreement among legal scholars that the basis for determining whether an offence is one of specific or general intent is incoherent. The characterizations are largely historic and reflect broad (and sometimes changing) assessments of what is just and fair in specific contexts. So, murder, as discussed above, is a crime of specific intent, while sexual assault has always been considered a crime of general intent. As a result, intoxication could not provide a defence to a charge of sexual assault. This changed in 1994 with the decision of the Supreme Court of Canada in *R v Daviault*. The accused, an alcoholic, was charged with the sexual assault of an elderly woman. The evidence was that on the night of the offence the accused had consumed eight beers and a 40-ounce bottle of brandy. Experts testified that for many people this amount of alcohol would result in a coma or death. Contrary to the conventional belief that intoxication could not operate as a defence to sexual assault, the trial judge found that the accused had consumed so much that he had entered a state that was like automatism, and that he was not able to form any degree of intention with respect to his actions. The Quebec Court of Appeal overturned the decision and substituted a conviction. On further appeal, the Supreme Court allowed the appeal and restored the acquittal.

In its 1994 ruling, the Court was guided by the *Charter* values with respect to a fair trial and justified a small and narrow exception to the general unavailability of intoxication as a defence. The Supreme Court emphasized that the level of intoxication would have to be so great that the accused essentially was in a state where no intent could be formed, and that scientific and medical evidence as to the impact of intoxication on the accused would be necessary. The decision, however, was extremely controversial and went contrary to the general trend to emphasize the protection of victims, and particularly women, in sexual assault cases. Changes to the laws regarding consent, for example, had clearly emphasized the vital importance of men to confirm whether their partner was consenting, rather than simply assuming it (McNabb & Baker, 2021). The decision in *Daviault* seemed to run counter to this trend, and women's groups and advocates for victims of sexual assault condemned the decision. Considerable pressure was brought to bear on Parliament, which subsequently passed section 33.1, an amendment to the *Criminal Code*, removing self-induced extreme intoxication as a defence.

Over the ensuing two decades, courts in several provinces found the new section both unconstitutional and constitutional (Baker & Knopff, 2014), leaving the viability of the defence uncertain. In 2022, the Supreme Court of Canada attempted to settle the controversy in the cases of *R v Sullivan* and *R v Chan*. In these cases, the accused both took drugs and then had unusual and highly unanticipated reactions to them. In the *Chan* case, he ingested narcotic mushrooms and had an extreme reaction. As a result, he believed he was a deity and that his father, who was present, was a devil. As a result, he stabbed and killed his father. In the *Sullivan* case, he overdosed on prescription medication to commit suicide. The suicide attempt failed, but Sullivan entered into a state of extreme psychosis in which he believed he had been captured by aliens. In this state, he stabbed his mother repeatedly, who survived her injuries.

Both cases are tragic but fell within the broad parameters of section 33.1 of the *Criminal Code*. Both accused voluntarily took the substances that led to their extreme state of psychosis, and while in that state committed criminal acts. The Court found that the section violated the accused's *Charter* rights under section 7 of the *Charter* and section 11(d), the presumption of innocence. Essentially, the Court found that the legislation was overbroad in the sense that it allowed for people to be convicted of a criminal offence when they acted involuntarily, and thus section 33.1 potentially convicts the morally innocent. Justice Kasirer invited Parliament to come up with a revised law that might satisfy the constitutional requirement of fundamental justice but still protect Canadians from the dangers of self-intoxicated individuals (Baker, 2022). He suggested that a constitutionally valid law might be one that used the standard of criminal negligence to hold offenders accountable when the loss of control and bodily harm were reasonably foreseeable at the time of intoxication. Shortly after the 2022 decisions of the Supreme Court, Justin Trudeau's Liberal government responded with new legislation regulating self-intoxication along the lines suggested by Kasirer, but they did not go further in restricting this defence to drug-induced intoxication (much medical evidence suggests that alcohol alone cannot induce automatism, as the *Daviault* Court believed). Legal practitioners and academics continue to be concerned that any such intoxication defence will continue to disadvantage and harm women complainants who have been sexually assaulted (Froc, 2022). The question of whether one ought to have reasonably known that some intoxicants could lead to bodily harm is likely to be a point of intense contention, and perhaps medical experts will be unwilling to draw such a stark causal connection. The effects of the new legislation will be known only as new cases emerge and new defendants attempt to use the defence as it is now regulated by the new law.

The *Sullivan* and *Chan* cases demonstrate the difficult balance between justice in particular cases and broader societal interests. We certainly agree that intoxication should very rarely be used as a defence and that protecting women from violence is a critical and vital objective of the criminal justice system. From this perspective, it is hard to justify the impact of the *Daviault* decision, and Parliament was well within its rights to overturn the decision and remove the defence. At the same time, finding Chan and Sullivan guilty also seems unjust as they are arguably individuals who unwittingly became enmeshed in a tragic set of events in which they killed and injured loved ones. Of course, in such cases judges also have considerable discretion to consider such circumstances through sentencing. The correct approach to dealing with these complex circumstances is an example of how criminal law often invokes public controversies that go well beyond the actual criminal prosecution.

## CONCLUSION

Criminal law is classically understood as a critical area of public law. It sits at the intersection of state authority, the regulation of private behaviour, and the definition of the acceptable limits of both private action and public control. It is through the criminal law that we see most visibly the state's capacity to regulate its citizens and to exert the potential of coercive force upon them. Of course, while we can define crimes, enforcing them and implementing policies that support the investigation and successful prosecution of offences is a complex task. In this sense, the criminal law is far more than just the promulgation of a list of offences and their constituent elements.

This chapter provided an overview of basic principles of criminal law. This is the context in which a multitude of policy decisions take place. Everything from the decision of the patrol officer to lay charges or to merely issue a warning to the Crown's decision to appeal a case depends on an assessment of the principles discussed in this chapter. Complex issues such as intoxication, assisted suicide, pornography, and obscenity will be assessed and potentially answered by policies, all within the context of how the criminal law defines offences and how the judicial process operates to prove the elements of the offence. The law of evidence is also critically important for determining the efficacy of criminal law policy, but its details are well beyond the scope of this volume. The criminal law operates at the intersection of state power and personal behaviour and responsibility. It is at the centre of concepts of social order, morality, and normative understandings of how society operates. An understanding of its operation is critical to understand the potential and limits of policy choices, as well as the study of the causes of crime and what options the state possesses to address these issues.

## REVIEW QUESTIONS

1  Why is *mens rea* sometimes a controversial element of a criminal offence?
2  What justifications would there be for including drunkenness as a defence to a criminal charge? What are the arguments against this?
3  Should individuals be criminally liable for negligence or carelessness? Why and why not?
4  What are the advantages to codifying the criminal law?
5  Should it be possible to convict someone of a crime on a balance of probabilities rather than proof beyond reasonable doubt?

## MOOT COURT TOPIC

Robert agrees to be the getaway driver for his two friends, Sam and Angie, who are planning to rob a convenience store. He initially tells them he isn't comfortable with doing this and expresses concern that someone might get hurt. They assure them that nobody will get hurt, and that they aren't using real guns, only replica toy guns. Robert believes them, but in fact, they are using real guns. The robbery goes well, but as they are making their getaway, they encounter a police cruiser that attempts to pull them over due to Robert's erratic driving. As the police officer approaches their car, Sam gets out and fires his gun. He misses the police officer but hits and kills a nearby pedestrian. The police officer returns fire, and shoots and kills Angie, who had also gotten out of the car and was about to open fire on the officer. Sam flees the scene and was later arrested. Robert is charged with homicide for both the killing of the pedestrian and also for the death of Angie. Does Robert have the *mens rea* to be convicted of murder? Does it matter whether the shots fired were from one of his accomplices or the police officer?

# Administrative Law

## LEARNING OBJECTIVES

- Understand the relationship between administrative law and the role of the state.
- Be able to explain the evolution of administrative law as part of the development of the modern welfare state.
- Understand and be able to articulate the grounds of judicial review.
- Be able to apply the grounds of judicial review to public policy case studies.
- Understand the role and function of privative clauses.
- Be able to articulate the differences between how courts and tribunals function.

Administrative law is an important element of public law, but its doctrines are rarely the subject of social science inquiry beyond the legal academy. Broadly defined, "administrative law" refers to the legal processes and accountability structures that facilitate and regulate the exercise of state power over the administration of its programs and policies. It involves a complex structure of judicial accountability and oversight mechanisms. These often seem to be characterized by a dizzying array of rules, regulations, and details, and are frequently associated with bureaucratic complexity. Administrative law helps us define and ascertain the limits and scope of the state's legal authority. What gives a health and safety inspector the right to enter a workplace, what sort of workplaces can they inspect, and what can they do while they are there? What discretion do inspectors have to issue citations or even potentially close a business down for unsafe workplace practices?

Beyond simply defining the scope of state administrative authority, however, administrative law is critically important for understanding state power. In general, the public sector has responsibility for implementing a vast array of policy directives. While the executive and legislature (cabinet and Parliament) might play lead roles in the creation of policy directions and the legislation that brings those policies into existence, it is the administrative state that implements and carries out those policies. It also generates the ideas behind those policies, as well as the parameters of policy options under consideration. For most ordinary citizens, it is through the vast machinery of government that most of their interactions with the state take place. As a sphere of public law, then, administrative law sits at the nexus of politics, public policy, public administration, and law.

## STATE ACCOUNTABILITY

Administrative law is central to our notions of state accountability and provides a means of operationalizing forms of accountability. The history of administrative law, both in Canada and elsewhere, provides a window into the internal struggles and dynamics of the state. As the responsibilities of the state grew in the post–Second World War period, governments attempted to develop new mechanisms for adjudicating claims and new processes of regulation that often mimicked judicial processes. At the same time, courts were reluctant to cede jurisdictional authority to government. The result was a back-and-forth jockeying for position as governments and courts both sought to establish their predominance as the vehicles by which accountability would be ensured.

At the heart of this debate is the question of how to hold state officials accountable and within the limits of their authority. If they are free to act as they choose, or to ignore the limits of their authority, then the exercise of that power can be arbitrary and capricious. This was the underlying rationale behind the very important Canadian case of *Roncarelli v Duplessis* (1959). In Chapter 1, we discussed this case in relation to the concept of the rule of law, but it is also an administrative law case. Decided in the 1950s, it involved then premier of the province of Quebec Maurice Duplessis and Frank Roncarelli, the owner of a Montreal restaurant. The case stands for the important principle that state authority must be used in accordance with the limits and intent underpinning its grant. During the 1950s, Duplessis' Union Nationale government had passed several draconian pieces of legislation to attack political and religious groups. One of these laws prohibited the distribution of pamphlets without a permit. The law was used to persecute Jehovah's Witnesses, who are known to distribute such literature on the street. Roncarelli was supportive of those who had been charged under the law and had posted bail for arrested individuals. To stop this, Duplessis used the power under the province's liquor licensing legislation to remove Roncarelli's licence to sell alcohol at his restaurant. This effectively put Roncarelli out of business. Importantly, the legislation governing the liquor licensing regime provided broad discretion to the premier to issue permits and provided virtually no guidance as to what criteria should be employed in making those decisions.

The Supreme Court found that the actions of the premier were outside of his legal authority to direct the chairman of the Liquor Licensing Board. While the chairman did have the discretion to cancel a liquor licence, the Court ruled that it must be for reasons that were related to the intention and purpose of the legislation. In other words, he couldn't use his legal authority for purposes that were unrelated to that legislation granting him that authority. In this case, it was clear that Duplessis was using his control over liquor licences to punish Roncarelli and to prevent him from helping members of a religious minority that were being incarcerated. As such, the premier's reasons had nothing to do with the sale and distribution of alcohol to the public and constituted an unlawful exercise of his discretionary authority.

In some ways, *Roncarelli v Duplessis* is an easy case. It is the "right" outcome, in that Duplessis was using his authority in ways that were clearly offensive to the intention of the legislation and our modern rights-based values. However, it needs to be kept in mind that this case was decided long before the adoption of the *Canadian Charter of Rights and Freedoms* and its protection of religious values. As an administrative law matter, it was highly significant for the Court to say very clearly that a grant of discretion to state officials, even if it appears broad and unconstrained, is subject to limits and is never completely unfettered. For our purposes, it reminds us of the importance of administrative law and judicial oversight as vehicles by which the boundaries and limits of state authority are maintained.

State officials have no special authority to do anything beyond what the law authorizes them to do. This was the insight of A.V. Dicey, the great constitutional legal theorist. Dicey was famous for his articulation of many important constitutional concepts, including the rule of law. (For an excellent overview of Dicey's constitutional theory and its applicability to administrative law, see Arthurs, 1979.) For Dicey, this was a straightforward proposition, but it has many significant implications for administrative law. Dicey's understanding of the rule of law was simply that the law applied to everyone in the same way, even – perhaps especially – those tasked with enacting and administering the law. The rule of law establishes the supremacy of law as the source of all state power and authority. In many ways, this is a restatement of Max Weber's notion of rational legal authority; namely, that power gets transformed into legitimate authority through the institution of law.

A second related element of Dicey's notion of the rule of law, and one that has had profound implications for bureaucracies in Anglo-American legal systems, is the notion that individuals should have access to the ordinary courts of the land to adjudicate grievances. In other words, where there are disputes about the authority of state officials, it is the independent judicial branch that hears the case and decides the matter. The courts, as the arbiters of law, were, in Dicey's view, the appropriate body to decide matters about the scope of the state's legal authority. It is important to keep in mind that Dicey, writing in the nineteenth century, was no fan of the expansion of state power (Arthurs, 1979). He was writing at a time when the state was growing with expanded responsibility for regulating such things as public health and employment and workplace standards. Law, in this context, served as a check on state power, which Dicey saw as potentially leading to arbitrary decisions that threatened individual freedom.

The origins of the rule of law as a concept, and the development of administrative law as a doctrine, is deeply embedded in this understanding of the state. Law acts as a sort of red light that prevents incursions by the state into the private realm (Harlow & Rawlings, 2009; Leyland & Anthony, 2013; see Box 5.1 for more on this approach). The growth and expansion of the state throughout the twentieth century has very much been in a contradictory and often conflictual relationship with law and courts (Arthurs, 1979; Daly, 2022; Sheldrick, 2009). This is a theme that will be explored more fully throughout the rest of this chapter. Before we move onto that discussion, however, it is necessary to map out the range of administrative bodies that exist, their functions, and the basic grounds under which they can be reviewed by courts.

---

**BOX 5.1. RED, GREEN, AND AMBER LIGHT THEORIES OF ADMINISTRATIVE LAW**

**Red light theories** understand judicial oversight as an important check on administrative power. To that extent, law is considered superior to administration and courts should be empowered to overturn decisions of administrators. This approach is generally consistent with classical liberal understandings of the public-private dichotomy and views government action as a threat to individual liberty and freedom. It asserts the primacy of law over politics.

**Green light theories** are more critical of judicial intervention/oversight and are more supportive of the role of the state and administration. While recognizing judicial review as necessary, it is seen as oriented towards enabling and promoting good administration, rather than as a check or block on administration. Green light theories recognize the need for public administration and do not prioritize law over administration. Green light theories do not ascribe superiority to courts and allow for there to be alternatives to the courts for making decisions and resolving disputes. For green light theorists, alternatives to legal rules can provide a more-than-sufficient basis for decision-making.

**Amber light theories** provide a middle ground, recognizing the need for public administration and alternatives to courts, but also recognizing that courts play an important oversight role in preventing abuse of power by state officials.

## THE ROLE AND FUNCTION OF ADMINISTRATIVE AGENCIES

The modern state is composed of many administrative agencies that operate much like courts – they hear cases, receive evidence, decide disputes, and issue rulings. They are often called boards or tribunals, but they should not be thought of as courts by a different name. Many boards operate with a degree of autonomy and independence from the line departments within which they are housed, but they are very much part of the state. Their level of independence falls short of judicial independence, in that the very existence of the agency is dependent on their grant of authority from the state. They lack the inherent authority that is constitutionally granted to Canada's superior courts. Consequently, scholars of administrative law often refer to these agencies as **quasi-judicial** in nature. The importance of the prefix "quasi" in this designation should not be underestimated.

Administrative boards and tribunals are considered quasi-judicial rather than judicial for two reasons. The first relates to the structure and form of these agencies. The second relates to their function and purpose. Courts are remarkably uniform in terms of their operation. While there may be differences in jurisdiction and the types of matters they are authorized to deal with, courts are structured in largely the same fashion.[1] The typical formulation of a judge (or panel of judges), along with counsel tables, space for a jury, etc., all contribute to a familiarity in terms of the formal structure of the judicial process. Courts are clearly adversarial, with two parties directly opposed, and a judge who acts solely as an impartial decision-maker, with no pre-existing expertise in the matter or stake in the outcome. A court in the United States looks very much like a court in Canada, the United Kingdom, Australia, or any number of other countries.

Administrative boards and agencies, by contrast, take a wide range of forms as set out in their **enabling legislation,** the statutory instrument that creates the entity and describes its functions and powers. Many boards and agencies, as indicated above, mimic judicial processes, but others do not. Some administrative agencies are small, meet periodically, and have only part-time members, and their processes lack the formalities of a judicial process. Others, by contrast, perform important regulatory functions, meet regularly, and have a panel of members that function like judges but possess full-time staff and have a policy and research capacity that courts do not have. Administrative boards and tribunals are established within specific policy domains and are designed to bring specialized knowledge and expertise to complex regulatory and

---

1   While this picture of the courts remains largely true, we acknowledge the rise of specialized "problem-solving courts," like "drug courts," that offer non-traditional approaches to adjudication (Hausegger et al., 2025, pp. 81–4).

policy problems. Judges, by definition, tend to be generalists, and need to be able to hear cases covering a wide range of legal topics. Members of administrative agencies, by contrast, are frequently appointed precisely because of their specialized expert knowledge. Administrative agencies may also have research staff, which provide additional support to panel members. Judges are not permitted to seek information outside the material filed by the parties. Some administrative boards may actually have their own legal counsel who question witnesses with the express mandate of "representing" the policy area and the board, rather than a particular viewpoint.

The specialized and policy nature of administrative boards and tribunals is a common feature of these agencies. Even within this context, though, administrative boards may perform a range of functions. Some operate within a limited and narrow policy framework. They may hear applications on a particular issue, or for a particular program, or they may hear appeals of the decisions of front-line administrative staff. These sorts of boards may possess relatively little discretion, and the implications of their decisions are limited in scope. Other administrative agencies, however, have been granted a large degree of policy responsibility and autonomy. A significant portion of a policy field has been delegated to these agencies. Labour relations, for example, is an area where a tremendous degree of responsibility for managing and regulating collective bargaining has been given over to labour relations boards (see Chapter 9). Similarly, the Canadian Radio and Telecommunications Commission has significant authority over the development and regulation of telecommunications policy. While the standards and principles governing a particular policy field may be set by a board's enabling legislation, the board itself often has a significant policy development function.

As a result of diversity of form and function of administrative boards and agencies, Ted Hodgetts (1973), a founding scholar of Canadian public administration, referred to them as "structural heretics" (ch. 7; Sheldrick, 2009). They stand apart and operate at arm's length from line departments, yet perform a wide array of functions, some more akin to the functions of other regulatory and policy bodies than to the functions of a court. They combine the independence of courts with specialized knowledge and a policy development function. Some boards may even have an explicitly political and policy-focused responsibility to consider a broader set of circumstances and a broader government-set agenda.

Administrative agencies also serve to represent both state and non-state interests. They provide an opportunity for those affected by policy formulation and implementation decisions to make representations and submissions about those plans. At the same time, they establish a degree of accountability for state officials, in that the development and implementation of policies are subjected to scrutiny and challenge. These boards provide both an opportunity and a requirement for state actors to articulate the rationale and principles underpinning policy decisions. Keep in mind, though, that as boards "represent," they might also exclude. Regulatory boards, for example, might provide a meaningful forum for large corporations and other governmental bodies to be heard, but it might be much more difficult for consumer groups or members of the public to have a voice in proceedings. Boards and agencies serve as a forum in which networks of governance between state and non-state actors come together. This is inherently a complex process, and one which is made even more complex by processes that are quasi-judicial in nature and subject to oversight by the courts.

To better understand these boards and tribunals, the first step in our analysis is to examine the principles that courts employ in reviewing administrative decisions and mapping these onto our traditional understanding of how states are organized. From there, we can examine the limits of this model and look at how administrative law has responded to attempts to reform and rethink the administrative structure of the state.


## JUDICIAL REVIEW


If we are to understand the intersection of law and politics within the administrative sphere, we need to understand the ways in which courts can oversee administrative decisions. This is more than just examining how courts ensure boards operate in a proper/appropriate fashion, but rather gives us insight into the ways in which courts and judges can interfere with the decisions of boards, and indeed substitute their own preferred outcomes for those of agencies. This is critically important, as courts and judges operate from a very different decision-making paradigm than administrative boards and state decision-makers. That paradigm, founded in the Diceyan notion of the rule of law, operates to not only define the parameters of administrative decision-making but also constrain and limit that decision-making power. Essentially, it operates to ensure the primacy of "judicial" approaches over administrative approaches to decision-making.

As suggested above, the starting point for understanding the relationship between judicial and administrative decision-making starts with the work of A.V. Dicey (see Box 5.2). Dicey approached his understanding of the state and state power from a very formal and legalistic perspective. He was also deeply committed to classical liberal principles, including the notion that state power should be strictly limited and that the law should operate to clearly delineate a sharp boundary between private and public spheres. The late nineteenth century witnessed a previously unseen expansion of the state authority and state capacity, as governments began to assume responsibility for such matters as basic public health, sewage, and occupational health and safety. These measures were a response to the social problems that characterized the industrial revolution, particularly in Britain, which included increased urbanization, poverty, and associated public health challenges. For Dicey, the increased role of the state represented

> **BOX 5.2.  A.V. DICEY AND THE FOUNDATIONS OF BRITISH CONSTITUTIONALISM**
>
> A.V. Dicey lived from 1835 until 1922. As a constitutional theorist, he is most famous for his book *Introduction to the Study of the Law of the Constitution*, which was published in 1885. His understanding of the rule of law has shaped much of Anglo-British constitutionalism. He is also widely cited for the articulation of the principles of parliamentary supremacy and the notion that the locus of sovereign power rests with Parliament. He was the Vinerian Professor of Law at Oxford University and was one of the first professors of law at the London School of Economics. Politically, he subscribed to laissez-faire economics and was supportive of Jeremy Bentham's principles of utilitarianism and radical individualism. He considered the twin principles of the rule of law and parliamentary supremacy as the bedrocks of the English constitution. It is all too common nowadays to see those principles in tension – how stable is the rule of law if it can be changed with a new political alignment in Parliament? – but Dicey rightly saw them as complementary, recognizing the ultimately political origins of law. To the extent that Anglo-British constitutional systems are largely unwritten, Dicey's articulation of these principles have become deeply engrained in our understanding of parliamentary constitutional systems.

the unwarranted adoption of what he called "collectivist principles" and a threat to individual freedom (Arthurs, 1979). The expansion of the administrative state meant increased discretion and power for state officials, which in the classical liberal framework threatened the autonomy of the individual. It raised the spectre of an arbitrary and capricious state, as well as the erosion of individual liberty and autonomy.

Dicey's approach to this problem was to insist on the primacy of the rule of law. The basic formulation of this principle is that all actions are permissible unless prohibited by law, and that state officials have no special privileges or powers beyond those of any other citizen. This principle informs many of our basic understandings of the relationship between state and citizen and how law operates to constrain both the actions of individual citizens and also the actions of the state. If we think back to Chapter 4 on criminal law, we can readily see this principle at work. Police officers, as representatives of the state, require legal authority to arrest and detain an individual. If they don't possess that, their actions constitute an assault on the individual and that person may be legally entitled to resist the police officer. Similarly, the search of an individual's private dwelling generally requires a search warrant as an indicator that the normal rules of trespass have been suspended to authorize the police to conduct what would otherwise be an unlawful intrusion onto someone's property.

The application of the rule of law to the growing power and authority of the administrative state establishes some of the key foundational principles of our understanding of both administrative law and state authority. In effect, Dicey was giving voice, in legal terms, to Max Weber's concept of authority. For Weber, the most stable form of authority was grounded in law – what he called rational-legal authority. For Dicey, this meant that every state action needed to be defined by and limited by the "jurisdiction" of the actor. That jurisdiction, to Dicey, should be clearly and explicitly defined by law – whether that be legislation, regulation, or judicial decision. Disputes about legal authority, by extension, should always be decided by the courts. For Dicey, the courts were the obvious and logical vehicle for safeguarding the "rights" of individuals from the dangers of arbitrary state power. The courts had long been the protectors of what he termed "ordinary law." The common law, with its emphasis on individual private property rights (see Chapter 8), was well-suited to resist the incursion and growth of a state that Dicey saw as fundamentally flawed and potentially dangerous to the interests of individuals. Moreover, the courts, according to the common law, already possess an inherent jurisdiction and authority to decide disputes about the meaning of "law." By the time of the rise of the administrative state, the independence of the judiciary was well established and understood to be outside of traditional state authority, meaning that there was a strong argument that law, as applied by the courts, should have primacy over administrative decision-making. Much of the historical development of administrative law jurisprudence has involved a pendulum swing between more restrictive and more permissive approaches to understanding this question of jurisdiction. While administrative law has certainly become more flexible and accommodating of administrative practices than Dicey would have preferred, his understanding of the rule of law and state authority nevertheless continues to have considerable influence and frames much of the ongoing debate (Arthurs, 1979).

## GROUNDS OF JUDICIAL REVIEW: THE LIMITS OF STATE AUTHORITY TO ACT

There are three broad grounds of judicial review that have been developed by the courts: **procedural error, error of law,** and **jurisdictional error.** Failure to adhere to the judicial standards established for these categories results in administrative decisions being quashed and invalidated by the courts. The grounds of review establish core principles of "good administration" that courts are prepared to impose on administrative bodies. The principles themselves are broad in nature and centred on concepts of due process and reasonableness.

It is worth noting what is meant by a decision of an administrative body being "quashed." Judicial review is different that an appeal. When a higher court hears an appeal from a lower court, it can either uphold the decision or overturn it. Overturning a lower court decision allows the appeal court to effectively dictate what the "correct" decision should have been. When an administrative decision is "quashed" because of judicial review, however, the court does not substitute its preference for that of the administrative agency. Rather, it declares the decision of no force and effect, and the issue is remitted to the original decision-maker to redo its decision. In other words, the case is sent back to the agency to rectify the errors they made and come to a new decision that is supported by their authority.

This reflects a fundamental balance between law/courts on the one hand, and politics/administration on the other. The ability to judicially review administrative agencies is inherent to the powers of superior courts, but it is, in theory, more limited than the power of a court of appeal. In some instances, however, the enabling legislation creating an administrative body grants a "right of appeal." This is an important signal that courts may have greater scope for intervening in administrative decision-making than in those cases where their authority is limited to just "judicial review." Finally, while "quashing" a decision on judicial review theoretically means the administrative agency could come to the exact same decision on rehearing the case, the judicial opinion often sends a very strong signal about what sort of outcome/result would survive a future challenge. So again, while there are clear distinctions between appeals and judicial review, sometimes these distinctions are not as great as they might first appear.

## PROCEDURAL ERRORS

Review for procedural errors attempts to ensure administrators follow sound and fair decision-making processes. Historically, the courts interpreted this to require a full oral hearing if an individual's rights were adversely affected by a state's decision. The hearing itself was to look as much like a judicial process as possible, reflecting a preference for a judicial model as the most appropriate mechanism for adjudicating rights and entitlements.

This was termed "natural justice" and resulted in many administrative boards developing an increasingly formalized and "quasi-judicial" model of decision-making. Procedural protection, under this model, was an all-or-nothing affair. Either a full hearing was required, or the individual received no procedural safeguards at all (see Box 5.3).

Over time, courts developed a more flexible approach to reviewing procedural errors. As the number and range of administrative decision-makers increased, it became clear that natural justice's all-or-nothing approach was inadequate. The procedural protections, for example, that apply in determining whether someone should be released from a psychiatric institution must necessarily be different than the adjudication of a grade

**BOX 5.3.  *STATUTORY POWERS PROCEDURES ACT* (RSO 1990)**

The *Statutory Powers Procedures Act* was enacted in Ontario in 1971 (see Atkey, 1972). It set out to create a comprehensive list of procedures that were to be followed in administrative proceedings. It very much followed an "all or nothing" approach to natural justice (see Chapter 1). It applied to all proceedings where there was a requirement to provide parties with a "hearing" and included a minimum list of procedural requirements that were very much like the processes of a court. These included the following:

- The right to reasonable notice of the hearing
- The right to reasonable information about any allegations or complaints about a one's behaviour or conduct
- The right to a public hearing
- The right to be represented by a lawyer or agent
- The right to call and examine witnesses, and to cross-examine the witnesses called by other parties
- The right to protection against self-incrimination and the use of anything from the hearing being used in subsequent criminal or civil proceedings
- The right to reasonable adjournments of the hearing
- The right to a written decision, including reasons if requested

appeal in a university course. While procedural safeguards are necessary in both, a full judicial-style hearing would be impractical. Indeed, if a judicial hearing were required for almost all administrative decisions, the state would quite simply grind to a halt. As a result, the doctrine of natural justice was supplanted by the notion of **procedural fairness**. At the core of this is the notion that someone subject to an administrative decision has the right to "know the reasons" for the decision, as well as a "right to respond" to the decision (*Nicholson v Haldimand Norfolk Police Commrs Bd.*, 1979; see also Box 5.4). The range of procedures necessary to operationalize the right to know and respond can vary. In many cases, a full oral hearing will not be required. In some cases, written submissions will be sufficient, while in other cases, an informal meeting might suffice.

In general, the more significant the decision being made by the administrative board, the greater the need for enhanced procedural safeguards. As the seriousness of the decision increases – often involving questions of livelihood (hearings held by professional societies regarding the right to practise for lawyers, doctors, or other professionals), issues of liberty (mental health assessments), or financial matters (securities commission hearings, CRTC hearings, labour board hearings, municipal/local planning hearings) – the greater the likelihood that procedural requirements will look increasingly court-like in nature.

**BOX 5.4.  MAVIS BAKER, THE DUTY TO GIVE REASONS, AND REASONABLE APPREHENSION OF BIAS**

*Baker v Canada (Minister of Citizenship and Immigration)* (1999) is one of the most important Supreme Court of Canada cases regarding procedural fairness. Mavis Baker, a Jamaican citizen, entered Canada in 1981 as a visitor but stayed for 11 years while working illegally. During that time, she had four children (all Canadian citizens) and was diagnosed with mental illnesses. She applied for an exemption from a 1992 deportation order pleading for "humanitarian and compassionate considerations" related to her illness and the need to remain connected to her children. A letter from an immigration officer in 1994 found insufficient grounds for the exemption but provided no reasons.

Upon the request of Baker's lawyer, Immigration and Citizenship Canada produced the notes made by the immigration officer reviewing her case. The notes included a number of potentially inflammatory and derogatory comments about Baker, including comments regarding the number of children she had, and speculation that she would be a strain on the Canadian welfare system for her entire life. The notes concluded by stating that "Canada can no longer afford this type of generosity."

The Supreme Court recognized that "in certain circumstances, the duty of procedural fairness will require the provision of a written explanation for a decision" and "in cases such as this where the decision had important significance for the individual ... some form of reasons should be required" (para. 43). In this case, the officer's notes were sufficient to qualify as "reasons," but their content did give rise to a reasonable apprehension of bias on the part of the decision-maker. Note that the question is not whether the decision-maker is biased (a higher standard to prove) but simply whether one might reasonably perceive the decision-maker as having a bias. And here, the officer's notes did "not disclose the existence of an open mind or a weighing of the particular circumstances of the case free from stereotypes" (para. 48).

While *Baker* is a clear statement that decision-makers must not only be unbiased, but also be seen to be unbiased, the case stands largely for the proposition that when important interests are at stake, decision-makers must give a rationale for the outcome to those affected. While the actual form the reasons can take is flexible and accommodating – accepting the "notes" produced here as "reasons," for example – procedural fairness requires that an administrative decision with serious consequences be accompanied by the reasons that led to the outcome. This is an important burden put on what might otherwise be an opaque process governed by an unaccountable administrative state.

# ERROR OF LAW AND JURISDICTIONAL ERRORS

Review for errors of law and jurisdictional errors are interlinked. At one level, error of law is exactly what the name suggests: The administrative decision-maker makes an error in either the interpretation or application of a legal principle. This can involve misinterpreting a statute, misapplying rules of evidence, or misapplying statutory provisions to the facts of the case. Jurisdictional error is, in one sense, simply a type of error of law, one that involves the board overstepping its authority. For all administrative boards and tribunals, their decision-making authority is defined by statute. This is called "enabling legislation," in the sense that the statute creates the board, defines its scope of authority, and authorizes it to act. In some instances, it is necessary for the decision-maker to determine whether they have the authority to decide a case. This may involve an interpretation of the enabling statute. One might think questions of jurisdiction would normally be self-evident, but in many instances it is not. Can a labour board or any other administrative tribunal, for example, apply the *Canadian Charter of Rights and Freedoms* or a human rights code when deciding a case? (Those are questions that the Supreme Court has answered in the affirmative but with considerable qualifications and complexity; see *Doré v Barreau du Québec*, 2012; *Tranchemontagne v Ontario*, 2006; and *British Columbia v Figliola*, 2011; see also Said, 2023). In other words, do tribunals have the jurisdiction and authority to apply other laws beyond their own enabling legislation?

For both error of law and jurisdictional error, then, a critical question is the degree to which courts will defer to expertise and decision-making choices of the administrative board. Interpretation is never an exact science. There are many different approaches to interpretation, which can produce very different outcomes. Over time, courts have moved from a "strict approach" when considering what constitutes an error of law to one that is more deferential, and which respects the autonomy and expertise of administrators. In some ways, this shift mirrors what happened with procedural review – namely, a move away from rigid dichotomous categories to a more nuanced and fluid approach. In this case, it is an approach which reflects a more complicated understanding of the relationship between courts and the broader state, as well as a deeper understanding of the complex role of modern government. This shift was necessary as state administration moved into more complex and difficult areas of regulation. When enabling legislation provides a broad mandate to an agency to "make decisions necessary for the public good" or for "the effective management" of a particular policy area, it is difficult to define the scope of jurisdiction with any precision. Moreover, such broad grants of authority suggest a legislative intention to permit the agency a broad scope to answer these questions. In such cases, should the court attempt to constrain the scope of decision-making authority or permit the agency the discretion to regulate as it sees fit and in accordance with its expertise? Having said that, this has also made judicial interpretation more complex and less predictable. As courts moved from determining whether administrative bodies are "correct" in how they interpret legislation to assessing the contextual reasonableness of their interpretations, predictability and consistency in judicial review cases became much more difficult to achieve.

## PRIVATIVE CLAUSES AND STANDARDS OF REVIEW

The interplay between error of law and jurisdictional error, along with very differing understandings of the role of courts and administration, is evidenced by the historical development of what are sometimes termed **privative clauses**. As the regulatory state expanded, courts were frequently hostile to administrative boards and tribunals and sought to limit their scope of authority. Courts sought to restrict the scope of administrative decision-making by employing a very narrow interpretative framework. Since they tended to value the expertise and efficiency gains that administrative tribunals could bring, governments were frustrated by judicial interference that presented an obstacle to administrative agencies fulfilling their mandate (Daly, 2022; Laskin, 1952). As a result, they sought measures that might limit the ability of the courts to overturn administrative decision-making.

---

**BOX 5.5. PRIVATIVE CLAUSES TO RESTRICT JUDICIAL OVERSIGHT: ONTARIO'S *LABOUR RELATIONS ACT*, 1950, C. 34, S. 69**

"69. No decision, order, direction, declaration or ruling of the Board shall be questioned or reviewed in any court, and no order shall be made or process entered, or proceedings taken in any court, whether by way of injunction, declaratory judgement, certiorari, mandamus, prohibition, quo warranto, or otherwise, to question, review, prohibit or restrain the Board or any of its proceedings."

"Certiorari," "mandamus," "prohibition," and "quo warranto" are known as "prerogative writs." These writs (orders) were based on the inherent authority and powers of the superior courts as granted to them by the Crown and provided very specific forms of remedy. They formed the basis of early forms of judicial review. In early judicial review cases, an applicant would be required to stipulate the actual writ they were seeking. Eventually these were replaced by a generic application for judicial review.

The instrument of choice for governments was the "privative clause." These clauses are inserted into the enabling legislation of an administrative agency to insulate decisions from judicial review. Effectively, they instruct the courts not to review for error of law and declare the decisions of the board to be final and binding and not subject to review for any reason. Box 5.5 provides an example of an early and very expansive privative clause that was included in the *Ontario Labour Relations Act*. One can readily see the broad nature of the language and how the Ontario legislature was clearly trying to cover off almost every potential ground of judicial review, thereby preserving the autonomy of the Ontario Labour Board to make decisions on its own. Indeed, it was in the field of labour relations that the courts had been particularly aggressive at striking down the decisions of labour boards, especially in cases where decisions seemed to favour trade unions over employers (for commentaries on this period of administrative law and the judicial review of labour relations, see Hogg, 1973; Weiler, 1971). It is worth noting that, at common law, trade unions were considered illegal as a "restraint on trade." Systems of labour relations, which we now accept as a fact of modern economic relations, were legislatively created explicitly to overturn the common law as developed by judges (see Chapter 9).

Despite this clear legislative direction to courts to not intervene in the decisions of labour relations boards, courts were quite willing to ignore privative clauses. This was achieved by an interpretative trick in which "errors of law," which were covered by the privative clause, were effectively turned into what courts called "jurisdictional errors," which courts deemed outside the scope of the privative clause. Essentially, the judicial argument was that while the legislative privative clause might protect "ordinary" errors of law from review, the administrative board had to have the actual authority (jurisdiction) to make the decision in the first place (see *Anisminic Ltd v Foreign Compensation Commission*, 1969). Following this line of argument, some errors of law (mistakes) might go to the jurisdiction of the board to decide the matter in the first place. Those sorts of errors, the courts reasoned, could never be protected from judicial review, for to do so would give administrative agencies carte blanche to determine their own authority. Authority had to come from legislation, and so long as that legislation stood unamended and in-force, courts were the final decision-makers as to how that legislative grant of authority should be interpreted. Once again, note the traditional Diceyan concern with state authority run amok.

While that line of argument might be uncontroversial, the determination of what constituted a jurisdictional issue was far from clear. At one level, if a board has the authority to make zoning decisions within a particular geographic municipal boundary, it seems a simple task to determine whether a property falls within that boundary or not. But take the example we gave above, where an administrative board has the authority to make decisions for the "effective management" of a particular policy realm.

Reasonable people might disagree as to what constitutes "effective management," and arguably a privative clause should insulate the administrative agency's decisions on that topic from judicial review. However, the court could now argue that, logically, the first question to determine jurisdiction is whether a decision was necessary for "effective management." If it was not, then the board had no authority to decide the issue in the first place. This interpretative approach places the question of effective management back within the scope of judicial oversight.

If we think of jurisdictional authority as a metaphorical box, review for errors of law relate to issues that clearly fall within the four walls of the box. Within the box, the existence of a privative clause meant that boards had the "right to be wrong," or more accurately, the discretion to determine, without interference, what they considered to be the correct answer. Review for jurisdictional error, however, effectively allowed courts to move an issue from "within the box" and place it on the boundaries of the box itself. Now the court no longer had to defer to the expertise of the board and had the full right to substitute its judgment for that of the agency decision-makers.

This technique was so successful that it operated to gut the effectiveness of privative clauses in insulating boards from judicial review. Privative clauses were introduced in labour relations throughout Canada during the 1940s. By 1952, however, Bora Laskin (1952), who would later go on to become chief justice of the Supreme Court of Canada, wrote that privative clauses were "futile," with courts ignoring these legislative attempts to limit judicial review. The courts were able to turn anything they felt to be a mistake in interpretation into a jurisdictional error.

Of course, this is not the end of the story. Just as with procedural review, the interpretative approach of the courts to jurisdiction also changed and evolved over time. The courts, over time, developed a more contextual approach to review for error law and jurisdiction, in which greater deference to the decisions of administrative decision-makers was extended. This developed into an approach by the courts where a privative clause provided effective protection against judicial review, except in those instances where a decision was considered "patently unreasonable." Decisions of a board were considered fully protected by privative clauses, unless they could be considered so unreasonable that it was virtually impossible to justify the decision. If Bora Laskin had considered privative clauses a futile tool in protecting administrative integrity, by the 1980s it was possible to say that they had become a full protection to judicial oversight, with only the most unreasonable decisions subject to being overturned (Goudge & Sheldrick, 1988). In the absence of a privative clause, however, or where right to appeal was legislatively provided, courts retained complete jurisdictional authority to overturn board decisions.

A full exploration of all the twists and turns of this jurisprudential journey are beyond the scope of this chapter, and indeed, many scholars have tried to rationalize the many judicial decisions on this topic. Nevertheless, we will attempt to provide a brief outline of the broad contours of how the courts thinking on this subject has changed.

The evolution of judicial review led to a shift away from categorizing types of error – procedural error, error of law, and jurisdictional errors – towards what **standard of review** should be applied by the courts. Standard of review can be thought of as a short form for the degree of deference a court should extend to an administrative board. If no deference is shown at all, the court is free to substitute its decision for that of the board. If a great deal of deference is shown, the court will interfere only in egregious cases where the board's decision cannot be justified. The first step in this process was acknowledging that only in the most unreasonable cases would a court interfere where there was a privative clause. But, as we know from our discussion, the difference between true jurisdictional errors and true errors of law is difficult to rationalize and explain on a consistent basis. As a result, it quickly became clear that similar types of cases, across multiple boards, could be treated very differently by the courts. If the presence or absence of a privative clause could rationally be explained, this might not be a problem, but as we also know, legislative drafting is also far from an exact science, and in many instances, the presence or absence of a privative clause appears somewhat random and not necessarily a good guide to legislative intent.

We should also note that while legislative drafters might often wish to protect administrative decision-makers from judicial oversight, there may also be instances where they might seek it out. This is reflected in those instances where legislators, rather than including a privative clause in enabling legislation, include an explicit **statutory right of appeal** to the courts. In these instances, the legislature appears to be stating very clearly that the courts are fully entitled to employ a standard of "correctness" in the review of an administrative body and do not need to demonstrate any degree of deference. But should they extend some degree of deference regardless? Given the overall trend to deference for administrative decisions, should this also apply where there is an explicit right of appeal? Arguably, at least in some instances, it might very well be appropriate, even where there is a right of appeal, for the court to recognize that the administrative decision-maker possesses specific expertise that makes them particularly well placed to make the decision they arrived at.

In the 2008 case of *Dunsmuir v New Brunswick*, the Supreme Court of Canada tried to simplify and rationalize the approach to standards of review. It attempted to do this by first reducing the standards of review from three (patent unreasonableness, reasonableness, and correctness) to just two – **reasonableness** and **correctness**. Under the first, an administrative tribunal's decision would be overturned only if it were considered by the court to be unreasonable; the second standard is more exacting and requires the tribunal's decision to be correct in the view of the court. While these standards are conceptually distinct, they are often hard to apply in practice. The reasonableness standard requires courts to do something they will always find difficult: to allow a decision to stand – indeed it may be "incorrect" in their judgment – simply because it was a reasonable outcome. This difficulty is an inherently human one; parents experience it when they decide to let their children "learn from their mistakes" rather than deciding a matter for them. It is always a challenge to watch someone proceed in a direction you think is wrong, especially when you might intervene.

The *Dunsmuir* Court postulated a contextual approach to determining which standard of review should be applied. Just as a parent might allow their child to make their own decisions in some cases (usually where the stakes are low) but not in others (where it might be a matter of life and death), context matters. The Court acknowledged that the presence of a privative clause was a strong indication of legislative intent that a standard of reasonableness should be applied, but the existence of such a clause was not conclusive. Rather, the Court could also consider other factors, including such things as the purpose of the tribunal as determined by the legislation creating it, the nature of the questions at issue, and the expertise of the tribunal. In short, the Court attempted to develop a set of principles that might apply to any administrative decision-maker, and arguably any type of administrative decision, regardless of any idiosyncrasies of legislative drafting. The explicit hope of the Court in *Dunsmuir* was to "develop a principled framework that is more coherent and workable."

Despite this, the *Dunsmuir* framework proved to be no more workable or coherent than frameworks that preceded it. Indeed, it took very little time for a body of incoherent and often contradictory judicial decisions to arise. As with frameworks that preceded it, the analytical approach provided by *Dunsmuir* offered little guidance as to how those principles should be applied. The result was a growing body of academic commentary that was critical of the decision and its subsequent application.[2]

Eventually, the Supreme Court of Canada agreed with the growing chorus of disenchantment with *Dunsmuir*. In 2018, it granted leave to appeal in three judicial review cases. Normally, the Supreme Court does not issue reasons for granting leave to appeal, but in this instance it explicitly stated that it was doing so to reconsider the issue of standards of judicial review and directed the appellants to devote a significant portion of their arguments to this question. The decisions in those cases were released in 2019 and the primary articulation of the Court's reconsideration of its approach was contained in its decision in *Canada (Minister of Immigration and Citizenship) v Vavilov* (2019).

---

2   Paul Daly (2018) has conveniently collated a list of commentary on the *Dunsmuir* case that has been published on his very useful administrative law blog; for a particularly compelling critique, see David Stratas's (2018) contribution.

**BOX 5.6.  THE FACTS OF *VAVILOV***

The Court's restatement of Canadian administrative law is, of course, the important aspect of *Canada (Minister of Immigration and Citizenship) v Vavilov*, but the facts of the case are interesting and worth recounting as an illustration of how administrative law works and affects Canadians. Alexander Vavilov was born in Canada and lived the life of an ordinary teenager until he discovered, at the age of 17, that his parents were actually Russian spies operating in Canada. If you think this sounds like the plot of a TV show, you'd be right – the show *The Americans* was based on this real-life case! The revelation of his parents' work put Vavilov's citizenship in question, since section 3(2)(a) of the *Citizenship Act* denied citizenship to people born in Canada if either of their parents were "a diplomatic or consular officer or other representative or employee in Canada of a foreign government." The provision was a corollary to the usual advantages given to diplomats ("diplomatic immunity" from domestic laws) and reflected the idea that the children of diplomats should not be considered Canadian just because they are born there. Vavilov's parents were not diplomats, however – they were spies. But should they be considered "employees of a foreign government"? The Registrar of Citizenship thought so and cancelled Vavilov's citizenship on that basis. The Supreme Court decided that the registrar's decision was to be adjudged against the standard of reasonableness, but that her judgment was ultimately "unreasonable." The intention of the statute was clearly to apply to those granted diplomatic privileges and immunities, not the clandestine activities of spies. As a result of the Court's decision, Vavilov was given his Canadian citizenship back.

In *Vavilov*, the Court departed from the approach laid out a decade earlier in *Dunsmuir* (see Box 5.6). First, the Court did endorse a "presumption of reasonableness" as the appropriate standard of review, which meant that, unless shown otherwise, the default standard of review would be "reasonableness." But it then went on to reverse its earlier articulation of a contextual approach to determining the appropriate standard of review. Rather, it articulated a set of factors that could rebut the presumption of reasonableness and lead to a standard of correctness. The first of those included a statutory right of appeal, which now means that in those cases courts can exercise much closer scrutiny over decisions of administrative boards. The Court delineates a non-exhaustive list of factors that can lead to a correctness standard, including constitutional questions, questions of law that are general and have wide applicability, and jurisdictional questions that involve delineating the jurisdiction between two or more administrative decision-makers. Once again, we can hear echoes of Dicey's insistence that it is the primary role of courts to interpret and apply the ordinary laws of the land. Significantly, the Court also stated that a reasonableness review must be "robust." It isn't sufficient for a decision to fall within a spectrum or continuum of what might be considered reasonable, but rather the courts can examine the reasoning of the administrative decision-maker to determine not just that the outcome is reasonable but also that the reasoning and decision-making process was itself reasonable. This has invited much and closer scrutiny of administrative decisions post-*Vavilov*, even within the framework of "reasonableness." Whether this latest restatement will lead to consistent and defensible jurisprudence is an open question, but many scholars suspect that there will be further "developments" as the post-*Vavilov* cases arise.

## THE FUTURE OF ADMINISTRATIVE LAW

It is not the intention of this chapter to explore in-depth the ins and outs of administrative law jurisprudence. As a result, the above discussion is tremendously simplified. Rather, our intention is to provide an example of how principles we discussed early in this book have played out in the administrative context. Courts employ a certain logic as to how they approach decision-making. That logic can change and evolve over time, but it has real impacts for actual decision-making and how states and governments act. The evolution of administrative law is principally the story of the evolution of the state over the last century (Daly, 2022). At the same time, the response of the courts to those developments needs to be understood and factored into the story of how the administrative state developed. However, vagaries of statutory interpretation, the uncertainly of language, and the difficulty of creating clear standards are clearly in evidence. As David Stratas (2018) pointed out post-*Dunsmuir*, one of the biggest difficulties of developing a coherent framework of administrative law is the ability of judges at the local level to interpret those frameworks to mean different things in different contexts. *Vavilov*, in many ways, seems to represent a return to a pre-*Dunsmuir* formalism. The Court is very clear that there is space for correctness review, and the evolution of reasonableness as a de facto standard for all administrative decisions has clearly been halted.

Is this the end of the story? Absolutely not. The same difficulties that plagued *Dunsmuir* will continue to present themselves as individual judges try to wrestle with the difficulty of operating within a governance system that extends beyond the judicial system. Courts must always balance what seems just and fair in the specific case before them, with context, legislative and regulatory language, past precedents, and the facts on the ground. For those who seek to understand state decision-making, administrative processes, and policy development, however, it is critical that the role of the courts in overseeing administrative decision-making is not ignored.

## CONCLUSION

In this chapter, we have explored how legal concepts have evolved and developed in relation to the expansion of the administrative state. Concepts such as judicial review, appeal, and standards of review all reflect historic principles that evolved through the common law. However, with the expansion of the modern state, they developed and changed to recognize a new political and legal context. This chapter outlines, in broad strokes, how administrative boards and tribunals function and how the courts have approached their task of providing judicial oversight. Courts have not always been comfortable with the growing importance of the administrative state and preferred to impose approaches to judicial review that were more consistent with the way in which courts have always functioned. At the same time, the administrative law jurisprudence has attempted to recognize the importance of administrative boards and to acknowledge the specialized expertise of quasi-judicial decision-makers. This has resulted in a back-and-forth approach to the development of administrative law jurisprudence. Understanding this is critical for an understanding of administrative law but also for understanding the intersection between law and administration and how law permeates and informs the modern state.

### REVIEW QUESTIONS

1  What are the reasons that underpin the creation of administrative boards and tribunals?
2  How did courts employ jurisdictional review to undermine the effectiveness of privative clauses? If courts are obligated to implement statutes created by Parliament, how can this be justified?
3  Why did courts display hostility to administrative boards?
4  Can you think of examples in which you've encountered principles of "procedural fairness" (or a lack thereof) in your day-to-day life?

# CHAPTER SIX

# Private Law with Public Dimensions: Contracts

## LEARNING OBJECTIVES

- Understand the difference between private and public law and how private law can have important public functions and consequences.
- Describe the difference between distributive and corrective justice, as well as their relevance to private law.
- Understand the fundamental elements of contract law: offer, acceptance, and consideration.
- Critically evaluate the application of contract law to public problems.

The focus of this chapter is **contract law**, which refers to the private law rules that govern legally binding agreements made between parties. Before focusing in on contracts specifically, however, it is useful to return to the general concept of private law in more detail since it frames the next few chapters and requires some additional exploration and discussion. As introduced in Chapter 1, private law concerns legal controversies between citizens whereas public law concerns those between a citizen and the state. This distinction has come under considerable scrutiny, with some claiming it is "old fashioned and undesirable in practice" (Harlow, 1980) and others arguing that it is "really very fundamental to Western legal thought" (Samuel, 1983). Central to this distinction is the special character of the state: "The invasion of one's house by the police is ... not the same as invasion by an irate neighbour" (Samuel, 1983, p. 583). This question of whether the state has special status or power in otherwise "private" actions – a theme we will return to throughout this chapter and the next – is only part of the story. Even strictly "private" legal controversies between individual citizens have clear public dimensions. In this chapter and the next few, we explore areas of private law that, once the basics of each is better understood, present compelling subjects for scholarship beyond legal study.

## PUBLIC CONCERNS AND PRIVATE LAW

Political scientists, even those interested in law broadly as a political institution, tend to focus on public law, especially constitutional law. This lack of attention is unfortunate, since private law is rife with elements of public concern and will likely impact more citizens than a typical constitutional case. While one is unlikely to bring a constitutional case, and hopefully one can avoid interacting with the criminal justice system, Canadians are much more likely to have some engagement with private law areas such as contract law, tort law, family law, and property law. Indeed, we use contracts almost every day since we make purchases, we likely own or rent someplace to live, and our family rights and responsibilities are defined within legal limits.

Moreover, the very idea of private law puts in play what might be called the meta-story of law in a liberal society: What value and limits can legitimately be placed on individual choice and individual responsibility? A key distinction traditionally observed between public and private law is the differential treatment in law of the legally empowered state from that of a free citizen. Consider this appraisal from English jurist Justice Laws: "For private persons the rule is that you may do anything you choose which the law does not prohibit.... But for public bodies the rule is the opposite.... It is that any action taken must be justified by positive law... (*R v Somerset*, 1995, p. 524; Sedley, 2015, p. 222). This asymmetry serves liberty from both directions: The state cannot assume its power to interfere with the citizenry, whereas the citizen can assume their freedom unless told otherwise in law. Moreover, private law can also enhance the power of citizens to order their own affairs. As legal theorist Hanoch Dagan (2021) argues, contract law offers "people a new power that enhances people's ability to be the authors of their own lives" because it "enables people to legitimately recruit others to advance their own goals, purposes, and projects, both material and social" (p. 25). Private law, in this view, *empowers* citizens and can maximize the effect of their freely made choices.

And yet the very idea of something being "private" immediately raises the spectre that such privacy can conceal and even justify "private" abuse, discrimination, and exploitation. A key critical insight of the feminist movement, for example, was the demonstration that notions of "private behaviour" were routinely used to shield domestic violence from legal repercussions and justify state non-intervention when such abuse was readily apparent. Similarly, a wide "freedom to contract," to protect your "right" to enter into transactions with whomever you please, has been invoked historically to create a space in law where racism and other discriminatory actions prevailed. The 1939 Supreme Court of Canada case of *Christie v York* is a vivid example of how private law can shield racist actions from legal consequences. In that case, Fred Christie was refused service at the York Tavern because he was Black and because there were concerns about potential rioting that might occur at the upcoming boxing trials at the nearby Montreal Forum. When Christie sued and took his case all the way to the Supreme Court, he was disappointed by the law's ineffectiveness in ensuring his equal treatment: After finding that Quebec's *Licence Act* didn't apply, the case fell "under the general principle of the freedom of commerce; and it must follow that, when refusing to serve [Christie], the respondent was strictly within its rights" (p. 145). For the Supreme Court of the time, freedom of commerce meant the freedom to racially discriminate.

The freedom and liberty private law happily bestows needs to be balanced against the societal need to prevent abuses of that liberty, like that experienced by Fred Christie. Once we accept that the state must play *some* role in the public regulation of private interactions, the question becomes, "to what extent?" Where and how that line is drawn is an inherently political issue and one that may evolve over time. Other interests and goals may also be factored into the development of substantive private law rules; for example, one influential movement of economists and economically minded legal academics has advocated for rules that prioritize "efficiency" (see Box 6.1).

---

**BOX 6.1. LAW AND ECONOMICS**

Since the 1980s, a "Law and Economics" movement has attempted – with considerable success – to transform private law to privilege *efficient* outcomes. The movement has had a significant impact on tort law, property law, and contract law. Questions about liabilities and damages, the Law and Economics line of thinking goes, are best answered by considering what the optimal outcome would be for the participants. Law and Economics proponents often seek what is called "Pareto efficiency," which is defined as the point where no individual can be made better off without making another party less well off (a sort of "win-win" situation that gives maximum advantage to all without disadvantaging anyone). Looking at law this way has generated many insights and led to significant reforms in legal processes, even if some of the grander aims of its promoters have proven unworkable or unwise.

An interesting application of the Law and Economics movement is the celebrated Coase theorem of liability. Ronald Coase argues that transaction costs are a key consideration when deciding legal entitlements. Transaction costs are the costs incurred through the process of transferring those legal entitlements: So, if you sell your house, you receive a sum of money less than the actual sale price because you might have to pay real estate agent fees, land transfer taxes, house inspection fees, etc., all of which are considered "transaction costs." Coase's insight was that, if transaction costs were free, the initial assignment of liability did not matter. In a classic example, consider a factory that makes a lot of noise, such that it provokes a noise complaint from the neighbouring property. If liability is placed on the factory, it will decide whether the products it makes are worth soundproofing the facility or ceasing production; in other words, it takes an externality (the noise) and incorporates it "internally" as part of its profitability calculations. If liability is not placed on the factory, the neighbouring property owner will itself put a value on the "quiet" and attempt to pay the factory to not make the noise. The decision whether to continue making the factory's products (and the noise) is market-driven and not subject to the assignment of liability. But, as Coase pointed out, there *are* transaction costs and bargaining is never as fluid as the "frictionless" examples assume. The space between the ideal assumptions and the real world is the space where we might see effective government regulation. This gives us a standard for assessing when to regulate and by how much. (It is usually less than regulation proponents assume, which is why the Coase theorem has become a favourite of most libertarians.)

"Law and Economics" is a variant of what are sometimes referred to as "instrumental" approaches to law. These "Law and ..." instrumental approaches suggest that law is the vehicle that can achieve some other non-legal aim or goal and depreciate law's own internal organization and goals. They effectively mean law is *used* to achieve something, rather than law having its own inherent utility. Such approaches deny or undermine the "immanent" idea of law – that law has its own internal rationality and perspective. It is common in non-legal disciplines to dismiss legal content as so much jargon and mystification, but doing so often creates additional confusion and frustration when the expected legal outcomes don't conform to what another approach might consider "rational."

Courts use the common law rules of private law to reconcile competing interests and goals, but sometimes the wrong balance is struck, and statutory authority must be used by the political branches to arrive at a new equilibrium more closely matching societal mores. Against the common law principle of "freedom of commerce" that permitted private businesses to discriminate against Fred Christie and others, the province of

Quebec eventually countered with legislation and enacted a provincial statutory *Charter of Human Rights and Freedoms* to combat "private" racial discrimination. These legislative schemes for the protection of human rights now exist across Canada and are clear examples of state regulation of private behaviour (the constitutional dimensions of such statutes are discussed in Chapter 3 with respect to equality rights).

Finding the right balance is a politically contested choice and, in our federation, what is considered appropriate can vary among the provinces. Since the provincial legislatures have power over "property and civil rights" in the province, by virtue of section 92(13) of the *Constitution Act, 1867*, private law is predominantly a provincial matter. For this reason, regardless of any of its other merits, the private/public law distinction has a significant operational importance for Canadian law. While there are most certainly federal private law matters and provincial public law ones, the vast majority of private law controversies are resolved according to provincial law because the provinces have the power to regulate contracts, property, and most of the interpersonal relationships in the province. This means that when we are considering private law rules and practices, we are often considering 10 different provincial variations and more in the territories (where federal authority makes the distinction even more complicated). Moreover, one province – Quebec – has an entirely different "civil code" approach to private law matters, which can result in legal outcomes that are markedly different to similar cases in other provinces. While there is a great deal of overlap in the common law provinces – where the underlying legal principles are often truly "common" – social scientists should always be aware of differences in provincial law, especially when particular provincial statutes are involved.

## CORRECTIVE AND DISTRIBUTIVE JUSTICE

Private law is traditionally associated with the idea of "corrective justice." Unlike the other formulations of "justice" canvassed in earlier chapters, corrective justice provides the foundation of the principles of private law and remains important to understand the normative dimensions of contract law and tort law. At the same time, some elements of a competing conception – "distributive justice" – have crept into those areas of private law, and thus the underlying philosophical foundations of private law are muddier than sometimes supposed. This dynamic helps explain the core tenets and evolution of private law, which is why it is worthwhile to introduce these two key conceptualizations of justice here.

The distinction between corrective and distributive justice was identified by the ancient Greek philosopher Aristotle in Volume V of the *Nicomachean Ethics*. Both forms of justice relate to the notion of equality but in very different senses. **Distributive justice** concerns itself with dividing a benefit according to some criteria. That criterion can, for example, be the fairness of dividing things equally among all or according to the participation or effort made to secure the benefit. The perennial question of whether a group-work mark should be given equally to all students in the group or apportioned to those who did the most is a question of distributive justice to which many readers might relate. At the level of the state, controversies about distributive justice are most germane to social welfare benefits: Should we provide a minimum guaranteed income or should benefits be tied to some other criterion? (Have you paid into the system via taxes or some other form of contribution? Do you need to prove you are actively seeking employment? These are two classic requirements to be granted Canadian Employment Insurance benefits.) Since it is mostly about apportioning benefits, distributive justice is, in our system, largely considered a political matter. In a well-known definition, Harold Lasswell (1936) describes "politics" itself as "who gets what, when, and how," which are the classic questions of distributive justice.

**Corrective justice**, on the other hand, is about "correcting" an injustice by putting parties back in the same position had the injustice not occurred. Instead of dividing a benefit, corrective justice addresses a *wrong* done by one party to another. It is "correlative" in that "the justification for regarding something as an injustice, and consequently for holding the defendant liable to the plaintiff, is the same from both sides" (Weinrib, 2012, p. 3). This symmetrical structure implies a strict adherence to the specificity of the wrong done by the offending party and the injury suffered by the other party. Importantly, it is the circumstances of the wrong, not the circumstances of the parties, that dictates liability and the possibility of a remedy. In this respect, aside from the specific wrong that occurred, the parties must be treated equally. For example, the relative wealth of the parties is not normally part of corrective justice; you may be rich and able to pay for the other party's injuries, but if you did not cause them, you should not be deemed liable. Similarly, a disreputable plaintiff is not precluded from receiving a remedy if their bad character was irrelevant to the legal matter under dispute. Corrective justice is not about "levelling the playing field," or other notions of "equity" (considerations that might be part of distributive justice), but solely about the wrong committed by one party that injured the other. In this context, "wrong" refers to a legal wrong that is not necessarily a *moral* wrong; for example, in many contract cases, there may be sound reasons to breach a contract that are morally defensible but which are, nevertheless, a wrong in law simply because they break the original agreement. In many cases, the demands of corrective justice place judges in a difficult position: Faced with a perhaps severely injured plaintiff and a deep-pocketed defendant who *could* pay to assist the plaintiff with those injuries, a judge must still deny relief if the defendant is not legally responsible for the wrong done. This is easier said than done, and it is not surprising then that we sometimes see judges stretching the law with novel judgments that extend private law beyond its traditional corrective basis.

## THE ELEMENTS OF CONTRACT LAW

The ability of individuals to "contract" with each other is the basis of our entire economy. As Scottish enlightenment philosopher Adam Smith explained in the eighteenth century, we can all benefit by concentrating on our particular talents and advantages: doing what we do best and trading for the rest. I might be very good at making shoes, for example, but not very handy at anything else. Faced with necessities beyond shoes, such as shelter and food, I could try to make everything – and live in a poorly constructed house and eat barely edible food – or I could concentrate on making more pairs of those excellent shoes and use them to barter for food and shelter from those better at producing them. With a diverse pool of talents, a system of free exchange is likely to be "non-zero sum," which means everyone is likely to benefit overall from the trading.

Trade can be a risky thing, however. What if I commit to a transaction but the other party does not fulfill its obligations? I can simply accept it as a loss and avoid dealing with that person ever again, but every time that happens, future trade is inhibited and the advantages created by trade are diminished. Another possible response is physical violence against the "cheater," but in addition to putting us on the road to chaotic anarchy, it too would diminish the benefits of a well-functioning system of trade. Concerns about unfulfilled promises might also make us more insular, leading us to trade only with our most trusted inner circle of friends and family. To facilitate secure trade among strangers, we need an external agent that can hold parties to their obligations or at least provide a remedy when obligations go unfulfilled. The state, with its monopoly on the use of force in the jurisdiction, is well positioned to provide the certainty of rules necessary to encourage trade on the widest stage possible.

As Dagan (2021) describes it, the set of state-enforced rules of contract "offers people a new power: to make credible commitments that can induce others to assist them in realizing their ends," and it "expand[s] the repertoire of secure interpersonal engagements beyond the realm of gift-based and similarly close-knit interactions" (p. 25). In order to do so, there needs to be a recognized means of identifying the creation of a legally binding agreement. Here, intention is key. A contract needs to be more than simply a casual offer ("I'll get the next round") or an ambiguous gift ("Take this now and you can get me back later"). In the common law rules of contract, there must be a real "meeting of the minds" between the parties, where the clear intention of both parties is to enter into a transaction with a level of specificity that makes it possible to be enforced (see Box 6.2 for a "contract" that really isn't one). The classic elements of a valid and enforceable common law contract are offer, acceptance, and consideration. All three elements each have a plethora of cases and controversies that fill contract law textbooks, but we can give only a brief description here.

**BOX 6.2.  NO, YOUR COURSE OUTLINE IS NOT A CONTRACT: THE TERM "CONTRACT" IN COMMON USAGE**

We use the term "contract" freely in contemporary language and its specific legal usage clearly does not exhaust the common usage of the word. This can create confusion and ambiguity. It is common at universities, for example, to refer to the course outline or syllabus as a "contract" between students and instructors. It is emphatically not a legally binding contract between those parties: One supposed party (the instructor) is a really an employee of the university and the other (the student) is essentially the customer of the university, and there is no direct contractual relationship between student and instructor in law (there is no "privity of contract," as the lawyers would put it). You will not have much luck suing your instructor in contract for a failure to meet the learning outcomes promised in the syllabus. At the same time, a course outline does set expectations and policies that govern the relationship between the instructor and the students, and it can be referenced in internal processes at the university (for academic misconduct procedures, for example), which may themselves be subject to judicial review. So, while a course outline is not a "contract" in law, its summary of obligations and expectations have a contractual character, which is likely why people mistakenly think of it as a "contract."

**Offer** and **acceptance** are easily understood from their everyday meaning, but, again, the legal requirements are more stringent than you might initially expect. And despite hundreds of years of development already, new issues continue to arise in the common law: Recently, the Saskatchewan Court of King's Bench decided that a texted "thumbs up" emoji sent in reply to the picture of a contract constituted a formal, legally binding "acceptance" (*South West Terminal*, 2023). When it comes to what counts as an "offer" in law, it must be distinguished from an "invitation to treat," which is considered only a prelude to negotiating a contract. This sounds complicated, but it has an easy-to-understand practical application since a "statement of price" is an "invitation to treat" and not an "offer." If, for example, a retailer has a mistake in their flyer that they are selling MacBooks for $200 and not $2,000, the retailer has not made a legally valid offer that you can subsequently demand from them. (It is important that the low price be *mistaken*, because otherwise, if it were done intentionally to drum up interest, it would be false advertising and punished according to the statutory *Competition Act*; see Box 6.3 for other ways advertising complicates the idea of an "offer"). A valid contract usually

**BOX 6.3. ADVERTISING – BINDING OFFER OR "MERE PUFFERY"?**

Advertising is generally not considered an "offer" for the purposes of contract law. This is a good thing because the advertiser might otherwise be making more "offers" than they have products! Moreover, one doesn't reasonably expect the Big Mac in the advertising to look as mouth-wateringly tempting as it appears in the commercial. In law, advertisements are generally treated as nothing more than "an expression of willingness to negotiate," but there are "unilateral contracts" that have been recognized as giving legal effect to advertising "puffery."

The famous case concerns the "Carbolic Smoke Ball" – a purported nineteenth-century influenza remedy that was advertised as guaranteeing its purchasers immunity if the Smoke Ball was used properly (three times daily for two weeks). The advertisement made the claim with a "£100 Reward" for anyone who got sick with the flu and noted that the money had already been "deposited with the Alliance Bank, Regent Steet, showing our sincerity in the manner." Lousia Carlill used the Smoke Ball properly, fell ill with the flu, and sued the manufacturer for her £100. In 1892, the English Court of Appeal rejected the manufacturer's claim that the reward was "mere puff" and awarded Carlill the money. The court found a "unilateral contract" had been made, supported by some of the highly specific characteristics of the advertisement: It was not an offer made to the world at large, but rather only to those who bought the product and followed the instructions; the reference to the money deposited in the bank was evidence of the seriousness of the guarantee; and the consideration was satisfied by the money paid for the Smoke Ball and the burden of following the instructions carefully. While this case (*Carlill v Carbolic Smoke Ball*, 1893) is still recognized as good law (and known by just about everyone who went to law school in the common law world), "unilateral contracts" of this sort remain rare, especially since advertisers are more cautious about making such specific, serious claims, and with other statutory and regulatory rules governing advertising in most jurisdictions.

A notable echo of the Carbolic Smoke Ball case occurred in the mid-1990s in the United States when Pepsi launched its Pepsi Points promotion with a television commercial that ended with the suggestion that a Harrier Jet (worth USD $33 million) would be the reward for seven million Pepsi Points. If they thought about it at all, Pepsi and their marketing department likely thought collecting seven million Pepsi Points would be a costly and time-consuming endeavour. Enterprising business student John Leonard spotted a loophole:

> The fine print of the Pepsi Points guide noted that if you had 15 Pepsi Points you could purchase more for 10 cents each. This was likely to comply with "no purchase necessary requirements," but it meant the Harrier Jet was ostensibly available for $700,000. With some funding from a family member, Leonard sent in an order form for "1 Harrier Jet," along with $700,008.50 to cover the cost of the extra points and $10 to cover shipping and handling! Pepsi quickly changed the advertisement to require 700 million points, but when sued by Leonard for breach of contract they argued the ad was meant to be humorous and not to be taken seriously. Judge Kimba Wood referenced *Carlill* but distinguished Leonard's case as not consistent with other "reward" cases (p. 125). The hallmarks of the *Carlill v Carbolic Smoke Ball* case were not present: There was no evidence that Pepsi had Harrier Jets at their disposal, personal ownership of such fighter craft is prohibited by US law, and the idea of a teenager flying one to school (as depicted in the commercial) was clearly meant to be a joke. After three years of trials and considerable litigation expenses, Judge Kimba Wood denied Leonard's claim finding that "no objective person could reasonably have concluded that the commercial actually offered consumers a Harrier Jet" (p. 127). Pepsi's ad, in other words, amounted to nothing more than mere puffery (*Leonard v Pepsico, Inc*, 1999).

contains the agreed-upon details, like the price, description of item or service, the date the transaction will be complete, and the date of payment (most sales receipts, you'll notice, have all of those details). Because a degree of specificity is required, most contracts are usually made in writing, but a valid contract can be made "by word of mouth or partly in writing and partly by word of mouth, or may be implied from the conduct of the parties" (Ontario *Sale of Goods Act*, s. 4). That said, there are rules of evidence that preclude evidence of oral aspects of the agreement if they "add to, subtract from, vary, or contradict a contract that has been wholly reduced to writing" (*Sattva Capital Corp*, 2014, para. 59). When it comes to contractual agreement, it is always better to have it in writing.

**Consideration** is often the most difficult element of a valid contract for non-lawyers to understand. The essential idea is that both parties of a contract must be gaining something of value. This may seem obvious, since, after all, "getting something" seems to be the whole point of entering into a contract. But unless there is some mutual benefit an otherwise valid contract may in fact not be legally enforceable. If your grandmother says she will give you money to buy a new car, and you happily and readily accept her offer, this is a gift, not a legally enforceable contract. Why? Because your grandmother did not get anything of value out of the supposed "exchange." This means that if your grandmother reconsiders and decides not to give you the money, you cannot sue her to uphold her promise. The requirement for consideration is the reason you will sometimes hear about employment contracts where the salary is $1 or some small amount is given to acquire a copyright; to hold a party to the terms of a contract, even where the contract is mostly "symbolic," exchanging something of value – even a paltry $1 – avoids any concerns that the contract is invalid and therefore unenforceable.

When a contract is breached, the remedy is to put the parties into the position they would have been in had the contract been performed. In most case, this means financial damages are awarded to the injured party at the expense of the party who failed to meet the obligations of the contract. Importantly, the injured party has a duty to *mitigate* the damages. So, if you were selling a car for $10,000 and the buyer contracted and then breached the agreement, you cannot sue the buyer for $10,000 and force them to take the car. Your duty to mitigate would require you to continue offering the car for sale, and (assuming it has *some* value) you might be able to sell it quickly at a lower price, say $7,000. In that case, you could sue the original (non-)buyer for the remaining $3,000, leaving you in the position you would have been had the original contract been performed: $10,000 richer and with no car. The other party is responsible for their commitment to overpay the fair-market value of the car (which has now been established at $7,000) – they end up with no car, but their liability is limited to the amount that was lost by non-performance (in this example, $3,000).

One of the goals of contract law is to give the parties the freedom to devise whatever arrangement they would prefer. Tellingly, this even extends to the power to decide what will happen if either side violates the agreement. Many contracts define the damages to be paid if either party breaches the contract. Courts will generally uphold these provisions even though the contract has been breached since it reflects the original intention of the parties on how to deal with contract breaches. This is particularly important for sophisticated commercial actors, who have the knowledge and capacity to make decisions about these matters as part of their negotiations. More generally, when sophisticated parties – such as large businesses, manufacturers, and governments – are contracting, the basic principles presented above are usually supplemented by more complicated rules (see Box 6.4 for the example of government "procurement").

## UNCONSCIONABLE CONTRACTS

Even a valid contract can be unenforceable if it is considered by the court to be "unconscionable." An **unconscionable contract** is one that cannot be said to be freely made and is not the result of a true "meeting of the minds." A classic example of an unconscionable

---

**BOX 6.4. GOVERNMENT PROCUREMENT AND CONTRACTING**

Modern commercial contracting can become extraordinarily complex, especially when governments are involved. The "legal personality" of the state allows for it to be a party to a contract in the first place, allowing it to engage in commercial activity as if it were not any different from an individual or corporation, but of course the scale of the government and its power to legislate makes it a party unlike any other. Given the public interest of spending tax money responsibly and for treating all interests fairly, modern governments hold themselves to onerous procurement rules. **Procurement** is the process of obtaining good and/or services, usually through a competitive bidding process, that is intended to ensure needs are met at the lowest possible cost. To do so, it is common for large organizations like governments to issue requests for proposals (RFPs) that producers answer with detailed submissions regarding their ability to meet the expectations and the price they would charge. The extent to which these RFPs are governed by ordinary contract law is sometimes difficult to discern and courts have often divided on key matters (see the Supreme Court's 5–4 decision in *Tercon Contractors Ltd. v British Columbia ( Transportation and Highways)*, 2010).

---

contract is one made under duress. If you sign a contract while the other party is holding a gun to your head, then we cannot say that contract was freely made and it would be unacceptable to enforce it afterwards (to say nothing of the criminal consequences of threatening someone with a weapon). "The courts," Chief Justice Dickson declared, "do not blindly enforce harsh or unconscionable bargains" (*Hunter Engineering Co v Syncrude Canada Ltd.*, 1989, p. 462). That extreme gun-to-the-head contract makes for an easy decision regarding its unenforceability, but the line between contract-vitiating duress and the normal pressures inherent in any commercial exchange is a blurry one, especially since contracting parties are rarely precisely equal in their economic and social power. In his influential article "Contract Law and Distributive Justice," legal scholar Anthony Kronman (1994) argued that such doctrines are best understood as a limitation on "advantage-taking," and he suggested that contract law needed to perform *some* role in securing distributive justice. The political-legal question is where that line should be drawn and inevitably draws courts into imposing public policy limitations on the freedom of contract.

The Canadian doctrine of unconscionability is "notoriously uncertain" (Hunt, 2021), perhaps reflecting the competing and irreconcilable values at stake. When should parties be bound by their agreement and when should it be considered so unfair that the contract is unenforceable? Canadian jurisprudence gives only very limited guidance. There are only two certain requirements: There must be (1) an inequality of bargaining power between the contracting parties, and (2) a "resulting improvident bargain" (*Uber Technologies Inc v Heller*, para. 65). In other words, a lousy contract negotiated between two parties that are not "equal" may turn out to not be a contract at all. But that creates ample scope for confusion: Your cell phone contract is between you and a large corporation, and the pricing of data is likely not to your liking (and well out-of-step with international comparators), but those contracts are enforced every day. As legal scholar Sarah P. Bradley (2007) notes, "it is a reality of business life that it is often to the advantage of one party to exploit another party's weakness or neediness, and such commercial pressure is common in mercantile negotiations" (p. 265). So, how unequal does the bargaining power have to be, and how bad does the bargain have to be, before the contract is unenforceable? That is a question of legal-political choice and one situated between the tensions of corrective and distributive justice.

## IS THE CONTRACTUAL FEDERALISM OF CHURCHILL FALLS UNCONSCIONABLE?

The decades-long legal battle between Quebec and the province of Newfoundland and Labrador over the Churchill Falls hydroelectric utility in Labrador illustrates the ambiguities of a potentially unconscionable contract – this time at the highest levels with power politics played through the medium of contract law. There can be little doubt that the contract to build and operate the facility was an "improvident bargain" for the people of Newfoundland and Labrador. The contractual term was long at 69 years (44 years, from 1972 to 2016, followed by an automatic renewal that would last until 2041), but it also locked in prices at a rate that was significantly below market value. By 2010, Quebec received $1.7 billion a year for the electricity generated by the facility, compared to $63 million received by Newfoundland and Labrador. At the renewal rates (2016 onward), Quebec would be able to purchase power from the facility for $2 per megawatt hour (MWh) while being able to sell it for $85 per MWh, at a time when power consumers in St. John's would be paying $104 per MWh (Blake, 2015, p. 61). In other words, to use power generated by a local provincial resource, Newfoundlanders would pay more than 50 times as much as Quebec and not even at the best price Quebec would sell it for abroad. The deal remains a persistent issue in Newfoundland and Labrador politics, where the general population certainly views the deal as profoundly unfair.

What about the other element of unconscionability, the imbalance of bargaining power? It seems odd to refer to a provincial government as anything but a sophisticated legal actor: After all, the province employs a team of lawyers to give it legal advice and even the poorest provincial governments have resources that dwarf those of individuals and private businesses. In this respect, Hydro-Québec's stated position is difficult to rebut: This was a contract "that was fairly negotiated between sophisticated commercial parties with ample legal and business advice" (Bradley, 2007, p. 259; see Feehan & Baker, 2007, for details of the negotiations). But consider Newfoundland and Labrador's position at the time of the contract in 1969: Quebec had made it clear that it would not allow Newfoundland and Labrador to transfer any power across its territory, the only route to Newfoundland and Labrador's potential customers in southern Ontario and the United States. The federal government, who might have otherwise played a role in guaranteeing provincial access to interprovincial trade, abandoned that responsibility for fear of stoking separatist sentiment in Quebec (Blake, 2015, pp. 59–62). In the words of one scholar, the contract was "a low, dishonest episode" that shows "Canadian federalism works best for bullies" (Blake, 2015, p. 62).

The Supreme Court of Canada has been called upon multiple times to address the injustice of the 1969 contract but, at every turn, has perpetuated it by applying private Civil Code rules instead of taking a broader view of an interprovincial arrangement to enhance regional economic development of a vital energy resource. At first blush, this might seem an unfair characterization of the Court's judgments – after all, impartially applying legal doctrines *without* an eye to politics might be considered the Court doing its proper job – but the *choices* the Court made in deciding the contract law issues show a remarkable disregard for how the politics of federalism led to an unjust outcome.

But is this truly a case of interprovincial relations? After all, as the style of cause for these cases indicate (*Churchill Falls (Labrador) Corp v Hydro-Québec*), this is a legal dispute between Hydro-Québec and something called the Churchill Falls (Labrador) Corporation Limited (CFLCo). In formal legal terms, this is not a dispute between provinces, but rather a commercial relationship between two privately owned corporations. The Court treats the parties this way, as private entities, which allows it to apply private contract law as if it were nothing more than a battle between Apple and Microsoft. But these entities are Crown corporations, meaning they are state-owned enterprises that have different incentives and functions beyond profit-generation, even if they are corporate entities subject to market forces and efficiencies. These particular Crown corporations are clearly public in a critical aspect: They hold monopolies on a utility (electricity) that citizens of the provinces cannot do without. Hydro-Québec is a Crown corporation whose sole shareholder is the Government of Quebec; CFLCo is a corporation that, since 1974, has been controlled by the Crown corporation Newfoundland and Labrador Power Commission, which is, in turn, majority-owned by the Government of Newfoundland and Labrador. To make it even more complicated, while Newfoundland and Labrador have a controlling 65.8 per cent share of CFLCo, the remaining 34.2 per cent is owned by Hydro-Québec. There are no private actors other than provinces in this entire "commercial" arrangement. In substance, this is an interprovincial conflict in the guise of a private contract.

In 2018, the Supreme Court once again sided with Hydro-Québec and rigidly upheld the terms of the initial contract. Justice Gascon, writing for seven of the eight members of the Court, declared that "this Court cannot change the content of the Contract, nor can it require the parties to renegotiate certain terms of the Contract or to share the benefits otherwise than as provided for in the Contract" (*Churchill Falls (Labrador) Corp v Hydro-Québec*, 2018, para. 6). In other words, the standard rules of contract apply: CFLCo made a deal with Hydro-Québec and they have to live with it. The majority's ruling, then, hews closely to the approach of corrective justice, with little regard for the distributive injustice.

Justice Rowe, the first and only Supreme Court Justice from the province of Newfoundland and Labrador, dissented from the Court's decision and its characterization of the contract. According to Rowe, the agreement between CLFCo and Hydro-Québec is "the *epitome* of a relational contract" (para. 142). Unlike a more standard contract, a relational contract like this one "establishes a long-term relationship between the parties premised on cooperation and the promise of mutual benefit," and instead of defining the parties' obligations "in rigid detail," it "assumes that the parties would work together to fulfill the aims of their contractual relationship" (para. 142). Such an approach to contract law would more directly incorporate elements of distributive justice. Also, by characterizing the contract this way, Rowe interprets the contract as more akin to the intergovernmental agreements routinely found in Canadian federalism than a strictly business contract.

Consider whether resource agreements between provinces are better construed as intergovernmental agreements or as private law contracts. The latter provides certainty and predictability, but its rigidity also has the potential to preserve an unfair outcome in a changing environment. One might argue, perhaps, that the Quebec Government would not have provided the debt financing sought by Newfoundland and Labrador for the project's original development if it were not assured of the substantial benefit that would accrue to them. Isn't that the very essence and advantage of contract law, as described above? From the perspective of interprovincial relations, however, it is easy to see that a "relational contract" could provide an incentive for Quebec to participate in the development of the resource but not lock in an excessive benefit that has only exacerbated interprovincial tensions and perpetuated an injustice.

In one sense, the Churchill Falls saga is a prime example where legal form – in this case, a contract between commercial entities – can command an outcome in law and allows for its enforcement in practice. Any political argument made for renegotiation can be answered by a lawyerly reply about the legal "certainty" of the contract's validity and the Court's steadfast enforcement of its terms. But the channelling of what is, in substance, an exercise in interprovincial power politics through the medium of law also demonstrates that the law itself conforms to that power distribution. Rowe's employment of the "relational contract" concept shows that, even in the frame of contract law doctrine, the Supreme Court always had a choice. It is perhaps telling that the Supreme Court has been unanimous in all of its Churchill Falls cases, over a span of decades, until the Bench benefitted from the appointment of a Newfoundlander. To what extent the cases were decided by the law or by the result remains unclear, but it is difficult to argue that politics played no role in the "private" matter of Churchill Falls.

## CONCLUSION

This chapter began with an introduction to the well-known classification of public versus private law. While this conceptual distinction has some uses (see, in particular, its importance to private law matters in Quebec, described in Chapter 1), it should not be understood as implying that private law legal controversies are without significant public dimensions. Certainly, as private law incorporates more elements of distributive, rather than corrective, justice, the political implications become clearer. But even if private law cases were strictly decided on a corrective basis, the state's authoritative determination of the substantive laws (whether it be directly through statute or indirectly by allowing existing common law rules to govern) and its role in enforcement would be reason enough to warrant greater consideration by political scientists. As seen in this chapter and the next, the state relies on private law and attempts to use it for its own ends in a fashion that can only be described as political.

Contract law, the topic of this chapter, illustrates this political foundation. Contract law might be thought of as especially private, with its doctrines envisioning a private exchange that simply includes an offer, an acceptance, and consideration. While Canadian law offers ample "liberty of contract," there is a public interest in preventing "unconscionable contracts" from being enforced. The Churchill Falls controversy presents a particularly compelling example of how this doctrinal debate can play out in a situation that is undeniably fraught with public concerns. There, the mega-politics of federalism play out through competing visions of what contract law entails. Whether you think the contract should continue to be enforced or not, it is clearly the sort of case that cannot be dismissed as a private matter warranting little public or scholarly attention.

### REVIEW QUESTIONS

1  What is the difference between public and private law? Does that distinction still matter?
2  What special considerations in contract law are necessary when the state is one of the contracting parties?
3  What is an "unconscionable" contract? Give some examples. Is it fair to make these contracts unenforceable?

## MOOT COURT TOPIC

An upper-year student offers to sell his notes to a junior student now taking the same class he once did. They arrive at an agreed-upon price of $100 and the exchange is made, but the upper-year student has neglected to tell the junior student that the notes are incomplete and the class has been substantially revamped since the notes were taken. Can the "contract" be enforced?

# CHAPTER SEVEN

# Private Law with Public Dimensions: Torts

## LEARNING OBJECTIVES

- Understand what defines a tort and how using tort law can address public problems.
- Be able to provide examples where the tort system has been used to address public problems and evaluate their effectiveness.
- Identify the conditions where a court might create a new tort.
- Understand the advantages and limitations of a damages regime that relies on financial compensation to address injuries.

At first glance, the issues presented by tort law might be dismissed as nothing more than the banal world of "slip and falls," car accidents, and frivolous lawsuits. Ignoring tort law, however, would mean missing a large part of the way in which we interact with the state and with other citizens. Tort law is rife with controversies that revolve around our relations with each other, the way we behave, and the way we expect others to treat us. The state role in devising and enforcing these rules means that tort law is part of our societal self-governance, and those rules can be considered public policies, even if they are initiated only upon private complaint. This chapter begins with a basic outline of how tort law works, and then describes how tort law can be used to improve the accountability of public actors and address public problems.

## LEGAL WRONGS

The conceptual basis of tort law is deceptively simple: A tort is a "legal wrong" committed by one party upon another. Obviously, this puts a lot of stress on which "wrongs" are recognized in law and which ones are not. Tort law distinguishes types of wrongs and decides what needs to be done about those wrongs identified as unlawful. A **cause of action** is the basis for any such lawsuit in tort and it can be established through common law or statute.

The classic understanding of tort law is that it is explicitly intended to deliver corrective justice, not distributive justice, as discussed in Chapter 6. Like contract law, tort law has been under pressure to address distributive matters too, and the notion that "those that can pay, should pay" has increasingly held sway over more formal designations of fault and responsibility. Still, like private law generally, tort law seeks to return the parties to the position they were in prior to the wrong, rather than punish the wrongdoer. This is an important distinction between tort law and criminal law. Tort law focuses squarely on the wrong done *between* parties and, in this way, distinguishes itself from the criminal law, which recognizes wrongs against the public order in addition to the impact on victims. As noted in Chapter 4, the **style of cause** – the "name" of a case – in the criminal context is therefore *R v the Accused*, where "R" is short for Rex, or the King, standing in for the public interest. By contrast, the style of cause in tort law, and private law generally, is *Party A v Party B*. Moreover, the consequences of tort law are not penal; the most common outcome is financial damages, not incarceration, even though some remedies might include some restraints on freedom (an *injunction*, for example, can prevent a party from committing or repeating a private law injury).

A vivid example of how tort and criminal law coexist is illustrated by the famous American cases brought against former Buffalo Bill and celebrity O.J. Simpson. Simpson was accused of murdering his ex-wife, Nicole Brown, and her friend, Ron Goldman. Despite ample DNA evidence of his guilt, the criminal case – *The People v O.J. Simpson* – ended up with Simpson being acquitted of the murder charge. While this was the end of the criminal trial, it was not the end of the legal story resulting from the murders. Goldman's family launched a successful private lawsuit against Simpson for the tort of "wrongful death" and were awarded $33.5 million in damages. How can the inconsistent verdicts be explained? In addition to there being two separate proceedings, the **standard of proof** was different in each trial: In the criminal trial, the much more stringent "proof beyond a reasonable doubt" was required to be met; in the private law action, only "proof on the balance of probabilities" was necessary (sometimes this is referred to as the "civil standard of proof"). This common standard of proof in private law simply asks whether the evidence makes it more likely than not – essentially more than 50 per cent certain – that a claim is correct. So, while Simpson was not found guilty beyond a reasonable doubt, he was deemed more likely than not to have committed the murders. This reconciles what might otherwise be two contradictory verdicts, but more importantly, it illustrates that one act – the homicide – can give rise to multiple independent legal paths (see Table 7.1).

**Table 7.1. Proceeding by Tort Law or Proceeding by Criminal Law**

| Key Differences | Crime | Tort |
| --- | --- | --- |
| Litigants | State v Accused | Private Actor v Private Actor |
| Standard of Proof | Beyond a reasonable doubt | Balance of probabilities |
| Purpose of Remedy | Deterrence, incapacitation, rehabilitation, justice | To put the parties back in the position they would have been if the wrong hadn't occurred |

The legal wrongs addressed in private law can be intentional or unintentional, unlike criminal law, which, for the most part, deals only with intentional wrongdoing (which is why *mens rea* is so important to that area of law, as discussed in Chapter 4). The most well-known tort, negligence, is unintentional, allowing private law to address behaviour which is *wrong* but also accidental. Sometimes the prominence of negligence in tort law eclipses intentional torts, but they too play an important role. Intentional torts include wrongs that also might be considered criminal (assault, battery, false imprisonment) but also non-criminal behaviour (defamation, nuisance, intrusion upon seclusion). So, while intention might be an element of a specific tort, it isn't required by all torts, and it certainly does not carry the importance that it does in criminal law.

## ELEMENTS OF NEGLIGENCE

The basic elements of the tort of negligence require the injured party to prove that the other party – called the **tortfeasor** – owed a **duty of care** to the injured party, that the **standard of care** was breached, and that the tortfeasor's actions **caused** the injury in both fact and in law. Each element of a tort enacts a political-legal choice that recognizes some behaviours and injuries but excludes others. Recognizing an injury in tort law can serve an important public purpose – like product liability, as discussed below – but also means committing to a court-based resolution of the public policy problem, as opposed to other means of resolution, like bureaucratic administration or mediation.

The elements of tort law can be better understood by observing the application and evolution of negligence claims in cases of product liability. The public interest in product safety and consumer protection have been greatly advanced by developments in tort law. Consider two negligence cases relating to product liability: the classic 1932 UK case of *Donoghue v Stevenson* and the 2008 Supreme Court of Canada case of *Mustapha v Culligan of Canada Ltd*. In *Donoghue v Stevenson*, a friend bought May Donoghue a bottle of ginger beer at a café that had been manufactured by David Stevenson. Donoghue had already consumed part of the ginger beer when she discovered a decomposing snail in the ginger beer bottle. Donoghue fell ill and was ultimately diagnosed with gastroenteritis and shock. A defective product could be the subject of a dispute in contract law, but here the contracting parties were not clear since the transactions were between Donoghue's friend and the café and between the café and Stevenson's company. The relationship between Donoghue, the injured party, and Stevenson, the party responsible for producing the snail-infused ginger beer, was not contractual and thus contract law offered no remedy. Could they have a relationship in tort law? That was the primary question for the Court in *Donoghue v Stevenson*: Does a manufacturer owe a duty of care to the ultimate consumer? This was a novel question in common law jurisprudence in 1932, but with an increasingly global and multifaceted system of industrial production, it became increasingly important to settle. Lord Atkin's famous passage in the case remains at the heart of modern tort law regarding the duty of care:

> The rule that you are to love your neighbour becomes in law, you must not injure your neighbour; and the lawyer's question, Who is my neighbour? receives a restricted reply. You must take *reasonable care* to avoid acts or omissions which you can *reasonably foresee* would be likely to injure your neighbour. Who, then, in law, is my neighbour? The answer seems to be – persons who are so *closely and directly affected by my act that I ought to have them in contemplation* as being so affected when I am directing my mind to the acts or omissions which are called in question. (p. 44, emphasis added)

Applied to the *Donoghue* case, it resulted in her favour. Stevenson needed to take **reasonable care** since he could reasonably foresee someone drinking his product and falling ill from his lax manufacturing standards. His omission of more stringent health and safety procedures was blameworthy and he should have had Donoghue, the ultimate consumer, in his contemplation even if his contractual obligations were limited to just his purchasers and distributors. Lord Atkin showed an awareness of how important this would be for the modern age of global trade and commerce – even though he surely would have marvelled at today's multinational supply chains – when he declared that jurisprudence should not "deny a legal remedy where there is so obviously a social wrong" (p. 46). This was an instance where the common law of tort could adapt to fulfill a socially useful purpose, in this case extending product liability beyond contracting parties and, instead, to consumers-at-large.

Flash forward 70 years later and Canadian judges were presented with the opportunity to reconsider this application of tort law as it applied to the case of *Mustapha v Culligan Waters*, with facts strangely reminiscent of *Donoghue v Stevenson*. Waddah Mustapha was a loyal customer to Culligan Waters for 15 years, favouring their advertised cleanliness and purity. That changed one day, when he was about to prepare a new bottle for drinking in his home machine and was dismayed to find a dead fly and part of another dead fly floating in the unopened bottle. While many of us would find that to be off-putting and demand a replacement, Mustapha's reaction was much more severe: Becoming "obsessed" with the incident and the "revolting implications" for the health and welfare of his family, Mustapha developed a major depressive disorder combined with a phobia and increased anxiety. The impact on his mental health was so acute that it impaired Mustapha's work life and ability to run his business. As a contractual matter, Mustapha's remedies were sharply limited, especially since Culligan had already offered to replace the defective merchandise. To provide for his ongoing medical expenses and for the loss of business, he sued Culligan in tort. After all, the fly-in-the-water-bottle doesn't sound too far afield from the snail-in-the-ginger-beer.

The Supreme Court of Canada rejected Mustapha's tort claim. Yes, Culligan Waters owed Mustapha a duty of care (just as Stevenson owed one to Donoghue) and the standard of care was breached (they should have ensured that water meant for personal consumption was free from foreign contaminants), but Mustapha's injury was too remote from the Culligan's wrong. In other words, the negligence in the manufacturing process was not closely connected enough to Mustapha's psychiatric condition. The need for a tort to be proximate to the injury is well known in tort law. Although an injury may be *factually* caused by a tortfeasor's wrongdoing, the standard for *legal* causation is much more limited. If this wasn't the case, any wrongdoing could result in liability even if the injury was at the end of a long sequence of events – think of the game of Mousetrap, where the boot kicks the pail that knocks the marble, and so on, until the mousetrap is dropped. If *legal* causation was equated with *factual* causation, liability for wrongdoing would be potentially unlimited in both time and space. But establishing a workable limit is a difficult legal-political task. The Court relied on a test of **reasonable foreseeability**: Could Culligan Waters have known that an injury like the one experienced by Mustapha was a reasonable outcome? Chief Justice McLachlin quoted an earlier English precedent that the "law expects reasonable fortitude and robustness of its citizens and will not impose liability for the exceptional frailty of certain individuals" (para. 14). Culligan Waters was entitled to assume that its customers would be of "reasonable fortitude," the Court decided, when it came to the issue of its liability for mistakes. If manufacturers were liable for every possible outcome, no matter how improbably but ultimately possible, the impact on commerce would be inhibiting and costly. On the other hand, the *Mustapha* decision, with its emphasis on mental "robustness," seems to be out-of-step with society's increasing concern with addressing mental wellness. Could this be an area where more distributive justice might be in order? The line the Court drew in 2008 might not be the one it would draw today. The balancing of a multitude of factors (legal, medical, financial, and societal) makes this a clear example of how tort law reflects but also operationalizes key political choices.

## NEW TORTS

Despite their jurisprudential innovations, *Donoghue v Stevenson* and *Mustapha v Culligan Waters* both employ the long-standing and well-recognized tort of negligence. This is not always the case and, since torts are part of the common law, new torts can arise whenever courts decide they are needed. For a new tort to be recognized, "at a minimum it must reflect a wrong, be necessary to address that wrong, and be an appropriate subject of judicial consideration" (*Nevsun Resources Ltd v Araya*, 2020, para. 237). The creation of the new tort "intrusion upon seclusion" by the Ontario Court of Appeal in 2012 provides a good example of when and how the court might establish a new tort to address a gap in public policy.

In 2009, Bank of Montreal (BMO) employee Sandra Jones discovered that another BMO employee, Winnie Tsige, had looked at her financial records 174 times over four years for no discernable work purpose. Since Tsige was in a common law relationship with Jones's former husband, the imposition on Jones's privacy seemed more than a little suspicious. The records not only contained all banking transactions but also other confidential identifying information like Jones's date of birth, address, and marital status. When Tsige was confronted by BMO, she admitted to accessing the records, claiming that she was doing so to make sure her partner was actually paying child support. While Tsige viewed the information, she claimed she did not reveal the information to anyone else and did not use it for any other purpose than satisfying her curiosity. Tsige was remorseful and apologized for her transgression. For violating their policies, she was suspended by BMO for one week without pay and denied a bonus. That may have satisfied BMO but offered no relief to Jones, whose privacy was infringed. Jones subsequently sued for $70,000 for "invasion of privacy."

The problem for Jones was that, at the time, there was no "invasion of privacy" tort known in Ontario law. While some provinces (like British Columbia, Saskatchewan, and Newfoundland and Labrador) had created an action for "invasion of privacy" by a provincial statute, Ontario's *Personal Information Protection and Electronic Documents Act* (PIPEDA) would have allowed Jones to sue BMO only for not adequately protecting her data, and BMO would likely have been able to defend that action by correctly portraying Tsige as a "rogue employee" acting against the company's policies. The Ontario courts were thus left with the difficult task of deciding whether to create a new tort of invasion of privacy and allow Jones's suit. On one hand, this appeared to be a clear gap in Ontario law – Jones's privacy was violated by Tsige's wrongful action, and it seemed to deserve some sort of legal response. But an "invasion of privacy" tort could also be potentially applied in a variety of other situations that were considerably different from Jones's case: What if the private information had been made public by Tsige? What if the information was more embarrassing to the injured party (perhaps browser history instead of purchase history)? What if Tsige had used the information maliciously, for financial fraud or identity theft, or facilitated others doing so? What if there was a public interest in the acquisition and disclosure of the information such that it might be considered protected and desirable speech?

In the Ontario Court of Appeal's decision, Justice Robert Sharpe approached the question of whether a new tort should be recognized with great care. Sharpe declined to find a broad new "invasion of privacy" tort. With only this particular case before it, the judicial capacity to address broad policy matters was clearly limited. "We were naturally reluctant about deciding more than was necessary," Justice Sharpe (2018) later wrote, adding "I feared that if we accepted the invitation to recognize a general right to sue for invasion of privacy, we might be biting off more than we could chew" (p. 197). At the same time, Sharpe and his colleagues rejected the argument that finding any tort here would "usurp the legislative role, as it involved a sensitive policy choice in a difficult area, affecting a wide variety of interests and institutions" (p. 198). Sharpe agreed that "issues raising difficult and contentious policy choices are ordinarily left to the legislative process," but here several factors pointed towards recognizing a new tort and it was "very much in the common law tradition to find a legal remedy to respond to a compelling individual claim" (p. 199). Given all the developments in law towards more seriously protecting privacy in both constitutional and statutory law, it made sense to develop tort law cautiously and carefully in this direction too. Sharpe noted that when jurisdictions did create a statutory cause of action, the statute did not give much detail and left the operational aspects to judges and the common law. And, instead of a broad tort of "invasion of privacy," the Court created a new narrower tort called "intrusion upon seclusion" that applied only to situations like *Jones v Tsige*, where someone intentionally or recklessly infringes upon another's private affairs such that a reasonable person would "regard [the intrusion] as highly offensive, causing distress, humiliation, or anguish" (p. 200) but where there was no further use or distribution of the private material. The tort would not be absolute and could be qualified by competing claims regarding freedom of speech and freedom of the press. By limiting the new tort and not attempting to solve all of the complex issues of privacy in one judicial decision, Justice Sharpe argued that the Court was "making law, not making up law" (p. 200), but even the circumscribed tort shows the judicial capacity to use private law to develop public policy.

## TORT REMEDIES

The remedies available in private law are intended to put the parties back in the position they would have been had the legal wrong not occurred. But courts have no magic powers to turn back time or an "undo" button for reality. In most cases, the only remedy the court has available to it is the awarding of financial damages. This needs to be kept in mind whenever tort law is used to address matters of public concern. Several problems arise from this monetary focus: How much is enough to remedy the infraction, and when can "punishment" be considered part of the remedy? Some of these problems relate back to the core issue of **commensurability**, the notion that all damages in law can be reduced to a common standard of dollars and cents. The private law system is deeply committed to fiscal commensurability, even as it sometimes bends to blunt or mitigates its effects.

Consider the tort of intrusion of seclusion discussed above. What remedy should Jones receive from Tsige? If the parties were put back into the position they were in before the wrong occurred, the information would have to be removed from Tsige's memory (like the devices used in the *Men in Black* movies), and even this might not be enough, considering that the violation was felt upon the discovery of the intrusion. The only real option for the Court is to have Tsige pay Jones a sum of money to make up for the intrusion. But how much? Jones asked for $70,000 at the outset. Was that a reliable self-assessment of how much she felt it impacted her or something more like an "opening bid"? The Ontario Court of Appeal ruled that, "given the intangible nature of the interest protected, damages for inclusion upon seclusion will ordinarily be measured by a modest conventional sum," and awarded Jones $10,000 (*Jones v Tsige*, 2012, paras. 71 and 90). Does this amount put the parties back where they would have otherwise been? Would $500 have been enough? Why was $70,000 too much?

Perhaps *Jones v Tsige* is just a particularly difficult case in which to assess damages. Many cases will have more easily quantifiable losses. In Ontario common law, damages where there is a readily identifiable cost are called (somewhat awkwardly) **special damages**. They include anything it is conceivable you would have a receipt for or damages that already have a dollar value attached to them: medical bills, actual lost wages, bills to replace or repair property damage, and out-of-pocket expenses are among the most common. While they still have to be reasonable, they are usually awarded in full to successful plaintiffs. These special damages are distinguishable from other types of damages that may be more speculative

**General damages** are perhaps the most controversial financial remedy since they are non-pecuniary and usually relate to the "pain and suffering" or general disadvantage that the plaintiff has suffered. They are thought to relate less to "compensating" the injured party and more to providing additional money to make their life more endurable. In the case of Waddah Mustapha, who suffered from the discovery of flies-in-the-water-bottle as described above, before the Supreme Court found no liability, the trial court awarded damages as follows: $274,000 for the loss of his salon business (a figure that could be arrived at by looking at the salon's pre- and post-injury revenue), $24,000 in special damages (likely composed mostly of medical and psychiatric bills to address his mental injury), and a further $80,000 for general damages. The $80,000 was meant to address the injury Mustapha suffered, the hardship it created, and its continuing impact on the quality of his life. Like the amount in *Jones v Tsige*, putting a precise dollar amount on this suffering is difficult, even though courts and juries try to find comparable cases to arrive at some consistency in damage awards.

The use of general damages creates a public policy danger. Remember that judges and juries are often going to be faced with a severely injured person and – being humans – they will sympathize with a successful plaintiff and be tempted to help them beyond the amounts established in earlier cases (which to them will be abstract, unlike the person in front of them in the courtroom). So, while arriving at a determinate figure is one problem, *escalating* damage assessments are another. In the United States, damage amounts are alleged to have inflated out of control, leading to a "litigation explosion" of claimants seeking supposed "pay days." Often these cases are misrepresented in the media – the famous McDonald's "hot coffee" case, for example, is one where the press doesn't reflect the reality (see Box 7.1) – but the damage amounts in most US states dwarf those awarded in Canada. In American politics, the topic of "tort reform" is a hot-button issue, but in Canada similar policies have been enacted and enforced by judges with virtually no political input or supervision.

---

**BOX 7.1. "HOT COFFEE"**

An American example often trotted out to show that tort law is "out of control" is the successful multi-million-dollar claim made against McDonald's for serving coffee that is too hot. The case appears absurd on its face – don't we want our coffee to be hot? That sentiment drove ridicule of the case in news reports, late-night television shows, and a famous parody on Seinfeld, where Kramer burns himself trying to smuggle a coffee into a movie theatre by hiding it in his shirt. The widespread mocking of the case resulted in it being the prime example for activists proposing "tort reform" in the United States. Susan Saladoff's documentary *Hot Coffee* reveals that the actual case, *Liebeck v McDonald's Restaurants* (1995), is more complicated than its media portrayal suggests. Seventy-nine-year-old Stella Liebeck was severely burned, requiring skin grafts and eight days of hospital care. Saladoff demonstrates that McDonald's practices with respect to coffee temperatures were problematic and that they had repeatedly settled many cases for similar injuries. As for the multi-million-dollar verdict? The jury likely wanted to send a message with a punitive damage award of $2.7 million – or two days of revenue McDonald's garnered from coffee sales alone. (The damage award was subsequently reduced by the judge to $480,000, further reducing the supposed "excessive" nature of the case.) McDonald's continues to be sued for the hotness of its coffee (Valinsky, 2023), including in Canada (Schmunk, 2023).

In the key 1978 case of *Andrews v Grand & Toy*, the Supreme Court of Canada effectively shifted the trajectory for general damages and averted the potential for high damage awards in Canada. Twenty-one-year-old James Andrews was injured in a traffic accident that was largely the fault of an employee of office supply company Grand & Toy. Andrews was rendered quadriplegic as a result of the injury and sued for the care that would be necessary for the remainder of his life. In addition to the monetary damages related to his care, which could be calculated and estimated accurately, the Court agreed that some amount was necessary to address Andrew's "pain and suffering" or, as an earlier court had described such amounts, as providing the injured "with reasonable solace for his misfortune" (p. 262). But how much? When it came to the exact amount, the Court recognized the limitations of their judicial capacity since "there is no medium of exchange for happiness…. The monetary evaluation of non-pecuniary losses is a philosophical and policy exercise more than a legal or logical one" (p. 261). As part of that "policy exercise," the Court noted that it would be useful if the amounts for such injuries should be standardized across the country and they "should not vary greatly from one part of the country to another" (p. 263). Justice Dickson was also clearly wary of damage awards in the United States that "have soared to dramatically high levels in recent years" and were "open to widely extravagant claims" (p. 261). Both factors suggested that a cap on general damages for "pain and suffering" was warranted. The Court noted that Andrews would be at the high end of such amount: "It is difficult to conceive of a person of his age losing more than Andrews has lost" (p. 263). It awarded him $100,000 for non-pecuniary losses (which, when combined with the special damages, amounted to a total award of $817,344). More importantly, it was ruled that "save in exceptional circumstances, this should be regarded as an upper limit of non-pecuniary loss in cases of this nature" (p. 265).

The rule in *Andrews* has proven to be one of the most durable examples of judicial policy-making in Canada. The $100,000 cap has been adjusted for inflation – approximately $400,000 in today's dollars – but over 40 years later, it is still routinely mentioned as the highest value that can be awarded for "pain and suffering" (and since that amount is reserved for the worst cases, like a young person paralyzed for life, most awards are considerably less). In 1995, the Supreme Court reaffirmed the *Andrews* limits and elevated them to a "rule of law" (*Ter Neuzen v Korn*, 1995, para. 114). Reflecting the pressures judges and juries are under to address the injured plaintiff before them, the cap has not been automatically applied to torts that are not accidental personal injuries: In *S.Y. v F.G.C.* (1996), the BC Court of Appeal rejected the imposition of such a cap in general damages for cases of sexual assault, and in *Hill v Church of Scientology* (1995) the Supreme Court ruled that no such damage limit was to be imposed in cases of defamation. Are these small cracks in the cap's application or will we slowly but surely see more torts be awarded higher and higher damage awards? The answer will depend on whether Canadian judges worry more about the inflationary potential of incommensurable injuries or the need to address what they see as the very real needs of the injured parties before them.

Canadian judges have put strict limits on **punitive damages** in private law cases. Unlike the damages that are intended to restore parties to the position they were in prior to the wrong occurring, punitive damages are imposed to punish a party for its wrongdoing. Such an approach runs counter to the norms of corrective justice, which is why they are generally avoided in Canadian tort law, but in some circumstances they are unavoidable. The leading Supreme Court case of *Whiten v Pilot Insurance Co* (2002) demonstrates why they cannot be entirely eliminated. After their house burned down in 1994, Daphne and Keith Whiten brought a claim to their insurer, Pilot Insurance. Instead of paying for the claim in full, Pilot initially paid the Whitens $5,000 for temporary living expenses but "thereafter pursued a hostile and confrontational policy which the jury must have concluded was calculated to force [Whiten] to settle her claim at substantially less than its fair value" (para. 3). Pilot alleged that the family had set fire to their own home, an accusation that "was contradicted by the local fire chief, [Pilot's] own expert investigator, and its initial expert, all of whom said there was no evidence whatsoever of arson" (para. 3). Pilot's refusal to pay the Whitens for the damage to their house was deemed to be based on "wishful thinking" and bore no "air of reality."

In this sort of case, to apply only non-punitive damages would be inviting a moral hazard: If Pilot had to pay only the amount the Whitens were owed under the policy (placing the party the position they were in if the wrong had not occurred), why wouldn't every insurance company resist paying every policy claim in the hopes that some claimants would lose interest or accept that payment was hopeless? If the worst case for the insurer was to simply pay what was owed, such egregious behaviour, like unfounded accusations of arson, would be encouraged even if they only had a small chance of being successfully defended. In this rather unique circumstance – where the ordinary damages would not sufficiently address the wrong committed – the Court was comfortable allowing punitive damages, but even here they were cautious about their usage. In his decision, Justice Binnie noted that the *Whiten* case "raises once again the spectre of uncontrolled and uncontrollable awards of punitive damages in civil actions" (para. 1) and, while the Court upheld the $1 million punitive damages, it was clear that the jury award was more than the Court would have imposed (Binnie noted that $20,000 in punitive damages might have had a sufficient "sting"; para. 83). Once again, the commensurability problem comes into view: What dollar value is "punitive" enough? The overall tenor of the *Whiten* decision suggests that Canadian punitive damages should be very limited and used only sparingly. For the most part, this message seems to have been effectively delivered to lower courts as Canadian punitive awards remain the exception, especially compared to their widespread use in United States.

## TORT LIABILITY FOR PUBLIC ACTORS

As seen earlier in this chapter, with respect to product liability and protecting privacy, tort law can be used to ensure the accountability of public actors and as a mechanism for the achievement of public policy goals. Using it as such upends the notion that private law is strictly a "private" matter and presents both possibilities and perils for the state. Essentially, creating or recognizing causes of action or expanding state liability empowers individuals to use tort law to achieve some public purpose, including keeping the state itself accountable.

Opting for this choice – using tort law to advance a public purpose – carries consequences. The employment of tort law for these ends means accepting a form of what Robert Kagan (2019) calls **adversarial legalism**, which he defines as "policymaking, policy implementation, and dispute resolution by means of party-and-lawyer-dominated legal contestation" as opposed to alternative means such as "bureaucratic administration" or "discretionary judgment by experts or political authorities" (p. 3). There are benefits to this approach, especially since it is "open to new kinds of justice claims and political movements," since lawyers and courts can "serve as powerful (even if not always complete) checks against official intolerance, corruption and arbitrariness, as protectors of essential individual rights, and as deterrents to corporate heedlessness" (p. 4). Since it allows for law to be a weapon wielded by non-governmental actors, adversarial legalism potentially "operates as an essential check on governmental malpractice" (p. 20).

A reliance on adversarial legalism comes with costs. Kagan (2019) offers a clear-eyed assessment of its deficiencies: Adversarial legalism is expensive and inefficient; it "inspires legal defensiveness and contentiousness, clogging up the processes of government, business, and other spheres of activity" (p. 4). The burdensome and uncertain legal process can chill meritorious claims and encourages courts to make law "more malleable and less predictable" (p. 4). When it comes to adversarial legalism, "often the outcome is mixed," Kagan assesses, and sometimes "it produces generally desirable outcomes but at a disturbingly high price in time and money (p. 38).

A necessary condition for tort law to act as a check on "government malpractice" is to expand state liability for its actions. It may seem obvious now that one can sue the government for its "wrongs," but traditionally the common law had immunized the government against all such suits. The well-known statement "the King can do no wrong" encapsulates the notion of **Crown immunity** and reflects the idea that the sovereign could not be sued in their own courts. Until the mid-twentieth century, the Canadian federal and provincial governments could not be held liable, even indirectly. This created some difficult situations, since the state was increasingly playing a larger and larger role in society. With the government providing a vast array of services to citizens, often similar or identical to private services that were subject to liability, the need for some degree of state liability became unavoidable. Should an injury be recoverable when a negligently driven truck is delivering office supplies on behalf of Staples but not when it is delivering them for the Ministry of Finance? In recognition that some government functions legitimately attracted liability despite the common law protection, all Canadian jurisdictions have passed statutes to make the Crown liable. Federally, for example, the *Crown Liability and Proceedings Act* states that "the Crown is liable for the damages for which, if it were a person, it would be liable … in respect of a tort committed by a servant of the Crown" (s. 3[b][ii]). This general liability can be modified by a more specific statute.

Consider the case of the mangled Connor McDavid hockey card (*Clark v Canada Post*, 2016). David Wayne Clark won an auction of a card of the hockey super star on eBay and arranged to have it mailed to him through Canada Post. Earlier, Clark had discovered that his community mailbox slot would not lock properly, so he alerted Canada Post to the problem and was told that his mail would be held at the main post office until the mailbox slot could be repaired. Despite this assurance, mail continued to be negligently delivered to the mailbox and, after the card arrived in the mail, Clark found that the card had been delivered, opened, and mangled (Bresge, 2016; Rhodes, 2016). Clark sued Canada Post in small claims court to recover the $140 he had spent on the card. Could Canada Post claim that it was immune from such claims? On the basis of the common law alone, they might have been able to claim Crown immunity, but the statutory federal *Crown Liability and Proceedings Act* made Canada Post liable in tort, making its responsibility the same as FedEx or any other delivery company. But there is another wrinkle: The *Canada Post Corporation Act* includes a section (s. 40) that makes Canada Post "not liable to any person for any claim arising from the loss, delay or mishandling of anything posted." As a more specific provision that addresses the precise situation, the *Canada Post Corporation Act* section trumps the *Crown Liabilities and Proceedings Act* according to a rule of statutory interpretation (see Chapter 2). End of story? Not quite. The small claims court adjudicator said that "had this item been damaged at any time while in Canada Post's custody, the claimant would clearly be out of luck," but "at the point of delivery … it ceases to be 'posted,'" such that section 40 no longer applies (para. 14). In this view, Canada Post was "negligent in delivering the mail to an insecure mailbox where it might be vandalized" (para. 16) and Clark was awarded the $140 plus $100 in legal fees. The strained interpretation of "posted" might have been an overly narrow one to satisfy the specific and sympathetic circumstances of the case, but it was also an amount that made Canada Post unlikely to appeal the decision.

The hockey card case shows the ability of the state to control its exposure to liability using its statutory authority. This raises an interesting question: If the state can escape liability, why would it ever invite any liability at all? If you had immunity from lawsuits, would you give it up and expose yourself to the loss of income for no appreciable advantage? The difference here is that the state is responsive to public pressures, especially those rooted in principle, and a function of the state's internal complexity. The principle is simple: The state should not be immune to lawsuits for actions that would attract liability for everyone else. This reflects the rule of law notion that those making the law should be subject to those very same laws. To do otherwise would be to invite criticism, explaining why legislation like the *Crown Liability Act* might be popular among voters and thus attractive to the government (for more on Crown immunity, see Monahan et al., 2024).

Some aspects of "government" routinely and controversially attract liability: Government drivers, for example, owe a duty of care to other drivers and pedestrians to drive non-negligently. But this is qualitatively different from *decisions* made by public officials. Assessing liability for government decisions is challenging because such decision-making "occurs across a wide spectrum," as the Supreme Court has recognized in its jurisprudence (*Nelson (City) v Marchi*, 2021, para. 39). In general, the Court has been more willing to shield high-level public policy choices from liability since those typically involve assessing trade-offs between competing values and the sort of decisions that benefit from a broader view of the costs and benefits associated with any particular policy alternative. "Courts are reluctant to impose a common law duty of care in relation to these policy choices," Justices Karakatsanis and Martin write, because governments must "set priorities and balance competing interests with finite resources" (*Marchi*, para. 1). Furthermore, performing the "business of governing" means making "difficult public policy choices that impact people differently and sometimes cause harm to private parties" (para. 1). Consider some of the policy decisions that governments must make in terms of health care: Funding some treatments and not others may result in reasonably foreseeable harm to some, but without the fiscal capacity to fund all procedures – including the most experimental and costly – governments are left to draw lines and make difficult decisions. Elections, not courts, are the path to accountability for these choices: "Courts are not institutionally designed to review polycentric government decisions, and public bodies must be shielded to some extent from the chilling effect of the threat of private lawsuits" (*Marchi*, para. 1). Imagine if a government chose not to pursue a policy in the public interest just because it might expose itself to a lawsuit from a corporation that might be impacted by the policy.

In contrast to those higher-level decisions, the Court has envisioned more "operational" policy decisions where liability is appropriate. The 1989 case of *Just v British Columbia* is illustrative. In that case, a boulder fell from a slope above a public highway and injured a driver below. The Court determined that the provincial government owed drivers a "duty to keep roads reasonably safe" and to ensure that highways are "reasonably maintained," but was tasked with the difficulty question of whether the policies regarding the inspection of roads for such hazards should invite liability. The Court reasoned that they should since they are *operational* decisions, not "true policy decisions" or "core policy decisions" that may warrant immunity. As Justices Karakatsanis and Martin would later acknowledge, "defining the scope of this immunity has challenged courts for decades" (para. 2; Marland et al., 2020).

This juridical attempt to separate implementation from the policy itself was always going to be problematic (Marland et al., 2020, p. 545). In public policy scholarship, it is well known that implementation is an essential aspect of policy development and ignored at the peril of misunderstanding the entire policy. Yet Canadian law continues to seek some means of distinguishing operational from "true policy decisions." In the 2021 case of *Nelson (City) v Marchi*, the Court dealt with an issue near and dear to Canadians: snow clearing. Taryn Joy Marchi parked her car in an angled parking space in downtown Nelson, British Columbia, after two days of heavy snowfall in the area. While the City of Nelson had cleared the parking spaces, they did not create a path to the sidewalk in front of the parking space that Marchi was seeking to access. Marchi crossed the snowbank and her foot sunk through the snow, bending her foot back and seriously injuring her leg. Marchi sued the City, arguing that to not make a passage from the parking spaces to the sidewalk was negligent. The City argued that "all of its decisions about extending snow removal hours were core policy decisions because they struck a balance between preserving the budget for future snow events and responding appropriately to the early January snowfall" (para. 78). A city policy for "Streets and Sidewalk Snow Clearing and Removal" was entered into evidence and noted that that plowing would be carried out "on a priority schedule to best serve the public and accommodate emergency equipment within budget guidelines" and prioritized different areas of the city. The Court ruled that the actual operational decision – to plow the parking spaces but not provide direct access to the sidewalk "bore none of the hallmarks of core policy," which would leave the state immune (para. 83). Since there was no evidence the decision "resulted from a deliberate decision involving any prospective balancing of competing objective and policy goals by the supervisor or her superiors," and since the supervisor herself was likely not "closely connected to a democratically-elected official," the decision not to plow the area where Marchi fell was one for which the state could be held liable. The decision was also subject to "day-to-day budgetary considerations" rather than "high-level ones," and because it could be assessed on objective criteria (how do other jurisdictions handle such parking spaces?), the Court found this to be an operational decision that invited liability. Importantly, the Court did not decide the case in Marchi's favour but instead ordered a new trial where the City would be able to argue that even without providing the direct access to the sidewalk, they had met the standard of care reasonably expected of a municipality removing snow (this is part of that objective assessment the Court relied upon).

The Court's decision in *Marchi* remains problematic in its continuing reliance on finding "operational" decisions that are subject to liability. For one thing, it simply shifts the difficult decisions to be made as part of the standard of care, which, despite its virtue of "objectivity," is subject to other biases: It may ignore important (subjective) differences of fiscal capacity and budgetary choices, but it may also encourage a race-to-the-bottom mentality where jurisdictions may collectively opt for low standards. It also, once again, relies on adversarial litigation as the accountability mechanism, a mode of dispute resolution that might be excessively costly – involving lawyers and courts – rather than a more bureaucratic or even electoral solution. One suspects that if the municipalities had the power to legislate immunity for snow-clearing decisions – regardless of whether they fit the Court's view of whether they were operational or policy – they would do so. That power, however, lies with the provincial governments and they seem to be content with the municipalities being exposed to this liability.

When it comes to the liability of public actors, it is important to realize that liability can be shared among multiple parties (public and private). Liability is shared through the rules of comparative negligence. **Comparative negligence** means the liability is apportioned according to the relative fault of each party and even the injured party bringing the case can be found partially responsible. While it can be applied to private parties too, the concept of comparative liability creates dynamics when public actors are involved because governments are thought to have the "deep pockets" necessary to pay very high damage awards. Its capacity to always pay makes the state an attractive party to include in any lawsuit, especially since other parties may be unable to pay or be capped to certain amounts by insurers (the standard $1 million insurance coverage in auto and home insurance plans is something judges and juries are acutely aware of in damage assessments). Given its size and fiscal capacity, the state effectively has no limit on the damages it can actually pay, even if those funds are actually derived from taxes collected from all taxpayers. If there is even a remote possibility the state can be connected to the wrongdoing, plaintiffs are encouraged to include it as a party to the suit.

## USING TORT LAW TO ADDRESS PUBLIC PROBLEMS

Another "public policy" application of tort law is for the government to leverage the private law system to address a public goal or need. Facing a public problem, the state might choose to not remedy it directly – for example, with a new public program and/ or an administrative, bureaucratic solution – but instead create a cause of action that will allow citizens to sue parties who fail to meet expectations. The implementation of disability policy in the United States is a classic example. In 1990, the *Americans with Disabilities Act* (ADA) required all businesses open to the public to be accessible and to make "reasonable modifications" to reach that standard. It did not set up an agency to monitor compliance, however, and instead allowed citizens to sue a business if it were not accessible. This "grassroots" approach allows for self-empowerment, since it allows the directly impacted to take action regardless of whether a bureaucrat deems it meritorious. One of the downsides is that it places the burden of enforcement on disadvantaged groups and individuals who may or may not be able to pursue legal action to vindicate their rights. Moreover, the system of dispute resolution is the ordinary court system, which is not known for its speed, affordability, and ease of use. It essentially leverages litigiousness, which carries with it attendant costs and dysfunctions. The *New York Times* profiled one activist, Albert Dytch, who had filed more that 180 ADA claims in California (Markham, 2021). The answer to the question posed in the article – "Is it profiteering – or justice?" – is left for the reader to decide, but it demonstrates the ambiguous nature of using private law in this manner. Canadians have a more bureaucratic means of resolving such disability claims – typically through claims to the Human Rights Tribunals – and even though this process is more client-friendly than a private lawsuit, it still imposes the burden of initiating the claim upon the already disadvantaged.

The use of private suits to obtain some sort of public policy goal is pervasive in Canadian governance. Other recent and innovative uses of private causes of action to address public problems can be seen in the novel torts of "negligent investigation," the tort against "family violence," and the "social host" liability for drinking-and-driving offences. All three are judicial creations in the common law that have attempted to address a public policy problem.

The Supreme Court of Canada established the **tort of negligent investigation** in the 2007 case of *Hill v Hamilton-Wentworth Police*. By doing so, they helped fill a gap in police accountability. With some very limited exceptions (like undercover operations), police must themselves obey the law, and they may also be subject to disciplinary procedures for misconduct. Both of those avenues of accountability can sanction an offending officer, but neither do much to address the victim of the misconduct. Here, private law can offer some redress, but it historically has done little. The existing tort of "malicious prosecution" can be used against police officers, but it is an intentional tort that requires plaintiffs to meet a very high standard (the officer must be motivated by some animosity or bias beyond the intent to carry out the lawful investigation). What about a simply poor police investigation where there was not malign intention? That was the case in *Hill*, where an Indigenous man was held in custody for a series of robberies that he did not commit. During the investigation, the police held a faulty line-up where Hill was the only Indigenous person in the array of suspects for witnesses to identify. Moreover, subsequent crimes with the same pattern continued to happen while Hill was in custody, a sure sign the police might have had the wrong man. The police work was sloppy but not intentionally bad – something that, prior to Hill's case, would have gone unaddressed. Hill had already served 20 months in prison, so dropping the charges or appealing the conviction was of little use to him. Hill sued the police force for "negligent investigation" and was successful in establishing the new tort as part of Canadian law. The new tort would find police liable where they departed from the standard of care of the reasonable police officer; unfortunately for Hill, his case did not meet this standard and he was unsuccessful in obtaining monetary damages as compensation for the impact of the faulty investigation on his life.

The dissenting judgment in *Hill* worried that the existence of this new tort might inhibit police from investigations in the public interest and open the floodgates to lawsuits against the police. The former is difficult to track, but when it comes to the latter, it seems the swell of lawsuits has not emerged. A study by McLellan (2020) reviewed the cases of "negligent investigation" and found an average of 10.2 cases per year in the wake of *Hill* (from 2008 to 2019), with plaintiffs winning only 28.6 per cent of the cases compared to 71.4 per cent for the police service. In this respect, the *Hill* case and the tort of negligent investigation appear to meet the majority's expectations for it: An avenue to address police accountability has been established without unduly burdening police forces with claims against them. That said, scholars have continued to find that police accountability measures in Canada overall need to be improved (Puddister, 2023; Roach, 2022), even with the possibility of private action for negligence.

Can private law play a role in the pressing public policy objective of stopping domestic violence? In 2022, Ontario Supreme Court Justice R.J. Mandhane recognized a **tort of family violence** in *Ahluwalia v Ahluwalia*, 2022. While deciding the property distribution and child and spousal support in the marital breakdown of Amrit Pal Singh Ahluwalia and Kuldeep Kaur Ahluwalia, Justice Mandhane awarded Kuldeep $150,000 in damages for the tort of family violence even though "making such a significant damage award is well-outside the normal boundaries of family law" (para. 4). Mandhane recognized that the *Divorce Act* specifically prohibits "misconduct" as a consideration for awarding spousal support and that "the Court must be careful not to arm family law litigants to overly complicate the [divorce] litigation through speculative and spurious tort claims" (para. 41). In this case, however, the marriage was "not typical," but rather "characterized by the father's abuse, and a 16-year pattern of coercion and control," such that it warranted a separate tort award (para. 5). According to Mandhane, the marriage was "not just 'unhappy' or 'dysfunctional'; it was violent" (para. 5). Tort law has a role to play, according to the justice, because the *Divorce Act* "does not create a complete statutory scheme to address all the legal issues that arise in a situation of alleged family violence," (para. 44). While the tort of assault is a long-standing and well-recognized one, it focuses largely on individual incidents of harm; the new tort of family violence would address "the pattern of coercion and control that lays at the heart of family violence cases and which creates the conditions of fear and helplessness" (para. 54). Moreover, this tort would be aimed at helping women leave these abusive relationships. It was possible that the "promise of significant financial compensation could make it more realistic for some women to leave violent relationships" (para. 68). Finally, establishing the tort would bolster other strong societal messages that such violence is unacceptable (para. 70). In sum, the new tort would leverage the system of private law to address a serious gap in Ontario's public policy regarding family violence. "While trial judges must be cautious about developing new foundations for liability," Mandhane proposed that we should do so "where the interests are worthy of protection and the development is necessary to stay abreast of social change" (para. 50). Mandhane's decision was overturned by the Ontario Court of Appeal, as that court decided that existing torts would be sufficient to deal with cases like Ahluwalia's, but the Supreme Court of Canada granted leave to appeal that decision in May 2024. The common law evolution of new torts is rarely a smooth progression and, given the public interest of increasing access to justice for vulnerable people, we may see the common law eventually recognize the tort again or in other jurisdictions.

## CONCLUSION

As a form of private law, tort law is usually conceived as the means by which individual citizens can sue each other for legal wrongs done to them. With respect to one of the most common torts, negligence, this means suing someone who is responsible for an accident that harms you, even though that accident was unintentional. But the law of torts clearly fulfills public functions, and its doctrines both reflect and shape the relationships that constitute society. As we have seen, the state's responses to significant public problems – product liability, police accountability, and invasions of privacy – rely at least in part on the state leveraging the system of torts. Doing so is consequential, not least in part because it utilizes a system of adversarial legalism that is often costly and inefficient but also allows for a claimant-initiated process that can be more responsive than a call for political action. Moreover, tort law provides some means for holding the government to account for its negligence. This form of accountability needs to be treated with care – while the government might rightly be responsible for its errors, the act of governing often creates winners and losers, and without the space to govern in the public interest, we may find our governments less willing to embark on initiatives that might incur liability. The balance between Crown liability and Crown immunity is one that needs careful calibration and should – like so much of tort law – be the subject of social science scholarly attention.

## REVIEW QUESTIONS

1  What are the key differences between a tort and a criminal offence?
2  How can torts be adjusted to meet modern societal demands? Should they be? In what sorts of cases?
3  Do torts provide an effective means of addressing social problems? Why and why not?
4  What sort of limits are there to prevent unlimited liability for all wrongs that may occur?

## MOOT COURT TOPIC

A professor miscalculates a student's final grade by forgetting to include an assignment submitted two days before the deadline. When the mistaken final grade is reported, the student (not realizing the error) contacts the professor and a program advisor but does not receive a response for three weeks. During those weeks, the student is despondent, develops a severe depression, quits his job, decides not to apply to law school, and makes a life-changing decision to move to California to pursue his passion for surfing. Upon learning of the miscalculation – finally – the student decides to sue the professor and the university for negligence.

# CHAPTER EIGHT

# Property Law

## LEARNING OBJECTIVES

- Understand the fundamental elements of property law.
- Critically evaluate the application of property law to public problems.
- Identify the cultural assumptions of property law and understand how they are challenged by rival conceptualizations.

The law of property has been described as "the most commonly encountered area of law but perhaps the least understood" (Chambers, 2021, p. 1). Property law is therefore an obvious target for more social science research. As this chapter demonstrates, controversies in property law routinely reflect conflicting and complex visions of how our society is constructed, and the role of the state in reconciling those conflicts. These issues are complex and require in-depth consideration beyond what can be described in this chapter. So, while we attempt to begin some discussion of these ideas and raise challenging questions, mainly we invite future social scientists to continue this conversation at an even deeper level.

## WHAT IS PROPERTY?

It is commonplace for students to think of property as "things": your house, your computer, your backpack. When pressed, some might include more abstract, intangible "things": money in your bank account can be considered property, for example. Both lawyers and non-lawyers distinguish between **real property**, which refers to land and everything permanently attached to it, and **personal property**, everything else that is not attached to a particular location. But, in law, property isn't just about the actual "things" themselves but more about the legal *relationship* between people and organizations that might make a claim to something. Property rights are often pluralized because these rights are rarely an absolute, singular claim but better conceived of as a **bundle of rights**. This formulation is derived from Justice Cardozo's memorable metaphor of property rights being a "bundle of sticks" (Ellickson, 2011 explains the origin of this metaphor at p. 215). Construed this way, property consists of powers and privileges that can be wholly maintained ("bundled" together) or separated ("severable"). As the "bundle" metaphor suggests, you can have multiple claims to the same "thing" – one person might hold the property rights to the minerals below land, another might have the right to build a structure on the land, and perhaps another can claim rights to the airspace above. Similarly, you can own a condominium and rent it out – both the owner and renter have some property rights in the same physical space. Property law is a "way of managing resources" and "as such, property law must contain rules about who can use what things for what purposes and for how long they may use those things" (Hamil, 2015, p. 682).

To manage and sort through often competing claims, property law provides recognizable rules for ordering those claims, giving protection for those with priority and establishing how we can share or transfer property to others. Two key foundational concepts in the modern property rights framework found in Canada and other Anglo-American jurisdictions are "ownership" and "possession."

**Ownership** implies the broadest bundle of rights related to something and typically includes the right to possess it, the right to use it (and even deplete or destroy it), the right to manage it, and the right to transfer it to someone else (as a gift or by selling/trading it). For the most part, as discussed below in its historical-cultural context, ownership in Canadian law is an individual, alienable right protected by law. In other words, the law recognizes when *you* choose to *transfer* it to someone and, within legally defined limits, it otherwise remains *yours* to do with *as you choose*. In this sense, property allows people to "exercise their freedom by controlling external objects of choice" (Dagan, 2021, p. 9; Weinrib, 2012, p. 275). Understood this way, property law is central to liberal notions of self-determination and autonomy (Dagan, 2021).

**Possession**, as you can probably tell from its inclusion as part of the ownership rights above, is a narrower set of rights related to immediate control and usage. It is often remarked that "possession is nine-tenths of the law," but this is at best a gross exaggeration. If your friend takes your laptop without your permission, she isn't entitled to ownership – indeed, she is a thief and you can have the police return your computer to your possession. It is true that some forms of possession (like "adverse possession," discussed below) can give rise to property rights (like "easements"), and some forms of possession rights can appear almost indistinguishably close to ownership (a 100-year lease, for example, might appear indistinguishable to full ownership), but the formal claim of ownership remains relevant in law. The separateness of possession and ownership expands the options that property rights give us over things: I can continue to own my laptop and have final authority to determine its use, but I can also loan it to you – this time with permission – and give you possession. The latter can itself give rise to rights identified in law: If you rent it from me, I will still own the laptop, but our rental agreement may restrict me from reading your email while you possess it. The possession/ownership distinction is a prime example of the multiple ways that property law gives us the freedom to structure our relationships to things and each other.

These notions of "ownership" and "possession" are deeply engrained in the human psyche. One of the first concepts toddlers understand and articulate is "mine!" and sharing is often one of the first socializing lessons that a child needs to learn. "From our very early days we are encouraged to share our toys," Sir William Fraser (1997) writes, "but the sharing presupposes the possessing" (p. 80). The word "property" has its origins in the Latin and Old French terms for "one's own," and the idea is strongly connected with the very notions of what is "proper." Because of its deep roots in human nature and society, the sense of property can be a bit mysterious. For example, economist Richard Thaler (1980) has described the "endowment effect": the sense that once you possess something, it increases in value to you and, as a correlative, you may therefore insist upon some form of "right" to it. A clear illustration of this effect is to consider how you would feel if, while standing in the checkout line, someone started taking items from your shopping cart. Since you haven't yet paid, you clearly don't have any "ownership" over them, and you could easily replace them with identical items from the shelves. Still, most people would feel violated by the stranger's new possession of what were once *your* groceries (Heller and Salzman, 2021, p. 48). Because of the importance of possession – and its endowment of greater value – we think we have a superior right to the items in our cart against all others, saving the grocery store itself (which retains the legal right of ownership until it is transferred by the actual sale of the items).

Heller and Salzman (2021) rightly insist that ownership is "a legal conclusion, not an empirical fact" (p. 104). This might sound strange to you: How can, say, home ownership not be an empirical fact? After all, there is usually a document (a "deed") indicating ownership and physical possession of the land that seems respected by all. If someone "trespasses" by entering our property without an adequate justification, we are likely to phone the police, who, in turn, are legally empowered to remove that person. That certainty of ownership seems to be a sound basis for concluding that it is an "empirical fact." But it is really a legal conclusion that you own a space (your "dwelling") and have the "right to exclude others" to the extent that the state will recognize and act upon your ownership.

A "right" to any form of property can arise from a variety of sources: You might have been the first to find it, the person who created it, the person who improved upon it, or the person who was making the most productive use of it. We've already seen these factors compete against each other in Chapter 2's discussion of *Pierson v Post*, where Pierson's possession of the fox won out over Post's first-in-time claim (he saw the fox first) and productive labour (he put more effort into chasing the fox). The privileging of some factors at the expense of others is a political choice that both shapes and reflects property law principles.

The ultimate playground rule, "I was here first," has some application in law, as first-in-time possession or first occupation can be a source of property rights. The notion appeals to our inherent sense of fairness – think also of "first come, first served" and all the ways in which we decide that someone gets something simply because they are the first one to claim it. But that is often only the beginning of the question of resource allocation, and the privilege of being first is often limited (you might be first in line for concert tickets, but you may find that you can buy only four tickets and not a whole stadium's worth of tickets).

A source of "new" property rights results from the application of labour. The most well-known theory of property rights arising from labour was articulated by seventeenth-century English philosopher John Locke. The starting point for Locke was the right inherent in one's own body. This right was, for Locke (1690/2003), literally God-given and, even though the world was given to "men in common," "every man has a property in his own person" (Chapter 5, ss. 26–7). Locke extends that right to the "labour of his body" and "the work of his hands" to arrive as a crucial foundation for a right to property: Whatever "he hath mixed his labour with, and joined to it something that is his own, and thereby makes it his property" (Chapter 5, s. 27). Combining one's labour with an external possession creates a right to it as property. Locke recognized limits on this acquisition, arguing that there must be "enough and as good, left in common for others"; furthermore, that which is taken cannot be more than used without waste (Chapter 5, s. 27). These limitations are intended to prevent individuals from taking an undue share or even *all* the resources to the detriment of others.

At its core, property law attempts to manage a central and vexing problem: We share a common physical world but cannot resist attempting to make part of it our own. Denying either the necessity – and sometimes joy – of sharing or the human need to possess usually leads to trouble. Those most opposed to sharing in any capacity would have to confront the undeniable interconnectedness of our well-being. A system of property that focused entirely on absolute individual ownership would undermine itself by not ensuring the basic advantages of that ownership: What good is it to have land that has been thoroughly contaminated and rendered unusable by a polluting neighbour? On the other side, those who imagine a utopia of unlimited sharing run into some predictable problems regarding human nature and human rights. The well-known "tragedy of the commons" suggests resources held by all will be maintained by no one, meaning the most productive use of the resource will never be achieved; to the contrary, the resources may be quickly depleted by the very same self-interest that cooperation was intended to avoid.

There is obviously ample ground between an absolute individual right to property and a world where no one owns anything. Property law commands this space and allows us to recognize *some* rights to *some* uses of *some* things *some* of the time. Not only are property rights limited, but they are also not static. Property rules will vary according to context, place, and time. Modern property rights in the Western European sense are typically characterized by three foundational characteristics: (1) They can be transferred (they are "alienable"), (2) they are individual, and (3) they are prescribed by law and enforced by law. One might question whether this was the best property system for colonial states such as Canada and Australia, both of which were characterized by vast tracts of land, nascent settler communities, and, of course, a diverse set of pre-existing Indigenous occupants with very different property systems. That consideration arose only in hindsight for the English settlers of Canada, who accepted that the English legal system of land was "received" in the New World (Quebec continued the French seigneurial system, which has a different approach to land ownership). In this conception, the state would play a key role as both the ultimate source of property and as guarantor of the "legal conclusions" determined by property law.

In the English conception of property, it is the Crown that grants permission to hold property and recognizes land ownership. In this view, the Crown holds something called "radical title" to the land, meaning it is the ultimate "owner." This does not mean much in day-to-day property ownership, but it is an important background assumption that frames the rights we hold and, in certain extreme situations, it can have important consequences. One practical effect of the Crown's radical title is that for property owners who die without a will ("intestate") and with no relatives to be beneficiaries, the property "escheats" to the Crown (meaning the state gets it). The Crown's radical title also underlies its power to expropriate (take) private property if it has a compelling public reason to do so (for example, to build a new highway). Under the common law, the Crown can even take private property without compensation if it does so explicitly through legislation (the common law presumption is that compensation *will* be given, so it must be explicit if it chooses not to compensate; in the United States, compensation is constitutionally guaranteed, a policy choice not followed by the Canadian founders). For the most part, however, the state's role is ensuring that the "titles" in law that it has granted citizens are maintained.

Recall the examples earlier in this chapter about someone taking your laptop without asking or with "trespassers" who enter your home without permission. The next step that occurred to you might have felt almost inexorable: If someone stole something from you or invaded your home, you would phone the police, with the expectation that they would restore your property right by returning your property to you or removing the intruder. "What distinguishes property from mere momentary possession," Macpherson (1978) notes, "is that property is a claim that will be enforced by society or the state, by custom or convention or law" (p. 3). The certainty of ownership and its enforcement is crucial for a system of property law, and is one of the core justifications for having a state at all.

## INDIGENOUS LAND CLAIMS

The account of property described so far has been one familiar to readers living in the modern Western European tradition. This is not the only conception of property possible. Some Indigenous Peoples in North America, for example, have very different understandings of the environment and the relationship between themselves and the land. The diversity of Indigenous views makes it difficult to generalize about any "Indigenous approach" to property, with some Indigenous lands being held communally and "other Indigenous societies hav[ing] laws governing forms of land ownership, use, access, inheritance, trespass … and definitions of private and public, as well as those who view land as a relation rather than an object of ownership" (Cameron et al., 2020, p. 9). Anishinabek law considers land as "held by the present generation for future generations," and thus "land does not ultimately belong to a person or people in the sense that they have absolute discretion or control" and is "provisionally held for (con)temporary sustenance and for those unborn" (Borrows, 2010, p. 246). The elements of the modern Western European tradition of property that are in tension or conflict with Indigenous notions of property result in some of the most difficult questions presented in Canadian law and politics today.

As noted earlier, "first-in-time possession" is a source of property rights well recognized in Anglo-American common law, even if it is not always definitive. The idea that law should privilege the earliest claim presents an obvious problem *within* common law thinking: The existence of Indigenous North Americans prior to European claims of sovereignty over the land means it is unfair to privilege those later European claims. This is not a new problem, and the common law has struggled for centuries to resolve it or, more often, to obfuscate it. The discussion below details some of those common law contortions, but it should be recognized that this is an argument *within* the Western European tradition. It should not be assumed that Indigenous Peoples see their relationship with the land to be one where land is "possessed" and that their earlier presence on the land has the same significance that the common law might attribute to it.

A common misconception – or at best, a simplification – is that the common law allowed for the European taking of North American land on the grounds that it was "empty" when they arrived. The concept of *terra nullius*, literally meaning "land of no one," has been recognized in international law but its application in the Canadian context is complicated and contested. According to Chief Justice McLachlin in the 2014 *Tsilhqot'in Nation v British Columbia* case, *terra nullius* has "never applied in Canada" and thus could never be the source of the Crown's right in Canadian land (para. 69). "If only this were deeply true," legal scholar and Indigenous law expert John Borrows (2015) writes, since "Canadian law still has *terra nullius* written all over it" (p. 702). What explains this discrepancy between Borrows and McLachlin? While McLachlin has the better technical legal argument about the workings of *terra nullius*, Borrows is right to wonder how the Crown's underlying property right was obtained without it. "Some kind of legal vacuum must be imagined," Borrows suggests before observing that "the emptiness at the heart of the Court's decision [in *Tsilhqot'in Nation*] is disturbing" (p. 703). The uncertain origin of the Crown's property claim is a function of both the misconceptions surrounding *terra nullius* and the confusion the Supreme Court of Canada has introduced in describing Canada's foundational property principles.

As Brian Slattery (2005) points out, the concept of *terra nullius* did not mean that any property claims of the Indigenous Peoples were transferred to the settlers: "Europeans could not appropriate America by mere discovery any more than Native Americans could appropriate Europe" (p. 51). "Discovery," in this case, meant a claim against *other European* nations, not against Indigenous Peoples. As Slattery notes, "the discovering nation had the exclusive right among European states to enter into relations with the Native peoples, to acquire lands from them, and to establish settlements" (p. 51). Under this approach, the land was not thought to be "empty," but no European state had yet established its "exclusive right" to negotiate with the Indigenous Peoples occupying the land. It is under this right that the British (and later Canadian) Crown entered into arrangements with the Indigenous Peoples then inhabiting that part of North America. Douglas Sanderson (2018) argues that these treaties "speak only to the transfer of interests in land and never to the acquisition of sovereignty," so they cannot be the source of the Crown's radical title (p. 320).

A key development in Canadian-Indigenous relations is the Royal Proclamation of 1763 made by the British Crown in the wake of the Seven Years' War, which ended French control over the land now known as Canada. The 1763 Proclamation recognizes that, unless the land is bargained for ("ceded" or "purchased"), any "ownership" of the land must also recognize the rights of Indigenous Peoples to at least use the resource as a "hunting ground." What the Proclamation does not do is clearly establish an Indigenous "ownership" of the land – something that, as noted earlier, would not be consistent with some Indigenous understandings of land and thus likely not something that would have been contemplated by any party at the time. From a European perspective, Indigenous inhabitants of North America lacked sovereignty because they were not organized into territorial states with recognizable (Western-styled) governments. As such, they were not "actors under the law of nations" as this was understood at the time (Flanagan, 2019, p. 54; Oguamanam, 2004). Consequently, without the characteristics of sovereignty, under British common law, the land would be "encumbered" with a necessity to respect to Indigenous use but not seen as being held in English property law by the Indigenous Peoples or as the land of a foreign nation. As a result, the Royal Proclamation sets out the Crown's responsibilities to Indigenous Peoples but falls short of declaring "ownership" and "property rights."

The approach of the Royal Proclamation of 1763 is reflected in the post-Confederation case of *St. Catharines Milling and Lumber Co v R* (1887). The federal Parliament gave a permit to St. Catharines Milling to conduct a logging operation in the disputed boundary of the northwest of Ontario, provoking the province to challenge the federal permit on the grounds that it applied to public land owned by the province. The case involves several disputes related to federalism, but it is notable for its articulation of "Indian title." According to the Court, the Royal Proclamation showed that "the tenure of the Indians was a personal and usufructuary right, dependent upon the good will of the sovereign" (p. 5). The "personal and usufructuary right" meant the Indigenous Peoples could "use" the land for "hunting grounds" and other activities, but that true ownership of the land rested with the Crown, even if it was encumbered by those personal rights. The fact that Indigenous Peoples could sell land only to the Crown and not to other settlers was seen by the Court as more evidence that the Crown held "radical title" on the land.

The framework of the Royal Proclamation of 1763 and cases like *St. Catharines Milling* made a patchwork mess of land occupied and used by the Indigenous Peoples in Canada. Some of the lands were ceded as part of negotiated treaties, some entirely unceded, and with variations across the country. Even when ceded by treaty, the treaties varied in their content and the process used to obtain consent, often with deception or miscommunication an element of the supposed bargain. Moreover, the treaty obligations themselves have often been unfulfilled or ignored over time. As the condition of Indigenous Peoples in Canada continued to be grossly unequal to non-Indigenous Canadians, the need to rethink the Canadian approach to property law as it applied to Indigenous communities became evident and imperative.

In 1973, the Supreme Court of Canada recognized an "Aboriginal title" that existed outside of colonial law in the case of *Calder v Attorney-General of British Columbia*. While the Court accepted that this title existed, it divided on whether the title was "extinguished" as a result of Confederation and the effective control of the land by settlers. While the case did not amount to a clear victory for the Nisga'a, who brought the case, it was enough of a milestone to encourage first the federal government and later the BC government to engage in a process for settling land claims. The opening presented by *Calder* was followed by the *Delgamuukw v British Columbia* decision in 1997 – which developed a test for Aboriginal title and permitted oral evidence to support claims – and further refined in 2014's *Tsilhqot'in Nation v British Columbia*. The test for Aboriginal title requires that the group asserting title must have "occupied" the land prior to colonization and, if present occupation is the proof of pre-sovereignty occupation, there must be continuity in the occupation and, at the time of sovereignty, that occupation must have been exclusive (*Delgamuukw*, para. 143). This exclusive occupation would obviously present an obstacle for Indigenous Peoples who were nomadic or semi-nomadic, a concern the Court addressed in *Tsilhqot'in Nation*, where the Court loosened this restriction to allow for "regular use of territories for hunting, fishing, trapping and foraging" to be sufficient for Aboriginal title so long as it "evinces an intention on the part of the Aboriginal group to hold or possess the land in a manner comparable to what would be required to establish title at common law" (para. 42). Once Aboriginal title is established, it gives "the Aboriginal group the right to use and control the land and enjoy its benefits," but "Governments can infringe Aboriginal rights … but only where they can justify the infringements on the basis of a compelling and substantial purpose and establish that they are consistent with the Crown's fiduciary duty to the group" (*Tsilhqot'in Nation*, 2014, para. 18). Any resource development on the land, for example, would impose upon the Crown at least a duty to consult with the Indigenous Peoples impacted. Significantly, however, this line of jurisprudence continues to assert that the Crown holds radical title to the land, despite it becoming increasingly difficult to ascertain how it acquired it in the first place, given the new emphasis and legitimacy placed on Indigenous rights and self-government (Sanderson, 2018).

Property law scholar Bruce Ziff (Ziff, 2019) notes the evolving nature of the Court's jurisprudence in this area, observing that over the last 39 years the Supreme Court has developed a whole new system of rules for determining Indigenous property rights (p. 403). He notes that Indigenous title claims must be based on "exclusive occupation at the time of the assertion of sovereignty," but this must not be applied in an "ethno-centric" fashion to deny claims of an "Aboriginal society that is fundamentally structured on hunting and gathering, without fixed settlements" (pp. 398–9). As seen above in *Tsilhqot'in Nation*, the Court continues to insist upon a claim "comparable" to the possession needed for title at common law. Ziff identifies this as a continuing tension in the Court's jurisprudence: "The resort to analogies reflects a perceived need to ground Aboriginal rights concepts in a lexicon that is intelligible by lawyers and judges operating within the framework of the Canadian legal system.… Aboriginal rights are at once treated as distinct from, but nonetheless similar to, generic Canadian property law" (p. 395). Given the necessity of accommodation, it is understandable that the resulting rules would be complicated and not wholly satisfying.

The majority's decision in *Delgamuukw* (1997) famously concludes, "Let us face it, we are all here to stay" (para. 186). For Ziff (2019), this admission "acknowledges that the law created by the Supreme Court of Canada is patently – overtly – a mediation of competing political positions" and a distinctive "blending of the common law and Aboriginal perspectives" (pp. 403–4). This is a task that cannot be achieved entirely *within* law, but rather a necessity imposed upon it by external conditions. It is a recognition that common law legal doctrines must ultimately yield to the reality of non-Indigenous and Indigenous Peoples living together in Canada but also to the imperfect and ever-evolving political reconciliation of different legal systems and approaches to law.

## THE POLITICS OF PUBLIC PROPERTY

While Indigenous conceptions of property are generally understood as being more communally oriented, one should not assume that the Western European approach is unconcerned with public uses of property. The right to exclude – a key component of private property – is easy to accept for a private residence, but for spaces that are ostensibly open for all to enter, the "right" to exclude quickly becomes problematic. Indoor shopping malls have bedeviled Canadian law for generations. Malls are unquestionably considered private property, but they also clearly invite the public to enter and arguably provide a much-needed public space akin to a town square. Despite being private property, shopping malls could not systematically exclude classes of people without running afoul of statutory human rights codes; but what about union workers wanting to picket a store in the mall or people the mall managers have deemed undesirable (which might include the homeless, the poor, or bored teenagers)? Canadian courts have given broad scope for mall operators to exclude but not without controversy (see Eric Tucker, 2012, for a discussion of litigation arising at the Toronto Eaton Centre).

And what about property owned by the state? Surely there are some public rights to access and use some of that property. Recent cases have denied injunctive relief and police enforcement to cities attempting to remove homeless encampments on state-owned property. For example, over 80 people in approximately 50 tents occupied two separate pieces of property owned by Prince George, British Columbia, without the permission of the City. After passing a resolution in June 2021, the City applied to the Court for an order to remove the encampments, while also coordinating with BC Housing to create more spaces for supportive housing. Chief Justice Hinkson of the BC Supreme Court denied the City's request in *Prince George (City) v Stewart*, finding that "the alternative housing options proposed by the City are not sufficiently low barrier and accessible to all of the occupants of the encampments" (para 96).

Recently the Region of Waterloo, Ontario, found itself in a similar predicament, and it too was denied the legal ability to remove an encampment on vacant city property. The municipality had passed a bylaw to prohibit "erecting any type of structure, including a tent" on land owned by the Region. But, in *The Regional Municipality of Waterloo v Persons Unknown and to be Ascertained* (2023), Justice Valente found that bylaw to be a violation of section 7 of the *Charter*, which protects life, liberty, and security of the person. Justice Valente noted that there were insufficient accessible shelter beds, meaning that "the Region's homeless have no alternative but to sleep outside" (para 92). Justice Valente's decision was controversial since the Region claimed to have enough shelter space, but the available spaces did not allow for the consumption of drugs, which made them "inaccessible" to many of those in the encampment, in Valente's view. As such, encampments continue to appear in communities across the country, and the legal and constitutional rules for living on public property will be under considerable pressure to develop further.

A related issue is the use of state-owned property that might function as a public forum. As discussed in Chapter 3, the right to free expression is not absolute, and restrictions on the time and place of expression are common. But some state-owned property has long been a venue for public expression, as illustrated by the idea of the "town square" as a forum for debate and sharing one's views. The notion of a public forum was the subject of three key Supreme Court rulings: *Committee for the Commonwealth of Canada v Canada* (1991), deciding a challenge to an airport regulation that prohibited soliciting and leafleting by an advocacy group; *Ramsden v Peterborough* (1993), deciding a challenge to a municipal bylaw creating an absolute ban on posters stuck to publicly owned hydro poles; and *City of Montréal (City) v 2952–1366 Québec Inc* (2005), where a municipal noise bylaw was upheld as a reasonable limit on freedom of expression. Initially, the Court struggled with the issues of access and limits: The *Commonwealth* case was heard by seven justices rendering six different opinions. "If the government had complete discretion to treat its property as it would a private citizen," Justice L'Heureux-Dubé notes in the *Commonwealth* case, it could "grant access to sidewalks, streets, parks, the courthouse lawn, and even Parliament Hill only to those whose message accorded with the government's preferences" (p. 192). In the same case, Justice McLachlin concedes that it would be improper for the state to deny free expression on those government-owned properties, but she suggested that there are other places where a citizen's right to free expression is not traditionally recognized: "The sanctum of the Prime Minister's office, an airport control tower, a prison cell or a judge's private chambers" are all government-owned places where one cannot barge in and start expressing opinions (p. 241).

The difficulties presented by expression on publicly owned property continued in *Ramsden*, where placing an advertisement on a utility pole was understood to be "a historically and politically significant form of expression" (p. 1107), such that a complete ban – instead of regulatory limits for safety and aesthetic reasons – was found unconstitutional. Finally, in the *Montréal* case, a majority of the Court decided to distinguish public property, "where one would expect constitutional protection for free expression" as proven by the "historical or actual function of the place," and determine "whether other aspects of the place suggest that free expression within it would undermine the values underlying free expression" (pp. 171–2). With respect to Montreal's noise bylaw, the City infringed freedom of expression since "streets are clearly areas of public, as opposed to private, concourse, where expression of many varieties has long been accepted" (p. 174). The infringement was justified under section 1, however, since the amplified noise the City was attempting to limit "may interfere with the activities of people using the streets and the buildings around it" (p. 177). While "people in urban neighbourhoods cannot expect to be free from the sounds of many activities ... they can and do expect that the level of this intrusion to be limited, so that they can enjoy a measure of peace and quiet" (p. 177).

The controversies surrounding expression and state-owned property continue to appear in Canadian law. Recent attempts to leverage the law to deal with pro-Palestine encampments on university campuses are likely to generate even more interesting jurisprudence. In general, as with many of the property dilemmas discussed in this chapter, it is likely that these controversies and others will be resolved by balancing and accommodating competing rights. That said, Canadian courts have also been very careful to recognize the important role property – and private property, especially – plays in the foundations of Canadian law. Even if property rights are not as clearly identified as they are in the American Constitution, Canadian property rights are secure and stable. Of course, the boundaries and limits remain subject to political contestation, and respecting and accommodating Indigenous approaches to the land continues to present a considerable challenge to the Canadian property law status quo. These ongoing controversies remind us of both the underlying importance of property and the capacity of our system to moderate competing claims in pursuit of an equilibrium that will allow freedom and industry to flourish in the context of greater justice.

## INTELLECTUAL PROPERTY AND FEDERAL REGULATION

Intellectual property presents a different set of problems than more traditional forms of property. Unlike materialistic "things," intellectual property concerns the property one can have in ideas. The scarcity that makes rules over land essential is replaced by an entirely different dynamic with respect to ideas, since once they are devised, their usage is potentially unlimited. Without regulation, the ease by which ideas can be copied would transform the principle "you reap what you sow" into "you sow, everyone can reap." Some form of protection is necessary to provide incentives for people to create and produce new ideas and inventions. On the other hand, too much protection can itself be stifling of creativity and innovation, since new ideas are often built on the foundation of existing knowledge.

In Canada, the federal government has the power to regulate intellectual property using its legislative authority over "Patents of Invention and Discovery" and "Copyrights" (*Constitution Act, 1867*, ss. 22–3). This means a uniform law across the nation for these matters – unlike most areas of private law, there is no provincial variation in how the law works. Three acts passed pursuant to these constitutional powers define the bulk of intellectual property law in Canada: the *Patent Act*, the *Copyright Act*, and the *Trademark Act*.

The *Patent Act* makes it possible for anyone to be granted a **patent** for their "invention" and creates a cause of action that allows for damages to be claimed if the patent is infringed. While it is a complex statute, its primary engine is startlingly simple: Section 55(1) reads, "A person who infringes a patent is liable to the patentee." Moreover, the act establishes an administrative process that includes a patent office, a patent commissioner, and an appeal process that resolves disputes before they become a matter for the federal courts (using the administrative law, described in Chapter 5). Despite this elaborate bureaucratic structure, the judiciary still plays an important role in developing patent law in Canada. Two remarkable cases before the Supreme Court in the early twenty-first century pushed patent law to adapt to new advances in biological science.

The 2002 case of *Harvard College v Canada (Commissioner of Patents)* posed a simple question for the Court: Can you patent a "new" form of life? At issue was the "Harvard Mouse" or "oncomouse," a genetically modified mouse that was more susceptible to cancer – which sounds incredibly ghoulish but is nevertheless a valuable tool for cancer research. Harvard sought to profit from their creation and was able to secure patents throughout the world, including in the United States and at least 15 European states. When the college applied for a Canadian patent, however, they were turned down by the commissioner of patents, who deemed the mouse to not be an "invention" for the purposes of the *Patent Act*. A majority of the Court upheld the commissioner's decision and suggested that if Parliament wanted higher life forms to be patentable it must do so explicitly.

This issue of patentable life was quickly before the Supreme Court again in the 2004 *Monsanto Canada v Schmeiser* case. This time the Court, with several new justices appointed, allowed a patent on genetically modified seeds. It was significant for most of the Court that the patent was not for the plant itself, but rather for the genes and modified cells that compose it. This meant that farmers, like Percy Schmeiser, could be deemed to be "using" the Monsanto seed even if it blew onto their fields or was subsequently replanted after an initial use. The *Monsanto* decision meant that, in the absence of a clear direction from Parliament, Canadian patent law will continue to distinguish between higher life forms (like mammals), which are not patentable, from lower life forms like bacteria and cells, which are patentable. In this regard, the Court-created distinction between lower and higher life forms for patents would benefit from greater consideration from Parliament. (Parliament did outlaw human cloning in its *Assisted Human Reproduction Act*, but it did not clarify any matters regarding non-human life.) As biotechnology continues its rapid advance, it is well past time for democratic input and thoughtful deliberation on these matters.

Where a patent protects the intellectual property of an invention, a **copyright** protects the intellectual property of an idea. In Canadian law generally, the copyright lasts for 50 years after the death of the creator. A copyright can apply to "every original literary, dramatic, musical and artistic work" and includes performances, sound recordings, and broadcasts (*Copyright Act*, s. 5). The *Copyright Act* protects the intellectual property from being used without the holder's consent but also subjects it to several exceptions, the most notable being the prospect of "fair dealing." According to section 29 of the act, "fair dealing for the purpose of research, private study, education, parody or satire does not infringe copyright." In *Alberta (Education) v Canadian Copyright Licencing Agency* (2012), the Court rejected the idea that Alberta school teachers who gave "short excerpts" of textbooks to their students for no cost went beyond "fair dealing." In a companion case decided the same day, *SOCAN v Bell Canada* (2012), the Supreme Court also decided that 30- to 90-second samples of songs as "previews" prior to sale also constituted "fair dealing" and did not violate copyright. While the Court has been respectful of the ownership of ideas that copyright protects, it has also been aggressive in ensuring that the protection granted does not stifle innovation and uses that don't directly impact the rights-holder financially.

The granting of a **trademark** does not necessarily involve any creative act (like a copyright), but rather simply needs to involve a name or "mark" that one does business under to "differentiate its wares from those of its competitors." The Canadian Intellectual Property Office (CIPO), an agency of the federal government, registers these trademarks pursuant to the *Trademark Act*. A trademark's "monopoly ... serv[es] an important public interest in assuring customers that they are buying from the source from whom they think they are buying and receiving the quality which they associate with that particular trade-mark" (*Mattel*, 2006, para. 21). In *Mattel, Inc v 3894207 Canada Inc* (2006), the Court reviewed the Trademark Board's decision to allow the Barbie's chain of Montreal restaurants to be trademarked despite the very famous Barbie doll sold by toymaker Mattel. The Court rejected Mattel's argument that the Barbie name was so well known that it should be protected even against other businesses that were unlikely to be confused with the doll in the minds of customers.

Do Parliament and the Courts strike the right balance in dealing with intellectual property issues? That is largely a matter of political judgment, so it is disappointing that Parliament has not been more active in responding to the Court's decisions. Perhaps our leaders tacitly approve of the approaches taken by the Court, but even if that is the case, bestowing some democratic legitimacy on the choices made could be helpful. Prime Minister Harper's *Copyright Modernization Act* in 2012 is illustrative; the uncertainties around digital piracy were mostly dispelled by implementing a $5,000 cap on non-commercial copyright infringement damages (a stark contrast to the multi-million-dollar lawsuits imposed on music-loving college students in the United States at the time) and instituting a notification regime where copyright holders notify the Internet service provider (ISP) of an infringement, which then requires the ISP to issue notice to the customer infringing on copyright. There is little doubt that intellectual property will become even more important in the years and decades to come, so it is an area of law that citizens of Canada will want to examine and shape in accordance with their values and preferences.

## CONCLUSION

The process for recognizing intellectual property rights is an obvious manifestation of the fact that property rights are inextricably linked to state power and enforcement. Indeed, the certainty of ownership and protection of private property is one of the classic justifications for having a state at all: "The great and chief end ... of Mens uniting into Commonwealths, and putting themselves under Government," John Locke asserted, "is the Preservation of their Property" (Chapter 9, s. 124). This Western European notion of property rights, with its emphasis on ownership and possession, fits awkwardly with other conceptions of property, especially those that are held by some Indigenous Peoples in Canada, and makes for political conundrums that Canadians continue to struggle with. Even within the common law legal perspective itself, controversies around the use of public property continue to erupt and traditional doctrines continue to be under pressure but may also provide the means to arrive at reasonable outcomes. Knowing those doctrines is an essential step to understanding these controversies, even if one ultimately arrives at the conclusion they need to be reformed.

With all this political contestation around the notion of property rights, it is worth reminding ourselves that the idea of property is one deeply rooted in human experience and recognized as a human right. Article 17 of the United Nations Declaration of Human Rights declares that "(1) Everyone has the right to own property alone as well as in association with others" and "(2) No one shall be arbitrarily deprived of his property." We express ourselves and author our story at least in part through things.

Think about the role your family home may have played in the story of your life, and your attachment to it. Think about how *your* clothes may define *you* and allow you to express yourself. While you certainly are more than the sum of your possessions, it is important to recognize the significance of your ability to possess. And securing that right connects you to the state in a way that is as profound and political as it is personal.

## REVIEW QUESTIONS

1  How does ownership differ from possession?
2  What are the three foundational characteristics of property in the Western European sense?
3  What are the sources of property rights? Are they in tension with each other? How is that tension resolved?
4  How do Indigenous concepts of property challenge Western European conceptualizations?
5  How can the expropriation of property serve the public interest and what limitations are placed upon it?

## MOOT COURT TOPIC

The City of Guelph would like to ensure that adequate greenspace is available to its citizens. A vacant lot is purchased by a developer that would like to build a new apartment complex that will appeal to Guelph's student population. Without authorization in the Ontario *Municipal Act*, and without an existing bylaw, the mayor and City Council tell the developer they will allow the lot – currently zoned for multi-occupant housing – to be used this way as long as the developer commits to 20 per cent of the land remaining greenspace open to all. If the developer refuses, the Council threatens to re-zone the land as a public park. The developer accepts and starts the project but now decides to only make 5 per cent of the area greenspace. What possible legal outcomes are there?

# CHAPTER NINE

# Labour Law

## LEARNING OBJECTIVES

- Understand why labour law is necessary and how it differs from traditional contractual relations.
- Be able to articulate the role of the state in mediating the employer–employee relationship.
- Understand the changing impact "freedom of association" has in the Canadian labour context.
- Be able to articulate the special dynamics that are in play when public sector unions are at issue.

It would be difficult to identify an area of law more obviously political than the laws governing the relationship between employers and employees. Labour law frames the employer–employee relationship, one traditionally characterized as a private one, within a broad spectrum of societal concerns: economic and industrial policy; worker safety and well-being; and social justice, to name but a few. Such political dimensions are even more pronounced when the employer is the state, making public sector unions and their potential for job action an always-pressing societal issue – few issues will rile up voters more than the health and safety threat of garbage not being collected weekly, or more seriously, a public sector strike impacting the delivery of health care or education. While a high-profile strike may capture our attention for a period, the effect of labour law (or its absence) is felt almost daily by everyone involved in the economic life of Canada. Employment is often seen as a core element of individual identity (it is common, upon being introduced, to be asked "… and what do you do?"), such that we should not be surprised that the laws governing its regulation can be the subject of considerable disagreement and deep legal-political contestation. This chapter introduces labour law as a vital subject for social scientists to further examine.

## IN THE ABSENCE OF LABOUR LAW

The importance of labour law is perhaps best understood by considering its absence, which largely characterizes the situation until the early twentieth century. Labour was once considered part of service owed to someone else under feudal systems, something that gave way to an understanding of labour as something that was self-possessed. The Lockean notion of the right to the labour of your own body meant that you have an interest in the product of your labour – something that is probably "obvious" to us now but a crucial milestone in the development of individual liberty. Labour law tells the next part of the story: Now that you should be paid for your labour, what is it worth?

The first answer – and the status quo prior to the advent of what we are calling "labour law" – is simply that it is worth what someone will pay you. In other words, the price of labour can be driven entirely by market forces. In a pure, unregulated labour market, that price will be determined by the purchaser's needs and the availability of people able to do the job. If you are the only person in the world who can produce what the employer wants, you can set the price of your labour close to the ultimate selling price of the product (or you might be better off selling it directly to the consumer). But that situation is rare and, in most situations, there will be an oversupply of labour for any given position. In addition, only larger employers may have the industrial capacity and capital to coordinate a team of employees to transform raw resources into products consumers want. In most workplace situations, employers will be in the advantageous position of dictating the terms of employment, including the crucial question of what wage will be earned.

The initial legal understanding of this relationship between employee and employer was that it should remain a largely private one beyond the "interference" of the state. There would always be some legal role for the state: After all, the principles of contract and criminal law would continue to apply, such that employers could not fraudulently refuse to pay wages for work done or deceive workers about their obligations, but these limits left ample scope for exploitation. It wasn't surprising then that unsafe working conditions, low wages, and often brutal practices emerged from a completely unregulated work environment.

The power imbalance between employers and employees can be addressed in three fundamental ways by the state: (1) The state can do nothing and let any imbalance continue, (2) the state can respond to the demands of its voters, recognizing that the many who are employees will have more democratic power than the few who are employers, and enact general legislation regulating labour practices, or (3) the state can facilitate negotiations between employers and their employees acting *collectively*, such that the relational power is better balanced. The third option is often thought of as the meat of labour law – with the state playing a role mediating between a collective union of employees and an employer – but the second option of general legislation is also an important aspect of labour law (sometimes in this context referred to separately as "employment law"). It should also be noted that these legislative regulatory schemes were not easily enacted. Rather, they came about due to the collective organizing of workers, economic disruptions, political action, and considerable sacrifice.

Such general legislation can have the virtue of enacting standards that protect employees across the entire jurisdiction, whether they are unionized or not. In Ontario, for example, the *Employment Standards Act, 2000* (ESA) guarantees some minimum protections for virtually all employees in the province. For example, section 17 of the ESA prescribes general working hours (eight hours a day and no more than 48 hours a week) and section 20 demands that no one work more than five hours without a 30-minute eating break. Another crucial section of the act – section 23 – requires employers to pay "at least the minimum wage," which is legislatively determined. All these legislated minimum standards protect workers, not just from predatory employers but from other workers who might have "voluntarily" agreed to exploitive conditions, effectively undercutting the interests of employees as a collective. So, according to the law, and aside from some specialized forms of employment, no one in Ontario can work 60 hours a week for $10/hour even *if* the employee and employer privately agreed to those terms; section 5 of the ESA even clarifies that no one can "contract out" of these standards and any employment agreement that purports to do so is void. This effectively overturns the classic traditional view where the relationship between employee and employer is a "private" one. What was once considered "nobody else's business" is now subject to publicly determined minimum standards. These minimum standards are important, but they only provide a basic "floor" for employee rights and may not even be realized in practice (see Box 9.1).

Statutes like the ESA can be found in all Canadian provinces. They are empowered by section 91(13) of the *Constitution Act, 1867*, which gives the provincial legislatures exclusive power over "civil rights in the province," which has been interpreted to include labour rights. These provincial acts cover the vast majority of employees in Canada, but that does not mean there is no role for the federal government in employment law. The federal government itself employs many public servants, with whom they are in an employee–employer relationship that is not subject to those provincial laws and regulations. The Government of Canada negotiates directly with the public sector unions representing many of those employees. More broadly, the federal government

## BOX 9.1.  WOMEN AND THE PAY GAP

A persistent public policy concern is the difference in pay between men and women, even when they are performing the same work. Such differences are explicitly illegal by virtue of section 42 of Ontario's *Employment Standards Act*, which reads that "no employer shall pay an employee of one sex at a rate of pay less than the rate paid to an employee of the other sex when they perform substantially the same kind of work."

Yet this "law on the books" has not translated into pay equity in practice. In 2021, women in Ontario made $0.89 for every $1 made by a man (Statistics Canada, 2022). In terms of average annual wages, where salaries and commissions are factored in, women make 75 per cent of what men make in Ontario. Even factoring in education leaves a substantial pay gap: A Canadian woman with a bachelor's degree makes an average of $69,062 annually, whereas a Canadian man with a bachelor's degree makes $97,761 (Canadian Women's Foundation, 2024). Gender gap disparity is even greater for Indigenous, racialized, and immigrant women.

One factor explaining the wage gap is that women and men tend to hold different types of jobs, and the occupations in which women work often pay lower wages. An Oxfam report cites the following example: Truck drivers (97 per cent of whom are male) make a median annual wage of $45,417 working full-time, while early childhood educators (97 per cent of whom are female) earn a median annual wage of $25,334 (Lambert & McInturff, 2016, p. 6). Women also make up a greater proportion of those who work part-time, which is another structural factor than explains some but not all of the discrepancy.

A persistent wage gap, even when the work performed is similar, may also be attributed to what is sometimes called the "motherhood penalty," referring to the loss of promotion and advancement due to career interruptions and obligations related to parenting. While parenting burdens do not fall exclusively upon women, they remain disproportionally carried by women, who also deal with the physical impact of pregnancy. Ontario's *Employment Standards Act* provides for a pregnancy leave of 17 weeks and a further 61 weeks of parental leave (which may be taken by either parent) and mandates that the employer reinstate the employee after the leave (it is illegal to fire someone for being pregnant or dismissing them while they are on leave).

Section 53(3) of the act stipulates that the wage rate upon reinstatement shall be the greater of the wage paid when the leave began or "the rate the employee would be earning had he or she worked throughout the leave." While this is the legal requirement, and it can be applied where there are clearly

> defined increases for seniority, it cannot easily account for the missed oppor-
> tunities to impress employers or the strengthening of relationships and senti-
> ments that occur when the employee is physically present in the workplace.
> This is where the "motherhood penalty" likely materializes, and it becomes
> difficult to counter with mere law alone, and instead may require a greater soci-
> etal appreciation of the demands of parenthood coupled with a better sharing
> of family responsibilities between men and women.

also has power over employment insurance (EI), a critical social benefit for those who lose their jobs and may require retraining. These matters initially fell within provincial jurisdiction, and, in fact, a national scheme of employment insurance was found to be unconstitutional in 1935. In the wake of the Great Depression, however, provinces found themselves without the fiscal capacity to provide the benefits needed, resulting in an agreement in 1940 to amend the constitution and assign the exclusive legislative authority over "Unemployment Insurance" to the federal Parliament in section 91(2a) of the *Constitution Act, 1867*. The power over this large social benefits program makes the federal government an important player in employment matters, a point dramati-cally illustrated by the response to COVID-19 and the introduction of the Canada Emergency Response Benefit (CERB) to ameliorate the financial impact of the virus.

## THE RISE OF UNIONS AND THE ROLE OF THE STATE

Any imbalance in power between an employer and an individual employee might be recalibrated if the employees were understood to be acting together. This is the essence of modern labour law: recognizing and facilitating the capacity of employees to work in concert to advance their collective interests. Any employer could likely push around a single employee, but could they do so when their entire workforce was on the other side of the ledger? The right to act collectively is constitutionally protected as the "freedom of association" found in section 2(d) of the *Canadian Charter of Rights and Freedoms*. This right to act collectively was initially restricted in its application to employment contexts, but it is now generally accepted that the "freedom of association" in section 2(d) protects some employment rights (as the next section will discuss). The twenty-first century constitutionalization of these rights, however, is only the latest stage in the much longer story of statutory protection for labour relations in Canada, which is why we are discussing that context before further delving into the constitutional politics. Until relatively recently, labour law was an instance in which legislatures provided better rights protection than courts, and statutes provide a pragmatic, political response to the pressing public policy problem of labour unrest.

Perhaps the key to understanding the importance of labour law is to know that it exists primarily to prevent violence and disorder. This may seem distant to us now, since instances of mass physical violence over labour relations are rare in contemporary Canada, but this is better understood as evidence of labour law's success, rather than its irrelevance. Coming out of the First World War, many Canadians struggled under difficult economic conditions, faced with runaway inflation, scarce housing, and record unemployment. Revolution was in the air – the 1917 Russian Revolution was a much commented-upon news event – and the potential for political action on employment matters and economic justice was evident in many parts of the country. The political moment crystalized in the Winnipeg General Strike of 1919. From May 15 to June 25 of that year, 30,000 workers in the city left their jobs in response to a call for a "general strike" from the Winnipeg Trades and Labour Council (WTLC). While essential services were maintained, Winnipeg was brought to an economic standstill. Winnipeg's political and business elites vociferously opposed the strikers and denounced the protests as part of a global conspiracy to overthrow the government (instead of recognizing some of the more moderate and reasonable demands regarding collective bargaining). Fearing that the Winnipeg Strike could inspire similar actions in other Canadian cities, the Government of Canada intervened on the side of the employers and sent in the North-West Mounted Police to break up the strike. On June 21, "Bloody Saturday," violence ensued, resulting in two deaths and dozens seriously injured. The mayhem – including shots fired, horses trampling people, and turned-over streetcars – left a permanent mark on the Canadian conscience.

While the 1919 General Strike did not directly lead to immediate legislation, the need to temper labour relations remained on the political agenda throughout the war years. With the return home of Second World War veterans and a rising consciousness about human rights, demands for state intervention in labour matters increased and led to the enactment of statutory protections that many hoped would prevent further violence, help maintain order, and facilitate better deals for employees with their employers.

While each Canadian jurisdiction's labour statute differs in the details, they share a common **tripartite** framework of three essential actors: representatives of employees, the employer, and the state. The state's role is predominantly played by an administrative tribunal, a labour relations board, as described in Chapter 5. Using the authority of law, the state's role is largely to provide a process by which the employees and the employer can **collectively bargain** and to ensure that whatever bargain arrived at is enforced. Unlike the contractual relationship between an employer and an individual employee, where an imbalance of power may be insufficient to address deficient working conditions, collective bargaining is a negotiation between the employer and all of the employees together, not just as individuals. This framework allows for employees to withdraw their labour altogether and negotiate with the employer on those terms; similarly, the employer remains free to hire an entirely new workforce (the so-called "scabs" or "replacement workers" – although some jurisdictions prohibit the employment of replacement workers), but this is difficult to do for large employers and fraught with the potential for disruption and violence. For this reason, the state plays an important facilitative role in encouraging settlements by setting out and enforcing a clear structure for negotiations.

The attractiveness of the collective bargain is that it provides labour peace for the time it is in effect. Section 46 of the *Ontario Labour Relations Act, 1995* (OLRA), for example, requires that the collective agreement "provide that there will be no strikes or lock-outs so long as the agreement continues to operate." Each side of the employment relationship is legally prohibited from using a key weapon: Workers cannot withhold their labour (a **strike**), nor can employers prevent employees from working (a **lock-out**). Instead of using those practices that are disruptive to the business, employees and employers agree to resolve any disputes that occur during the collective agreement period by using binding arbitration. Section 48 of the OLRA requires every collective agreement to have such a clause: "All differences between the parties" must be settled by "final and binding" arbitration "without stoppage of work." As discussed in Chapter 2, **binding arbitration** is an alternative means of dispute resolution in which the parties agree upon the appointment of an arbitrator who, after hearing submissions from both sides, imposes a resolution deemed, in the arbitrator's eyes, to be fair, reasonable, and consistent with the collective agreement. In sum, the combination of the OLRA and the collective agreement means there is guaranteed labour peace during the period the collective agreement is in force.

The existence of an in-force collective agreement is the enticing promise of labour law, but getting to that point is often a contentious process. Labour relations statutes also prescribe the rules for establishing a union of employees in the first place, as well as the framework for negotiating the collective agreement. Unions are established through a process called **certification**. The path to certification begins when some of the employees seek to unionize, a right of all non-management employees of any firm. Employers are usually opposed to the unionization of their workforce for the simple reason that the individual employer-employee relationship is likely more to their advantage than bargaining against their employees in unison. The beginning of a labour union is thus a very delicate period and legislation guards the process. The specifics for certification vary according to jurisdiction, but in general the rules require majority support among the employees (this is usually proven first by a petition that leads to a vote on unionization or by the "signing" of union membership cards). Employers are legislatively barred from retaliating against employees seeking to unionize, but they may communicate to their employees the costs and consequences of unionizing. When Walmart Canada was confronted with the creation of a union in one of their Quebec stores, Walmart threatened to close the branch and ultimately decided to do so, rather than create the precedent of a unionized store that might inspire others throughout the chain. This was ultimately deemed a violation of Quebec's labour code, but it shows the lengths businesses might take to oppose the establishment of a labour union.

Once a union has been certified, it becomes the **exclusive bargaining representative of all employees.** This is a key power of a union that is enabled by legislation. Even if an employee is completely opposed to unionization, votes against the union, and refuses to participate in any union meetings or activities, that employee is still represented by the union and cannot make a separate, individual deal with the employer. Individual arrangements between employees and the employer would obviously undermine the collective action – and the collective bargain – that would be essential to arriving at labour peace. Under what is referred to as the **Rand formula,** a dissenting employee can decline membership in the union in a formal sense (you don't have to carry a card, go to meetings, or have anything to do with union activities) but they still have to pay union dues and accept the union as their bargaining representative. Without the Rand formula, unions would attract free riders: employees who refused to pay union fees but who would still benefit from the gains the union secures in collective bargaining. All of these checks and balances result from a regulated relationship between employees, acting collectively, and the employer – regulation that can be productive for both sides but which inevitably involves some curtailing of individual freedom.

## COURTS AND THE FREEDOM OF ASSOCIATION

Courts have traditionally been hostile to collective actions of employees, instead usually privileging the individual relationship between an employee and employer. This approach meshed with an overall "laissez faire" orientation that sought to keep the state out of economic relations and industry. US courts in the early twentieth century were notoriously hostile to worker protection laws on this ground; *Lochner v New York* (1905) is perhaps the most prominent example, in which the US Supreme Court found New York's *Bakeshop Act* an unconstitutional infringement on the "freedom to contract" even though its "interference" was the meagre prohibition of working bakery employees more than 10 hours a day or 60 hours a week. In light of the North American history of judicial resistance to labour rights, as the *Canadian Charter of Rights and Freedoms* moved towards enactment in the early 1980s, some labour scholars feared giving more power to the judiciary on the grounds that decisions would undermine the statutory gains made towards protecting unions ("labour's experience with the judiciary had been uniformly bad"; Mandel, 1989, p. 185). The poor reputation of the judiciary in the labour context was one of the reasons that administrative tribunals, labour relations boards, were generally preferred in labour law statutes, rather than leaving the courts with the exclusive power to resolve disputes.

The inclusion of "freedom of association" in section 2(d) of the *Charter* was thus viewed with some initial scepticism by labour advocates. That scepticism was reflected in the early *Charter* decisions made by the Supreme Court interpreting section 2(d). The famous "Labour Trilogy" of cases interpreted the "freedom to associate" in a very narrow and somewhat perplexing manner, effectively transforming a collective right into an individual one. (The notion of an individual freedom to associate is a difficult one to comprehend, for the simple reason that association implies more than one person). The Court ruled that the *Charter* did not include a "right to strike" since it "has always been the subject of legislative control" and "has been abrogated from time to time in social circumstances" (*Re Public Service Employees Relations Act (Alberta)*, 1987, p. 232). Justice McIntyre appeared keen to avoid involving the courts in the "extremely sensitive subject" of the "political, social and economic questions [that] frequently dominate in labour disputes": "If the right to strike is constitutionalized, then its application, its extent and any questions of its legality, become matters of law" and "would inevitably throw the courts back in the field of labour relations and much of the value of specialized labour tribunals would be lost" (pp. 232–5). The "Labour Trilogy" approach reigned for more than a decade and few "freedom of association" cases were litigated in this period.

The judicial attitude towards protecting labour rights seemed to shift with the rise of austerity-minded governments in the 1990s. A key and early sign of this shift was the Supreme Court's 2001 decision in *Dunmore v Ontario*. Bob Rae's NDP Government of Ontario reversed the historic exclusion of agricultural workers from the *Ontario Labour Relations Act* with its 1994 *Agricultural Labour Relations Act*. When Mike Harris's Progressive Conservatives took power, they repealed Rae's act with their own *Labour Relations and Employment Statute Law Amendment Act* in 1995, once again excluding agricultural workers from the statutory scheme of protections. With no constitutional right at stake, this should have been a simple act of statutory repeal – one government choosing differently from the prior one, the sort of typical policy reversal one might expect when one partisan government replaces another. In reviewing this sequence of statutes in *Dunmore*, however, the Supreme Court found that the exclusion of one type of workers (agricultural workers) was now impermissible on constitutional grounds. Section 2(d) required some sort of protection for Ontario agricultural workers, even if the details of the precise scheme could be the subject of future legislation. The previous status quo – the one that existed for over 50 years (including 12 years under the *Charter*) – was now unconstitutional because of the Court's revised approach to section 2(d). *Dunmore* was followed up by the Supreme Court's 2007 decision in *Health Services and Support v British Columbia*, which required a "meaningful process" of addressing labour relations for health care workers, even if the specific tripartite form of collective bargaining of the traditional union context was not required (see Savage & Smith, 2017, pp. 146–65).

In a second "Labour Trilogy" in 2015–16, the Supreme Court essentially reversed the earlier trilogy of cases and found a constitutional right to collective bargaining and, crucially, a constitutional right to strike for the first time in Canadian law. In the first case, *Mounted Police Association of Ontario v Canada (Attorney General)* (2015), the Court ruled that RCMP officers – excluded from the federal Canada Labour Code, an exclusion once held to be constitutional in *Delisle v Canada* (1999) – now needed to be part of a "meaningful collective bargaining" process instead of a legislated "association" that gave employee input through staff representatives not elected by the employees. The Court did not require that the Mounties be allowed to unionize in the traditional labour law sense, but it was clear that in lieu of that structure they would expect a robust system of collective bargaining, even if it left the final details for Parliament to decide. In the second case, *Meredith v Canada* (2015), general "time-limited" salary freezes were found constitutional and did not infringe section 2(d) since the right guarantees "the right of employees to associate in a meaningful way in the pursuit of collective workplace goals" but "does not guarantee a particular outcome" (para. 25). In other words, it is more of a process right – a right to be heard – and not a right against the substantial outcomes that may be arrived at. In the final and most important case of the new "trilogy," *Saskatchewan Federation of Labour* (2015), the Court made its boldest step by denying the Saskatchewan government the ability to declare some public services "essential," such that those workers would be unable to strike. For the first time, the Court found a "right to strike" in the Canadian Constitution with Justice Abella declaring that "the right to strike is not merely derivative of collective bargaining, it is an indispensable component of that right" (para. 3).

Since 2015 – and especially since the *Saskatchewan Federation of Labour* case – Canadian labour law has been in a state of considerable flux. The Supreme Court did not unmoor all of its existing precedents, but it did increase uncertainty in an area of law that exists primarily to provide certainty as a means of facilitating successful negotiations. The Court has not required that all labour situations use the same traditional tripartite model, but it has required "meaningful processes" that allow employees to work collectively to advance their goals, even if the courts will not directly assess the outcomes that result from such processes. Governments may not "unilaterally with[draw] workers' right to strike without designating some sort of independent review process for resolving disputes" (Savage & Smith, 2017, p. 203). What that independent review process is, whether it is sufficient, and in what labour situations it can be imposed continues to evolve. The uncertainty of the current state of labour law is illustrated by the 2016 Supreme Court case of *British Columbia Teachers' Federation* (2016), which consisted of a one-sentence reversal of the BC Court of Appeal's judgment. In the always politically contentious world of the government's collective bargaining with public school teachers, the courts were asked to clarify how negotiations must be conducted in order to be considered "meaningful." The Supreme Court favoured an approach that required the government to "negotiate in good faith." That meant that even though the government is "allowed to take firm positions, even extreme ones," the government "must not be inflexible and intransigent" and "must honestly strive to find a middle ground." The tension in this formulation – "extreme" positions are allowed, but they must not be "inflexible" – is not only an invitation to future litigation, but it may derail future negotiations since parties unsure of their own legal limits are prone to otherwise unnecessary conflict. If governments become frustrated with their inability to define the precise limits of section 2(d), they will be tempted to use the notwithstanding clause (see Chapter 3 and Box 9.2) to restore the legislative power they have lost. Perhaps the only real certainty is that section 2(d) will continue to evolve for the foreseeable future.

## PUBLIC SECTOR UNIONS

The rudimentary sketch of labour law principles above apply generally to most employee–employer situations, but there are special considerations – and a different political dynamic – when they involve **public sector unions**, for which the employer is the state. The contexts of these two situations, with private and public employers, are dramatically different. In the private sector, where unions can be a drag on profitability, rates of unionization have sharply declined; in the public sector, where business competition is non-existent or limited, unions have thrived. In 1997, there were about as many private sector employees unionized in Canada as there were in the public sector, but by 2021, there were 5,000 fewer private sector union employees, while public sector employees increased by 1.2 million over the same period. From 1997 to 2021, the percentage of public sector employees rose slightly (74.7 per cent in 1997 and 77.2 per cent in 2021), whereas private sector employees became even less likely to be unionized (21.3 per cent in 1997 and 15.3 per cent in 2021). Unionization, in other words, has become more of a public sector concern and far less important for the private employment context.

The tripartite structure is also complicated in the public sector because the state is expected to be both the employer and the independent facilitator of labour peace. While the state as an employer is likely to jealously guard their resources, there is little competitive threat and many other factors substitute for profitability in its calculations.

**BOX 9.2.  THE FORD GOVERNMENT ATTEMPTS TO USE THE NOTWITHSTANDING CLAUSE TO LEGISLATE EDUCATION WORKERS BACK TO WORK**

The new constitutional status quo with respect to the "right to strike" was tested to dramatic new levels in Ontario in 2022. At issue was a labour dispute between the provincial government and educational support workers, represented by the Canadian Union of Public Employees' (CUPE) Ontario School Board Council of Unions (OSBCU). With lengthy periods of children having been home from school during the pandemic, Doug Ford's provincial government was adamant that a labour disruption should not lead to more missed school days, but it was also unwilling to meet the wage and work-condition demands of the union. After months of failed negotiations, CUPE issued its strike notice on October 30, with an intention to strike five days later. The next day, October 31, the government introduced Bill 28, the *Keeping Students in Class Act*, which mandated the employees back to work, proposed stiff fines for both the union and members for defiance, and – perhaps most notably – included an invocation of the notwithstanding clause in the likely event that Bill 28 might be found unconstitutional in light of the most recent Supreme Court of Canada decisions on collective bargaining. Several days of intense political contestation happened in the media, with the government's use of the "controversial" clause mixed with heightened public sentiment about the labour negotiations themselves. During this time, the possibility of a "general strike" day was raised, where all of the public sector unions might withdraw their labour simultaneously in sympathy and to protect their bargaining rights from similar treatment in the future. The prospect of such a widespread shutdown may have been the motivation for the government's backdown a few days later when they returned to the bargaining table and repealed the legislation containing the notwithstanding clause. If so, it demonstrates that even if the Supreme Court elevated collective bargaining to the constitutional level, and even if the government were armed with the notwithstanding clause to counter it, the real power was still in the ability of workers to act collectively. For all the changes in legal form, it was politics and social mobilization that dictated the outcome – even if it was a little messy and chaotic for parents scrambling to find childcare!

Elected actors, for example, may seek to avoid tax increases, but they are going to be far more responsive to citizen complaints about the garbage not getting picked up or if children are unable to go to school because their teachers are on strike. These electoral concerns might make the state-as-employer overpay for labour. At the same time, there is an inherent unfairness in the negotiations between employees and employer when the employer can unsettle or limit a collective agreement using its power over legislation. It is no coincidence that the Supreme Court decisions reinterpreting the "freedom of association" all arise from challenges by public sector unions, since the conflict between the state as employer and the state as lawmaker makes for a potentially greater power imbalance than a private employer negotiating with its employees. Many public sector unions are not governed by the general labour statutes that affect private employees but are instead subject to specific legislation regulating their employment relationship. The Ontario *Labour Relations Act*, for example, does not include teachers and college employees. With more specific legislation entirely under the government's control, the temptation to avoid genuine bargaining and simply legislate is always present (sometimes you might hear in the media about "legislating them back to work" – this is the means being advocated). It is hard to negotiate fairly with an actor that also has the power to alter the rules of bargaining whenever it pleases.

Consider the political dynamics of the 2004 case of *Newfoundland (Treasury Board) v N.A.P.E.* (2004). In light of pay discrepancies between male and female health care workers, the government and the union settled an ongoing grievance by signing a "pay equity" agreement that would make adjustments over a four-year period to help remedy the imbalance, amounting to a $24 million pay adjustment for the health care sector workers. Before any adjustments were made, the Newfoundland House of Assembly passed a *Public Sector Restraint Act*, which responded to a fiscal crisis in the province's budget by freezing the salaries of all public workers. According to the president of the Treasury Board, the act would helpfully "erase an obligation we had there of approximately $24M" (para. 9). Even though the *Public Sector Restraint Act* was general legislation aimed at all public sector workers, it is hard not to see the Government of Newfoundland and Labrador's actions as somewhat disreputable: settling a dispute and then legislating to free themselves from the commitments they made to settle it. In fairness, the government did ultimately offer some pay equity adjustment during the freeze, just at a smaller amount than it agreed to initially. Since this case occurred during the period when the "freedom of association" right in section 2(d) was largely neglected by the courts, the challenge to the *Public Sector Restraint Act* was grounded instead on the equality right is section 15. The Supreme Court did find a violation but upheld the act as a reasonable limit on the right (using section 1 of the *Charter*), largely because of the scope of the financial emergency Newfoundland and Labrador was experiencing.

Would a decision like *N.A.P.E.* hold up in the new era where section 2(d) has been reinterpreted? So far, in cases like *Meredith*, general pay freezes have been held constitutional, and a series of public sector restraint bills in Nova Scotia, Manitoba, and Alberta have all survived constitutional challenges at the lower courts (with the Supreme Court declining to hear appeals). But the Supreme Court's jurisprudence has increasingly put its emphasis on the temporary nature of such measures and reiterated the importance of employees having input into the conditions under which they work. While a fiscal emergency would likely still be given considerable weight, the newfound "meaningful" collective bargaining rights will surely provide more of a counterbalance in future cases. It also appears as if the Court is particularly mindful of the bargaining situation created when one party holds legislative authority and where public servants might not be able to strike because they are deemed in legislation to be "essential." It is less clear that the Court also recognizes the other dynamics at play in the public sector unionization context, especially the lack of competition and political imperative to maintain services even at higher-than-expected costs. By intervening more directly into the state employer–employee relationship, the judicial branch may have assumed a role it is not well-suited to manage. Moreover, the uncertainty their interventions have brought are not conducive to the stability that labour has as its primary goal. When applied to public sector unions, where "essential services" are at issue, the stakes are even higher and the uncertainty that might be bearable in private contexts may result in distortive prices, service limitations, and perhaps even further political demands for the "privatization" of public services.

## CONCLUSION

As demonstrated throughout the chapter, it is difficult to characterize employment relationships in Canada as strictly "private." At one point, it may have been possible to do so, but the history of exploitation and its potential for violence has made it imperative for the state to play a significant role. Today, even non-unionized employees receive at least some protection from the state in the form of provincial legislation governing almost all employment contexts (and where it doesn't, federal statutes usually play a similar role). This does not mean that labour law is a settled matter – far from it! As we have seen, the Supreme Court's recent reinterpretation of the "freedom of association" in section 2(d) of the *Charter* suggests that core labour rights – traditionally thought of as primarily statutory – are now more vigorously protected as constitutional rights. This has provoked attempts by provincial legislature to use the notwithstanding clause in section 33 of the *Charter* or threaten its use in response. This now overtly political battle occurs in a context of increasing controversy about the role of public sector unions and the difficulty of balancing the rights of civil servants with the public interest in the effective (and cost-effective) delivery of public services.

All these developments are likely to increase the legal aspects of Canadian employment, making an understanding of its nuances a fertile subject for social scientists interested in examining the work life of Canadians generally. In her provocative article,

"The Limitations of Pieces of Paper: A Role for Social Science in Labour Law," law professor Sara Slinn (2005) explicitly calls for more empirical social science evidence to be used to formulate labour policy and law in Canada. Legislated "cooling-off" periods, for example, are assumed to discourage strikes and lockouts, but, as Slinn notes, there is little evidence they actually achieve that end. Social science, she suggests, can help inform a more robust understanding of labour law and its actual, real-world operation.

Slinn notes that "labour law is broader and richer and more complex than what is contained in statutes and case reports" (p. 292). She describes assumptions in labour law that are seldom tested, including assumptions about politics and informal sources of law. With respect to the latter, she notes that legal scholars rarely consider the outcomes of grievances and the dynamics of negotiations, in favour of focusing on formal judicial decisions and administrative outcomes. For example, Slinn refers to research that shows that, despite claims of their expertise, labour relations boards, like the US National Labour Relations Board, have "no means of actually measuring the effect ... of different employer tactics on employee free choice" (Slinn, 2005, p. 296). Like other legal tests, the test of employer interference purports to be an "objective" test based on how a "reasonable employee" might behave. When labour boards judge whether employers have interfered with the unionization process, they must make a "best guess" about which practices might constitute unlawful interference. In Ontario, boards are left to hypothesize "whether the alleged conduct would likely affect the ability of employees of average intelligence and fortitude to freely express their true wishes in a representation vote" (*Capelas Homes*, 1998, para. 27; Slinn, 2005, p. 364) A social scientist could employ a variety of research methods to better discern the impact of an array of practices on employee behaviour: Experimental designs could track different forms of influence, survey data could explore the impact through responses, and even pre-existing data from election advertising could inform such analyses.

Slinn (2005) is clear that social science evidence itself has limitations. It cannot answer normative questions about law: "Social science research cannot tell us whether something is 'bad' or 'good,'" and there are always limits on the available data (p. 309). Still, social science is useful for measuring and describing effects, something that deserves more prominence in labour law and the formulation of labour policy. Slinn concludes by calling for more interchange between social scientists, legal scholars, and practitioners. One of the obstacles, however, is the lack of expertise that social scientists have with respect to the nuances of labour law: "In social science," Slinn notes, "researchers often ask questions and measure variables in ways that are not as helpful to the formulation of legal questions as they could be" (p. 310). In order to most effectively combine law and social science, and for empirical research to have its greatest impact on law, it is first necessary for social science researchers to be at least conversant in the law and be able to understand the legal questions that are most pertinent to their subject. This book is an effort to bridge those disciplinary boundaries, and we hope that this chapter will provide a foundation and inspiration to budding social scientists to engage more thoroughly with labour lawyers and legal scholars in their future research.

## REVIEW QUESTIONS

1  If we didn't have labour law, what problems might arise in employee–employer relationships?
2  What is collective action and why is it important for labour law?
3  How does the state deal with its conflict of interest in public sector labour disputes? Is it doing so fairly and effectively?

# CHAPTER TEN

# Law and the Environment

## LEARNING OBJECTIVES

- Understand how the division of powers impacts environmental law.
- Understand the structure and operation of environmental assessment legislation.
- Be able to articulate how "environmental crimes" are structured and how they differ from "true" crimes.
- Be able to articulate the strengths and limits of law as a policy tool to regulate the environment.
- Understand how the concept of "standing" limits who can access the courts in environmental matters.
- Understand how the courts and the logic of judicial interpretation can be politically employed against environmental activists.

There is no denying the serious environmental issues facing the planet, and environmental concerns have been long-standing public policy problems. On the one hand, these are issues of science, but they are also political issues that require us to address public policy, governance, and politics. They are also economic issues, as shifts to green energy, sustainability, and greenhouse gas reductions impact jobs and livelihoods and require changes to modes of economic production and economic priorities. Law plays an important role in environmental regulation. There are numerous policy instruments available to governments regulating pollution and environmental hazards. These instruments, such as tax incentives, carbon offsets, taxes on greenhouse gas emissions, the creation of approval processes for development projects, or the outright prohibition/criminalization of polluting, involve law to a greater or lesser extent. The adage "there ought to be a law against that" can be applied to environmental issues with mixed success.

An examination of law's role in the regulation of the environment permits an opportunity to revisit many of the themes explored in earlier chapters. Environmental regulation necessarily has implications for property and contract rights. Does an environmental spill affecting a river raise issues of torts and negligence? At what point does environmental pollution amount to a crime? Indeed, in many jurisdictions there have been attempts to define environmental pollution as a form of criminal offence. This, in turn, leads to questions of investigation, enforcement, and the application of criminal standards of proof to environmental questions. Governments have set up complex approval processes to assess the environmental impact of development projects. Environmental assessments employ boards and tribunals, raising the various administrative law questions we explored in Chapter 5. Environmental issues often cross borders – both territorial borders and constitutional/jurisdictional borders. Many issues of environmental regulation implicate federal jurisdictional responsibility but at the same time also raise issues that fall within provincial areas of constitutional authority (see the controversy over the "carbon tax" in Box 3.3 in Chapter 3). Such issues may also raise questions of international law, a topic not explored in this volume. Finally, environmental issues often provoke a wide variety of conflicts and political disputes, which find themselves before the courts. This raises a host of other issues about law, courts, and politics, including such questions as who can sue on behalf of the environment and how lawsuits can be used to potentially stifle political expression (for a fuller exploration of the complexities of environmental law and politics see Green, 2022). In this chapter, we provide an overview of these various issues, to highlight the way environmental issues intersect and overlap with legal issues and legal concepts.

## THE ENVIRONMENT AND THE CONSTITUTION

As discussed in Chapter 3, the Canadian Constitution divides jurisdictional authority between the federal and provincial governments. In 1867, when the original division of powers was formulated, the environment was not really considered, so it is not found in the heads of authority listed in sections 91 and 92 of the *Constitution Act, 1867*. As a result, federal and provincial authority over environmental regulation must be linked to other bases of jurisdiction in the constitution. Federal power to regulate the environment rests on a number of grants of authority, including control over crown land (s. 91 [1A]), fisheries (s. 91[12]), navigation and shipping (s. 91[10]), the criminal law (s. 91[27]), and the Crown's fiduciary obligations towards Indigenous Peoples and lands reserved for them (s. 91[24]). In addition, the federal government's broad jurisdictional authority over peace, order, and good government has been interpreted to include jurisdictional authority over marine pollution and interprovincial water pollution. Broadly speaking, if an area of activity is federally regulated (such as nuclear power or airports), environmental regulation associated with it can be claimed by the federal government. Furthermore, section 132 of the *Constitution Act, 1867* gives the federal government jurisdiction to make treaties with other countries and to enforce those treaties. This has allowed the federal government the authority to regulate boundary waters and migratory birds, both of which have environmental implications.

Similarly, there are numerous provisions in provincial grants of authority in section 92 of the *Constitution Act* granting provinces authority to regulate the environment. Most notably, this includes property and civil rights in the province (s. 92[13]), which allows provinces to regulate most business and commercial activities, including environmental consequences of those activities. Section 92(5) of the *Constitution Act* empowers provinces to manage provincial crown lands, which provides a basis for regulating mining and logging on provincial lands. Section 92(8) gives provinces jurisdictional authority over municipalities, which includes local authority to regulate a diverse range of environmental matters such as waste disposal, recycling, drinking water, and wastewater. Finally, section 92(16) includes a broad grant of authority over all matters of a local or private nature in the province, which potentially includes environmental concerns.

The above discussion provides a very abbreviated discussion of the bases of environmental jurisdictional authority for the federal and provincial governments. It should be apparent that there is considerable overlap between the two. Furthermore, both federal and provincial governments have the full authority to enforce their own laws, including the creation of penalties and offences. The federal government, however, has the exclusive authority to create criminal offences, which has been the basis for federal regulations over hazardous substances, toxic waste, etc. Both levels of government have created very similar approval processes for developments that might impact the environment, and the question of which assessment and approval process applies to a particular project is a question of jurisdiction that may need to be determined. These questions can become issues of constitutional disagreement between levels of government, although the challenge to jurisdictional authority may come from a private entity as a means of trying to escape regulatory decisions.

## ENVIRONMENTAL ASSESSMENTS AND REPRESENTATION

Every jurisdiction in Canada has some sort of **environmental assessment** process. These are administrative processes designed to evaluate the impact of development projects on the environment. They apply to a diverse range of projects, including new roads, construction of landfill sites, mines, hydroelectric dams, airports, and housing projects (see Box 10.1). The intention behind the assessment is to determine, with some degree of certainty, the actual environmental impacts of the project as proposed, and consider alternatives and/or proposals for the mitigation of that environmental risk. In assessing risk, a wide range of factors might be considered, including climate change, greenhouse gas emissions, destruction of habitat, species at risk, and the impact on the quality of life of those residing near the development. This has particular importance for Indigenous Peoples, whose traditional territories often are in proximity to proposed mining, forestry, and hydroelectric development projects. These developments often carry with them the possibility of economic development opportunities for Indigenous communities but at the same time pose risks to traditional hunting and fishing grounds and sometimes might require the relocation of entire communities. One of the challenges facing environmental assessments is how to incorporate Indigenous knowledge and understanding into a process that is often highly oriented towards privileging Western scientific knowledge/expertise and concepts of progress/development.

Environmental assessment procedures are an important procedural step that industry and government proponents for a project must navigate to get approval for their project to go ahead. It also means that a great deal of time and effort must be spent on preparing assessment documents and holding hearings to go over that evidence. Scientific experts need to be employed to document the environmental impacts of a project carefully and thoroughly. At the same time, these processes are far from neutral and value-free. Scientific experts employed by the proponent of a project may try to minimize environmental risks or propose mitigation strategies to overcome potential objections. Scientific evidence can be framed and organized in a fashion that is supportive of the project or in opposition to it. For this reason, assessment agencies will often have their own scientific and expert staff who are trained to evaluate the evidence presented to the board. In some cases, assessments may be done by agency staff, who make a recommendation, rather than through a full hearing process.

Of course, these processes become sites of political contestation. Environmental NGOs, Indigenous communities, and residents' associations may all wish to participate and provide evidence to counter the material presented by the project proponents. These groups may, in turn, employ their own scientific experts that will put forward positions counter to those of the proponents. Again, this is why it is important that agencies have the expertise to assess the quality of the information they are receiving

Assessment processes do provide opportunities for the opponents of projects to organize and intervene in the process. From the point of view of the proponents of a development project, this might create what seems like an overly bureaucratic, costly, and lengthy process. From the point of view of others, however, this is an important – and perhaps the only – opportunity to question the principles underpinning a project, query the environmental impact, and potentially stop a project from taking place.

Finally, it is worth noting that environmental regulation and assessment is a multi-level governance issue. As indicated above, these issues frequently raise constitutional questions about whose jurisdiction a particular project falls within. At the same time, though, even if a project clearly falls within a particular jurisdiction (federal or provincial), it may have implications that go beyond that particular jurisdiction. In the case of the Trans Mountain Pipeline, which is discussed in more detail below, while the project fell within federal jurisdiction, the provincial government of British Columbia opposed the project, as did the municipalities of Burnaby and Vancouver. As a result, all these jurisdictions engaged in litigation to stop the project, as did Indigenous communities impacted by the pipeline.

## THE FEDERAL ENVIRONMENTAL ASSESSMENT PROCESSES IN CANADA

The federal *Canadian Environmental Assessment Act* was enacted in 1992 and substantially revised in 2012. It provided a comprehensive administrative process, including the possibility of a hearing conducted by independent panels of experts, for projects that fall within federal jurisdictional authority. Assessments were conducted by either the Canadian Environmental Assessment Agency, the National Energy Board, or the Canadian Nuclear Safety Commission. The act was revised several times and ultimately replaced in 2018 with the *Canadian Impact Assessment Act* (IAA). The new legislation created a Canadian Impact Assessment Agency, which became the sole agency responsible for conducting environmental assessments. Box 10.1 lists the types of issues that are considered by the impact assessment process.

Under the old legislative framework, the minister of the environment retained considerable authority and discretion over the environmental assessment process, including managing timelines for assessments and having the final decision-making authority to accept or reject the recommendations of an environmental assessment. Under the new legislation, the discretion of the minister is considerably more limited. The independence of the agency was enhanced, and the minister now has no choice but to accept a negative recommendation. In other words, while the minister does not have to accept a recommendation to allow a project to proceed, they must accept a recommendation to not permit a project to move forward.

The IAA envisions two types of processes. The first assessment process is agency-led and is conducted by staff, which issue a report. The second type of assessment process involves a full hearing by an independent review panel. Hearings are required for certain types of development projects, such as those dealing with nuclear issues and those involving oil and gas/energy infrastructure developments. Agency staff support the independent review panel by providing technical, procedural, and logistical support. At the end of a hearing, the review panel issues a report to the minister that is also made public. The report outlines the environmental impacts of a project, potential alternatives, and possible mitigation strategies. It is within the authority of a panel to recommend that a project not proceed on the basis that the environmental impacts are too great. Hearings can be quite lengthy, and the IAA stipulates that generally a hearing should not last more than 300 days, although it could last as many as 600 days. For complex projects, a hearing can take several years.

One of the reasons hearings can take a long time is both the complexity of issues to be considered and the fact that these hearings provide important mechanisms for public participation. The legislation directs the agency to consider a wide range of environmental, social, and economic impacts. The intention is to provide a comprehensive assessment of a proposed development (IAA, s. 22[1][a]). The proponent, therefore, must provide a detailed and comprehensive package of materials that goes beyond simply the "environmental science" of the project but which addresses a broad range of socioeconomic factors. This includes an assessment of the advantages and benefits of the

---

**BOX 10.1. MATTERS REQUIRING AN IMPACT ASSESSMENT**

Pursuant to the *Impact Assessment Act*, the government has enacted regulations that set out the types of issues requiring an impact assessment. Furthermore, the minister of the environment has the authority to designate certain types of projects that do not fall within the list as requiring an assessment. (*Physical Activities Regulations*). These include the following:

- Development projects in national parks or protected areas
- Defence projects, including the construction of new military bases, low-level training flights of military aircraft, and the testing of military weapons for more than five days
- Mining and resource extraction activities
- Nuclear facilities
- Oil and gas and other fossil fuel facilities/projects
- Electricity transmission lines and pipelines that are international or interprovincial
- Renewable energy projects, including hydroelectric damns, offshore tidal energy projects, and offshore wind generating facilities
- Transportation projects such as airports, railways, canals, and interprovincial highways and bridges
- Hazardous waste disposal and storage sites
- Water projects such as dams, dikes, or water diversion projects

project, both to the local and broader economy, but also its impact on people's ways of life and the local community (see Box 10.2). The assessment panel is also directed to consider the broader implications of the project for Canada as a whole, including its international environmental commitments to the reduction of carbon emissions. Finally, reviews must also consider the implications of the project for Indigenous Peoples and incorporate Indigenous knowledge and ways of life into the assessment of the project. All of this must be considered in assessing the merits of the project, as well as assessing any mitigation strategies or alternatives to the proposed project.

The assessment process provides an important opportunity for members of the public to weigh in on proposals. As indicated above, this includes residents, those impacted by the project, environmental organizations, and Indigenous communities. One of the significant changes in the *Impact Assessment Act* was to both broaden the scope for public participation and increase and enhance the importance of consultation with Indigenous communities. As listed in Box 10.2, Indigenous knowledge, as well as the

---

**BOX 10.2. FACTORS CONSIDERED IN AN IMPACT ASSESSMENT**

- The purpose of and need for the project
- Alternative means of carrying out the project
- Positive and negative consequences of changes to the environment and to health, social, and economic conditions
- Measures to mitigate adverse consequences
- Impact of the project on any Indigenous group
- Indigenous knowledge when presented
- Considerations related to Indigenous cultures
- Any assessment of the project conducted by or on behalf of an Indigenous governing body
- Community knowledge when provided
- The extent to which the project contributes to sustainability
- The extent to which the project contributes to or hinders Canada's ability to meet its environmental obligations and climate change commitments
- The impact of the project on diverse groups of people, such as those identified by gender and other identity factors (age, ethnicity, ability, etc.)
- Any comments received
- Any other matter deemed relevant by the agency

Source: IAA, s. 22(1).

impact of the project on Indigenous culture and ways of life, must be considered by the agency. The IAA now explicitly prioritizes Indigenous issues and mandates cooperation and coordinated action with Indigenous governing bodies, promoting communication and cooperation with Indigenous Peoples, ensuring respect for the rights of Indigenous Peoples, and ensuring Indigenous knowledge and community knowledge are considered. This shift reflects the Government of Canada's fiduciary obligations to Indigenous Peoples in Canada. They are also reflective of the saga of the Trans Mountain Pipeline environmental case, where the government was found not to have discharged fully its obligations to adequately consult with Indigenous Peoples. Box 10.3 highlights the

---

**BOX 10.3. THE TRANS MOUNTAIN PIPELINE AND THE DUTY TO CONSULT**

The Trans Mountain Pipeline was originally completed in 1953 after large oil deposits were discovered near Leduc, Alberta. The pipeline was designed to transport oil from the oil fields in Alberta to the Pacific coast and refineries near Vancouver, British Columbia. In 2004, Kinder Morgan began the process for developing a second pipeline that would parallel the route of the original. This has been the subject of considerable debate, numerous environmental assessment hearings, and considerable protest and opposition. Opposition came from environmental organizations, Indigenous communities, and local governments. The application for National Energy Board (NEB) approval of the pipeline was filed by Kinder Morgan in 2013. The project was approved by the NEB in May 2016 and received federal cabinet approval five months later.

In 2018, the Federal Court quashed the approval of the project on the basis that there had been inadequate consultation with Indigenous Peoples. The essence of the decision was that the consultation plan established by the government permitted Indigenous Peoples to comment on the proposal but did not allow for real dialogue over the concerns of Indigenous communities. The government, to discharge its "duty to consult," had to demonstrate a genuine and bona fide willingness to engage with Indigenous communities. As a result, the government was forced to restart consultations.

As a result of this decision, Kinder Morgan decided to walk away from the pipeline project, because of increasing financial costs and a growing fear that the project would never receive approval. The Kinder Morgan shareholders voted to sell the pipeline very shortly after the Federal Court decision. The federal government purchased the pipeline from Kinder Morgan for $4.5 billion. The government explicitly decided to purchase the pipeline in order to save it.

Trans Mountain Pipeline case and its implications for environmental assessments that require the participation of Indigenous Peoples.

Under the *Canadian Environmental Assessment Act*, there was a "standing test" for public participation. **Standing** is a term that refers to those who are entitled to appear before a court. Usually, a party has standing because they have been directly affected by the matter being considered by the court. Under the old environmental assessment legislation, members of the public were entitled to participate in the review if they were directly impacted by the proposal or if they had "relevant information or expertise." Many environmental groups would be given standing to participate on this latter basis. Under the new IAA, this requirement has been altered, and the agency is given discretion to determine the scope and manner by which members of the public can participate. The removal of the standing test – combined with the broad direction to consider a range of societal impacts, including the impacts on Indigenous Peoples as well as gender and a variety of other identities – signals a much broader approach to public participation.

Public participation in environmental reviews is an important element of ensuring transparency and legitimacy of outcomes (Mikadze, 2016). At the same time, the politicization of assessment processes means the process can become bogged down and delayed due to participation by groups opposed to pipeline developments. It is not our intention to comment on the legitimacy of such tactics, but rather simply to note that they have often been effective. Under previous legislative schemes, there have been efforts to restrict the participation of public group. This has resulted in successful applications for judicial review effectively invalidating and quashing approvals that had been granted (Leach, 2021). The new IAA and its related statutes restore an emphasis on public participation, and this may result in difficulties moving large-scale projects, and particularly oil and gas projects, through the approval process.

The changes to the environmental assessment framework have generally been seen as positive by environmental organizations but are viewed in a much more cautious and/or negative light by some governments and the proponents of projects subject to assessment. This has been particularly the case in Alberta, where the United Conservative government of Jason Kenney pejoratively labelled the legislation the "no more pipelines" act (Leach, 2021). According to the Government of Alberta, the *Impact Assessment Act*, and particularly the obligations to consult, would mean that it would be virtually impossible to successfully get approval for major infrastructure projects, such as pipelines, in the future.

The Alberta Government challenged the legislation in court, and successfully argued before the Alberta Court of Appeal that the legislation violated provincial jurisdiction over natural resources (*Reference Re Impact Assessment Act,* 2022). The Court viewed the legislation as a serious threat to constitutional division of powers but also went on to endorse Kenney's view that the legislation would adversely impact the likelihood of investment in major capital infrastructure projects. The decision was subsequently upheld by the Supreme Court of Canada, agreeing that the legislation went beyond areas of federal environmental authority (*Reference Re Impact Assessment Act*, 2023). Chief Justice Wagner, while acknowledging federal authority over environmental matters, also emphasized that the government must stay within its jurisdictional limits. He recommended that the government negotiate with the provinces to jointly and collaboratively regulate environmental issues.

That case was a "reference case" brought by the Alberta government. These are cases where a government asks the court for a ruling about the constitutional validity of a case. Reference cases are "advisory" and not legally binding (for more on reference cases, see Chapter 2). Consequently, the IAA remained in force. However, the federal government has stated that it will listen to the Supreme Court's ruling and promised amendments to the IAA.

## CRIMINAL LAW AND ENVIRONMENTAL OFFENCES

The use of the criminal law is an important environmental regulatory mechanism. This means the creation of environmental offences and the development of enforcement mechanisms, including inspectors, prosecutors, and standards for establishing guilt/culpability. It also means the creation of penalties, including fines, and in some cases imprisonment. Given Canada's constitutional division of powers, it also means that both the federal government and the provincial government have the capacity to define and create environmental offences (but only the federal government can justify their laws using the jurisdiction over criminal law). The standards and procedures developed for true criminal offences (murder, for example) may need modification when applied to environmental offences.

The federal government has widespread jurisdictional authority to establish environmental offences related to areas under its jurisdictional authority but also has the authority to create criminal offences under section 92(27) of the *Constitution Act, 1867*. The *Canadian Environmental Protection Act* (1999) explicitly creates offences related to the management and control of toxic substances and hazardous waste. These offences include the failure to comply with regulations for the disposal of hazardous substances or chemicals into the water or the atmosphere or failing to comply with any orders to stop or correct a violation. Similarly, the *Hazardous Products Act* makes it illegal to advertise, sell, or import products that contain toxic or dangerous substances. The *Canada National Parks Act* creates regulations and offences related to the protection of animals and activities within national parks. The *Canada Wildlife Act* authorizes the federal government to designate wildlife protection areas to protect the habitat of migratory birds and species at risk. Within these areas, a wide range of activities are prohibited, including hunting, trapping, and fishing (including the possession of equipment for those activities); introducing other organisms that might harm wildlife or lead to a degradation of wildlife habitat; carrying on farming or agricultural activities within the area; and carrying on recreational activities such as hiking, swimming, or camping.

Provincial governments have a parallel and complementary jurisdiction to create offences related to environmental issues. This authority is generally related to the provincial authority over "property and civil rights" (s. 92[13]) and "local works and undertakings" (s. 92[10]) established by the *Constitution Act, 1867*. The provinces also have authority over provincial Crown land, which can be quite extensive. As with the federal government, the provinces can prohibit activities and create offences for the discharge of harmful substances into the environment. In general, provinces have wide-ranging authority over the management of waste, including its disposal. Provincial environment ministries have created complex regulatory frameworks for approving waste disposal, regulating the environmental implications of construction projects, and creating standards for the discharge of pollutants into the environment. Furthermore, most environment ministries have an investigative branch and enforcement officers that investigate environmental spills, oversee clean-up operations, and lay charges for violations of environmental regulations. In many instances, environment ministries have their own legal units that prosecute offences under provincial legislation. It should also be remembered that most municipalities also have broad authority over waste disposal and the management of garbage.

There are several important differences between environmental offences and offences more traditionally understood as criminal. In general, the criminal law applies only to individual behaviour and imposes individual responsibility. In most instances, you cannot be held criminally responsible for the actions of another person. This principle is difficult to apply in the environmental context, particularly where responsibility for pollution or environmental damage may not be directly linked to the actions of a single individual but are rather the result of corporate decision-making or a broader set of policies/decisions. To ensure environmental compliance, it is arguably necessary to be able to penalize the corporation. Even this, however, may be insufficient. If the CEO of a corporation authorizes a course of action that causes extreme environmental damage or even serious adverse health impacts and loss of life, then it is important that both the corporation and the individuals responsible for the decision be held accountable; otherwise, it might be possible for the corporation to assume the financial liability of an environmental spill, without any incentive to change its processes and decision-making.

As a result, many environmental regulatory frameworks allow for corporations to be charged directly but also officers of the corporations and, in some instances, members of the company's board of directors. The intent is to prevent the company and those who run it from escaping liability by hiding behind the identity of the corporation as a separate legal entity.

As we discussed in Chapter 4, the criminal law also requires a certain level of intentionality on the part of the accused in order for them to be found guilty. This is known as *mens rea* or guilty mind. This means that an individual cannot be found guilty of a crime for mere inadvertence or even negligence. There are, of course, exceptions, such as criminal negligence causing death, but usually it is a requirement that the accused intended to commit the offence. In environmental offences, however, it is very difficult to demonstrate the level of intentionality that the criminal law requires. For example, if there is an oil spill at sea, can we say that anyone on the ship, or even in the company, "intended" it to happen? This is not likely something that can be established, and certainly not to the standard of proof beyond reasonable doubt. Accidents happen and the likelihood might increase because of corporate decisions. Decision-makers might even understand this and factor it into their calculations of risk. Nevertheless, that doesn't mean that anyone intended to cause the accident. Consequently, there may need to be incentives for corporate officials to take all necessary steps to prevent oil spills and other environmental contaminations. Given the severity of some environmental accidents, criminal liability may need to be considered as part of that "incentive" structure to create environmental responsibility.

To achieve this, and to avoid some of the restrictions inherent in traditional criminal law, environmental offences often involve what is sometimes called **strict liability**. Essentially, this means that the commission of the act is sufficient to establish culpability. In other words, the fact of an environmental spill, or a violation of regulations, in and of itself is the basis for a finding of guilt. It does not matter, in this context, that a corporate CEO or the board of directors did not intend the environmental spill. This does not mean that directors of corporations are completely without a defence in these situations; rather, it is a defence to a strict liability offence to demonstrate that one took all necessary steps to ensure **due diligence** to avoid the environmental spill (without the availability of this defence, the offence would be an "absolute liability" offence, and these are used very sparingly in Canadian law). So, going back to our case of an oil tanker spill, the fact of the spill might be enough to trigger a finding of guilt, but the oil company and its executives can argue, in defence, that they took all the steps necessary to minimize the possibility of an oil spill. If, for example, there was evidence that regular maintenance schedules were not maintained or that the company was utilizing tankers that were old and should have been taken out of service, it would be very difficult to establish a defence of due diligence. But, if they had adhered to reasonable precautions and preventative maintenance, they might avoid a conviction. The intention behind the strict liability offence, then, is both to ensure that corporations and their executives can be held accountable and to demonstrate that an incentive structure is in place to ensure that corporations put environmental issues on their agenda and consider the environmental implications of their decisions. It is important to note the difficulty in establishing responsibility for the individual accused in what is a complex regulatory context. Similar issues are raised in host of corporate regulatory contexts, including corporate fraud and anti-combines cases.

Of course, no scheme of environmental offences will be successful in changing behaviour if the penalties associated with those offences are insufficient. In Canada, environmental protection legislation at both the federal and provincial levels allow for significant penalties on those who violate environmental standards. Penalties can range from warnings, compliance orders, orders to cease an activity, fines, and imprisonment. Several commentators have noted, within the Canadian context, a willingness of governments to increase the penalties associated with environmental damage (Atcheson et al., 2019; Parker & Wasylenchuk, 2021). Under the *Canadian Environmental Enforcement Act* of 2009, mandatory minimum fines were established for both individuals and corporations. As well, maximum fines were also increased. Under that legislation, the maximum fine for an individual was increased to $1 million with a mandatory minimum fine of $15,000. For corporations, the minimum fine was established at $500,000, and the maximum fine was pegged at $6 million. As well, if an individual or corporation is convicted for a subsequent similar offence, fines are automatically doubled.

In 2005, the Ontario government enacted significant increases to the penalty structure of the *Ontario Environmental Protection Act*. Maximum fine levels were nearly doubled with individual fines going from a maximum of $20,000 for a first offence, and $50,000 for a subsequent offence, to $50,000 and $100,000, respectively. More importantly, for particular offences under the legislation – those dealing with discharges of hazardous waste and failure to comply with environmental compliance orders or licence requirements – fines were increased substantially (s. 187[3]). For these offences, individual maximums were increased to a potential maximum of $4 million with a mandatory minimum of $5,000. For subsequent convictions, the maximum increased to $6 million, and the mandatory minimum was set at $20,000. Prior to 2005, there were no minimums, and the maximum penalty was only $50,000 for a first offence and $100,000 for a second offence.

It is, of course, one thing for governments to increase the fines associated with environmental offences, but judges need to enforce the legislation and be willing to impose those fines. Have courts been willing to impose higher fines? It does appear that the amounts of fines have increased subsequent to these legislative changes. According to Atcheson et al. (2019), between 1991 and 2009, the average value of fines was approximately \$1.4 million a year. Since 2009, that amount increased to nearly \$3.9 million in 2015 and has continued to steadily increase since then (Parker & Wasylenchuk, 2021). Perhaps more significantly than the total or average value of fines levied, the number of large fines levied has also been steadily increasing. This is a trend that has been seen across nearly every jurisdiction in Canada.

The *Canadian Environmental Protection Act* allows for imprisonment for up to three years for serious offences. Provincial legislation also allows for imprisonment as a possible penalty. As a rule, imprisonment for environmental offences is relatively uncommon in Canada, although it certainly does happen. At a provincial level, it seems that imprisonment is more likely to be considered by the courts in cases of repeated violations of provincial regulations, and/or repeated failures to comply with orders issued under environmental regulations. In extreme cases, it is possible that criminal charges might be brought by the Crown in relation to environmental issues. In these cases, however, the Crown must establish the very high standards of proof required by the criminal law. For example, if there were evidence that an individual or corporation knowingly discharged materials into the environment that were hazardous to the health of people, or even resulted in death, it might be possible to bring charges for manslaughter. However, the Crown would need to establish beyond reasonable doubt that this was done. For this reason, true criminal charges are generally reserved for the most egregious and catastrophic environmental disasters.

## QUESTIONS OF STANDING

This chapter has focused on how the state regulates environmental issues. We've discussed state regulatory frameworks, as well as the state's ability to create environmental offences. This leaves open the question of private litigation around environmental issues. If an individual, or a community, is concerned about environmental impacts, can they commence litigation themselves? Can they sue for damages, arguing negligence or some other tort (see chapter 7)? This raises the broader question of standing, or who has the right to bring a case before the courts. In general, one must be able to demonstrate that you have been directly impacted and incurred damages due to the actions of another. This may not always be possible to establish in a direct way in environmental cases. Of course, in some instances, establishing direct impact may be straightforward. If a community's drinking water supply has been polluted, the direct impact is self-evident. But what about cases where the impact may be less direct? If one is arguing that acts of pollution have caused long-lasting health impacts – such as cancer – that might only manifest themselves years after exposure, establishing causation may be problematic.

In other instances, however, it may be difficult to find anyone that has been directly impacted. Environmental degradation of wildlife habitats, for example, may not directly impact any single person but may have huge impacts on the environment. In these cases, the issue is one of broad public interest, and the impacts are felt by the public at large, but it may be impossible to identify any single individual or group of individuals who have been directly impacted. This has raised considerable debate about who has the right to go to court to protect the "environment" in its own right. Since animals and trees cannot launch lawsuits, can someone do this on their behalf? The law of standing is complex, and a full discussion is beyond the scope of this chapter. However, in Canada, the courts have developed a concept of **public interest standing**. Public interest standing allows groups or individuals to bring a case forward to the courts, despite not having been directly affected by the issue they wish to raise. One of the difficulties presented by such cases is that the court may lack a factual foundation on which to assess the claims being raised before it. This runs counter to the overall decision-making process of the common law, which tries to distill legal principles through their application to the facts of a case. For this reason, the courts are generally reluctant to grant applications for public interest standing. An interesting alternative to public interest standing, discussed in Box 10.4, is to actually consider the environment to hold a status equal to legal personhood.

Consequently, most public interest groups, such as environmental organizations, generally prefer to find an individual or group of plaintiffs who have experienced damages around which to build a lawsuit. Organizations can then support the litigants but also apply for **intervenor status** in the courts. Generally, it is far easier for a public interest group to obtain intervenor status in a case, rather than standing as a litigant. Intervenor status allows the organization to lead evidence and present arguments to the court on issues related to their expertise. This is a more limited role than when a public interest group acts as a plaintiff, but it can still result in significant influence over the outcome of the litigation.

While public interest standing might be relatively rare, it does potentially have a role in environmental cases. Again, it goes back to that question of who can speak for the environment, and in what ways can environmental issues get before the courts. The regulatory systems that we have already discussed in this chapter, however, mean that we rarely see private litigation as an environmental protection strategy. Rather, cases usually play out through the existing legislative and regulatory frameworks. As we saw earlier, those legislative schemes include broad public interest standing rules. This is important, as it demonstrates how the existence of mechanisms such as environmental assessment boards creates vehicles and institutional frameworks for the raising of important public issues. In the absence of those processes, those concerned about the environment might have to rely on private litigation as a strategy. Arguably, the regulatory and administrative framework is better suited than the courts to providing participatory opportunities.

**BOX 10.4. THE "PERSONHOOD" OF THE MAGPIE RIVER**

A liberalized standard for standing is one route for environmentalists to press their case in court, but a more novel approach has been tried – with success – in several jurisdictions: granting legal personhood to the environmental feature itself. Just as the law recognizes "corporations" as a legal fiction (Chapter 2), why not extend this status to rivers, trees, and animals? Having been granted legal personhood, the entity would be able to sue others in its own name in court for its own protection. Rivers, forests, and lakes in New Zealand and Colombia have been granted this legal status, and the residents of Toledo, Ohio, granted Lake Erie legal personhood in 2019 to address toxic algae that imperilled their drinking water, even though that attempt was ultimately struck down in US Federal Court (Hessey, 2021).

In February 2021, the Magpie River in Quebec became the first Canadian body of water to be granted legal personhood. It gained this status through a joint resolution of the municipality of Minganie and the Innu Council of the Ekuanitshit. This cooperation between settler authority and the local Indigenous Peoples suggests a path to reconciliation based on a shared understanding of the importance of environmental preservation. The joint resolution gives the river nine rights, including "the right to live, exist, and flow; the right to respect for its natural cycles; and the right to take legal action" (Hessey, 2021).

But, when it comes to taking legal action, who will really be calling the shots? Obviously, the river cannot make its own legal choices or express its own views. While environmentalists assume the river would seek its own preservation, perhaps the river would prefer to be productive and help generate electricity. This is, of course, all nonsense, but it demonstrates that the question of legal personhood is really a question of *who* speaks *for* the river. In the case of other legal persons who cannot express or exercise legal options (very small children and the severely disabled, for example), the legal rules about who can speak on their behalf are well defined. The joint agreement between the Innu Council of the Ekuanitshit and the regional government of Minganie carries with it a strong argument for its legitimacy, but there may be other interests that need to be considered. Other levels of government, industry, and even environmental activists may all have a claim to being able to say what is in the best interests of the river and its surroundings. The Magpie River joint resolution has yet to be tested in court, but a judicial determination is inevitable by design. When the cases arise, legal personhood is probably more likely to be a vehicle for contesting those claims, rather than a resolution of them. (See also Flynn, 2022.)

When private litigation does occur in environmental cases, it may be through a **class action lawsuit**. While a full discussion of class action suits is beyond the scope of this chapter, these cases involve identifying a "group" or "class" of litigants who have suffered damages. The actual case focuses on one or two litigants, who effectively stand as "representative plaintiffs." In other words, the facts of what happened to them, and the injuries they suffered, are used as a proxy for all the individuals who suffered damages. Typically, in these cases, a fund is established for the damages, and all members of the class are entitled to a share of the fund, pro-rated based on the extent of the injury they suffered. In many ways, class actions are a more effective way of bringing some environmental cases before the courts, as it allows the courts to dig into the factual context of what happened.

## STRATEGIC LITIGATION AGAINST PUBLIC PARTICIPATION (SLAPPS)

Strategic litigation against public participation, or **SLAPPs**, constitutes a unique category of cases that frequently occur around environmental disputes. SLAPPs are private lawsuits in which individuals, corporations, or even governments sue those who might challenge or object to their activities.[1] The intention behind the lawsuit is to effectively use the threat of litigation to either punish or deter individuals from engaging in public debate and activism around an environmental issue.

A developer, for example, might sue local residents who oppose a housing development. Demonstrators might be sued for trespassing, for participating in a protest or blockade, or for defamation arising out of things that might be said during a protest. Organizers of a boycott might be sued for inducing breach of contract or defamation. In some cases, residents and activists who seek to challenge development decisions before environmental regulatory bodies are sued because of that participation. That litigation might allege that the challenge constitutes an "abuse of process," or it might allege that the testimony presented to the regulatory board is defamatory (see Box 10.5).

As suggested, SLAPP litigation makes use of the tools of private litigation to prevent public comment and public participation. One of the reasons SLAPP lawsuits are so effective, is that they can take advantage of several well-established and deeply rooted principles of our litigation system. The first is that courts do not prejudge the likely outcome of a lawsuit. Most of these cases, if followed through to a final determination, are unsuccessful (Pring & Canan, 1989, p. 26; Sheldrick, 2014, p. 20). They also involve greatly exaggerated claims of damages that, if true, are far beyond what any court would order.

---

1   A great deal has been written on the subject of SLAPPs. See Landry, 2010; Pring, 1989; Pring & Canan, 1986; Sheldrick, 2014; Tollefson, 1994, 1996.

> **BOX 10.5.  CAUSES OF ACTION THAT COMMONLY FORM THE BASIS OF SLAPP LAWSUITS**
>
> · Defamation and slander
> · Invasion of privacy/exploitation of personality
> · Malicious prosecution/abuse of process
> · Interference with contract
> · Nuisance and Trespass
>
> Source: Sheldrick (2014, Chapter 2).

Nevertheless, because the system allows litigants to drive the process, it is only after a full exploration of the facts and evidence by the court that a decision is rendered. Accordingly, courts are generally unwilling to curtail these sorts of lawsuits. The court does not judge the reasonableness of a plaintiff's claims or the likelihood of them being substantiated.

Courts operate based on certain assumptions about the rationality of parties to a case. There is an assumption that plaintiffs will make their decision to bring a case forward based on an assessment of the damages incurred, the cost of the litigation, and the likelihood of success. The greater the injury suffered, the more reasonable it might be to bring a case forward, even if the likelihood of success might not be high. If the damages are less significant, but the likelihood of victory is great, again the decision might be made to bring a case forward. Similarly, if the chance of victory is less likely, and damages are relatively small, it would be irrational to pursue the litigation given the costs involved in a lawsuit. Ultimately, the assessment of these various factors will depend on the individual plaintiff, what injuries were incurred, and their financial resources. The courts also assume that once litigation begins, parties will be open to settling the case on a reasonable basis. Again, this determination will depend on the above factors. A settlement below the damages requested, for example, might seem very reasonable if the chances of success are mixed.

In SLAPP cases, however, the economics of these assessments and considerations are reversed. The plaintiff is not necessarily looking to win the case. Rather, the goal is to stop protest and activism that might be hurting business activities. As such, they might be willing to spend the money to pursue a case, as they are considering factors that go beyond the four corners of the actual litigation. If the objective is to tie activists up in a costly legal battle that starves them of resources, to create a chill that prevents others from joining their cause, or even to get a settlement that includes commitments from the defendants to stop their activities, then the logic of a typical lawsuit simply does not apply. The fact that the case will ultimately be lost may not be a significant consideration.

There has been much discussion, both in the academic literature and by courts, as to the potential abuse posed by SLAPP litigation. In particular, the concern is that courts, through the mechanism of private litigation, are being used to curtail freedom of expression, public debate, and participation in civic and political life. The courts, despite acknowledging the dangers of SLAPP litigation, have proven relatively ineffective at dealing with it themselves (Landry, 2010; Pring & Canan, 1986; Sheldrick, 2014). As a result, legislatures in many jurisdictions have stepped in to try to regulate SLAPP litigation. In the United States, roughly two thirds of states have enacted some sort of anti-SLAPP legislation. In Canada, British Columbia, Ontario, and Quebec have legislative frameworks governing SLAPP litigation. A key element of all these legislative schemes is the need to balance the rule of law so that courts are accessible to those who seek redress for injury and grievance, while at the same protecting freedom of expression and preventing abuse of the judicial process (Sheldrick, 2021).

The most successful regulatory schemes have sought to reverse the economic logic of a SLAPP lawsuit and overcome the underpinning judicial logic that has made addressing SLAPPs so difficult. This typically means a combination of the following types of initiatives:

- An **expedited review** process allowing for an early and speedy determination of the SLAPP question. This means that plaintiffs cannot utilize delaying tactics to starve defendants of resources.
- A shift of the **burden of proof** away from the defendant, to demonstrate that the case has no merit, to the plaintiff, to demonstrate that it does have merit. Typically, anti-SLAPP legislation places a burden on the defendant to show that their expression on a matter of public importance has been negatively impacted by the lawsuit. Once that is established, the burden shifts to the plaintiff to demonstrate that they have suffered injury and that there is a real case to try on the merits. This does not need to involve a full review of all the evidence that would be brought at trial, but it requires the plaintiff to demonstrate that there is a reasonable chance of success should the case proceed to trial.
- A shift in the normal responsibility for **costs** in the trial, with the provision that if the case is determined to be a SLAPP lawsuit, or if the plaintiff loses, they will bear a larger share of the defendant's costs in the case. In some legislative schemes, this involves requiring the plaintiff to provide resources to the defendant to help mount their defence, rather than waiting until the end of the case for a determination of costs.
- An explicit balancing of the impact of the case on freedom of expression and the merits of the case.
- Allowing the court to exercise strict management control over the case. This ensures that if the case is allowed to proceed, the parties cannot engage in delaying tactics or costly motions that are not required.

It should be clear that this sort of legislative intervention in the judicial process represents a significant departure from the norm. Courts are generally allowed to set their own rules and processes, particularly where it comes to the management of cases and preventing abuse of the judicial process. Of course, it is often the case that lawsuits are brought for political purposes. Almost every constitutional case, for example, involves some sort of political issues. In SLAPP cases, however, the lawsuit is brought under the veil of a private dispute, and the political motivations of the plaintiff are not readily clear in the substantive claims being advanced. This implicates the courts in a type of litigation that undermines the legitimacy and neutrality of the judicial process. As a result, a political solution, through legislative intervention, is necessary to both ensure that those who have suffered injury are permitted to seek redress in the courts, and limit and constrain SLAPP cases. Of course, this is not an easy determination, and it involves the courts in one more type of political assessment.

## CONCLUSION

In this chapter, we explored some dimensions of how law intersects with questions of both environmental protection and environmental regulation. Environmental policy has become deeply rooted in a variety of quasi-judicial administrative procedures. Environmental assessments, which are designed to subject development projects to scrutiny through a lens of environmental protection, do so through the application of legal processes and legal structures. At the same time, these quasi-judicial processes also become the locus for political contestation between developers, environmental activists, and those impacted (both positively and negatively) by development decisions.

Environmental issues, however, are also addressed through other dimensions of public law, most notably through the criminal law, as well as private law. The creation of environmental offences, the development of different standards of liability for these offences, and penalty schemes that involve both fines and the potential of imprisonment represent significant alterations of traditional criminal law. Finally, both environmental activists and lobby groups, as well as developers, have taken advantage of various dimensions of private law to advocate around their positions and to seek to influence environmental policy and issues. In this sense, law and the environment provide us with a case study that explores many of the theses throughout earlier chapters. It is an administrative law subject, a criminal law subject, and a private law subject. At the same time, most fundamentally, it is a political subject, through which law both shapes outcomes, with the application of legal principles, and is used and employed as a technique and a strategy by those seeking to influence outcomes. This has been a major theme of the book, namely that law stands on its own, and legal principles have an integrity as a system of knowledge that shapes the results of both legal and political cases. At the same time, it is a structure that parties and political actors operate within, and it can be both a constraint and an opportunity to shape political outcomes.

## REVIEW QUESTIONS

1  Environmental assessment processes are complex. What do you think accounts for that complexity? Do you think they are effective tools for protecting the environment? Why?
2  How have environmental assessment processes evolved to take into account Indigenous concerns and knowledge systems? Has this been adequate?
3  Given what you know about the criminal law, do you think environmental spills should be treated as crimes? How serious should environmental damage be before it can be considered "criminal"?
4  Should the law of standing be expansive, allowing many people to go to court, or should it be more restrictive? What arguments support expanding the rules of standing?

## MOOT COURT TOPIC

Acme Industrial has been operating in a small rural town for 30 years. Over that time, it routinely discharged chemical waste into the river running through the town. It has been charged numerous times with violation of environmental regulations and has always paid the fines that have been levied against it. It has not, however, fully complied with orders to fix its processes and stop discharging waste. More recently, the company was bought out by a major global manufacturing company. A new CEO was appointed with orders to clean up the company's operations but also to make the company profitable. The new CEO was shocked by the company's environmental practices and ordered an immediate review and resultant changes. The staff responsible for making those changes informed the CEO of how much it would cost to make all the required changes, and he instructed them to "go slow" on the most costly items. The CEO lied to the board of directors as to the progress being made on the environmental protections and their implementation. In the meantime, a major spill happened, contaminating the drinking water supply of the town, devastating a fishery in a nearby lake, and leading to many townspeople being hospitalized. How should liability for the spill be assessed?

# Afterword

As we noted in the Introduction, this a book about law but one that differs from conventional textbooks that introduce law to undergraduate students. Our goal is not only to provide students with a foundational understanding of law but also to encourage students to engage with law directly as a subject of research *in its own terms*, while also appreciating law's intimate connection with politics. This tension is really at the heart of the book: We believe that law has its own autonomous frame of reference, but that frame itself cannot be fully understood without also seeing it as embedded in the contextual reality of political institutions. The former requires us not only to acknowledge the important ways law is independent of politics (and to cherish those protections) but also to treat legal doctrines seriously, with a normative force of their own and with a complexity social scientists may be reluctant to embrace. The latter reflects the neo-institutional approach to law we have advanced throughout the book. It draws our attention to the myriad ways law intersects with matters of public concern and impacts public policy. The pervasiveness of law in modern public life is itself a reason to better understand law's intricacies. We wrote this text in large part because we think both that insights about law are complementary to public policy and that neglecting either one leads to an impoverished understanding of law's significant role in Canadian society.

In Part 1, to better understand the neo-institutional contours of law, we first explored foundational elements: sources of law and legal reasoning. As we demonstrated in Chapter 1, the question of defining law is really an invitation to join an ongoing debate about the nature of law. While there are simple answers – no one would deny a statute enacted by Parliament is "law" – capturing the full scope of what law entails is difficult. Law can be empowering (such as the power to write a will) in addition to restraining (like a criminal prohibition); positivists insist on law being separate from morals and "justice" in a way that natural law adherents might find objectionable; and the rule of law shields us against arbitrariness but clearly accommodates dramatic changes to law that reflect popular will (so long as it takes the form of a statute enacted into law). When it comes to law, easy starting points are open to contestation and quickly complicated.

Even the obvious "law" of an enacted statute will be "of no force or effect" if judges find that the act violates the constitution. To do so, judges engage in *interpretation*, a core part of legal reasoning. In Chapter 2, we introduced key elements of common law legal reasoning: the respect for precedent (*stare decisis*), how it is operationalized in the Canadian judicial hierarchy, and how the rules of statutory interpretation guide judges. Along with the sources of law identified in Chapter 1, Chapter 2 provided the basics that are necessary to understand law as it is understood by its own practitioners. These practitioners – Canadian judges and lawyers – operate in an institutional frame that is shaped by the politics of authority, democracy, and the rule of law. The constitution, the subject of Chapter 3, is the "supreme law" of Canada, but it is also the product and reflection of its politics. The *Canadian Charter of Rights and Freedoms* lists a collection of rights but makes them all subject to "reasonable limits" that are "demonstrably justified in a free and democratic society." Justified infringements, then, must be consistent with the politics we live by in a country that is free and democratic. Writ large, the constitution is emblematic of a relationship between law and politics that underlies virtually all of our legal controversies, even if others are less high-profile and more obscure.

Part 2 introduced and examined seven different areas of public and private law. In addition to providing the foundational knowledge for students to begin to engage with doctrines in each field, we applied our neo-institutional approach to show how those doctrines impact public policies and how the decisions and action of legal actors shape public outcomes and, more generally, delineated the role of the state in each area. With respect to criminal law (Chapter 4), the connections are most obvious and stark: here the state is charged with maintaining public order and it uses its coercive power to force compliance with its laws. But, as we described in Chapter 4, the *Criminal Code of Canada* is a complicated and nuanced statute – another product of an explicitly political process – that is nested in a system of criminal justice norms, as well as constitutional and common law rules, and which relies heavily on the discretion of actors who apply and enforce its provisions. If you didn't know the doctrines of criminal law, you'd be at a loss to explain what these actors were trying to achieve and how they interact with one another; at the same time, if you knew only the doctrines of criminal law, you would know very little about how Canada's criminal justice system actually operates.

The subject of Chapter 5, administrative law, generates less public attention and scrutiny than criminal law, but it governs a wide swath of the modern state's activity and impacts the lives of ordinary Canadians on a regular basis. Whether it be through the regulation of professions that serve them (the College of Physicians), the resolution of their housing disputes (landlord-tenant boards), or even the television they are allowed to watch or not (the Canadian Radio-Television Commission), administrative law governs a surprisingly large amount of Canadian day-to-day life. As government plays this larger role, the importance of subjecting bureaucratic tribunals and agencies to public scrutiny has become critical to ensure some degree of accountability and transparency. The neo-institutional lens offers insights here too: While independent agencies applying their expertise are useful and legitimate for governments to establish, the exercise of political power still needs to be lawful. The story of administrative law is largely the struggle of the courts to balance a healthy respect for the efficiency and expertise of non-judicial bodies with the demands of the rule of law. The grounds for judicial review and the tests for judicial deference are complicated and often arcane, but we believe they are essential to understanding modern Canadian public administration and the fragmenting of state power in the bureaucratic age.

Areas of private law are often neglected by political scientists since they are, by definition, not "public" and thus seemingly distant from the government activity they are usually interested in. As we argue in Chapters 6, 7, and 8, this is unfortunate, because the doctrines in these areas clearly have significant public dimensions. Branding them "private" simply means that the litigants to the case are non-state actors. The formality of who is a litigant to a case can be important, but it provides only a very weak justification for not paying attention to the often crucial public elements that arise in such cases. The Churchill Falls example is a telling one: In that "private law" contracts case between two "private" corporations (never mind that all the shareholders are governments!), matters of interstate federalism played out in a dramatic fashion, with the "normal" doctrines of contract law dictating a public outcome impacting an entire province of Canadians. Chapter 7 showed that tort law – normally understood as simply concerned with lawsuits between private citizens – can be used in two very important public ways: (1) to hold public actors to account by making them liable for their negligence and (2) by being the tool for states to address public problems. In areas as diverse as product liability, police accountability, and family violence, we see tort law being relied upon to mitigate public problems. Such approaches can be criticized as being reactive and incurring the costs of the cumbersome civil justice system, but they are also empowering in the sense that they allow ordinary Canadians to initiate legal claims and (sometimes) arrive at a just result.

Chapter 8 considers another area often deemed private: property law. The attentive reader might have noticed that we did not include "private law" in this chapter title, as we did with Chapters 6 and 7. We did this because the public dimensions of property law are truly inherent in the entire topic. We sometimes think of property solely in terms of private property, but even that type of property cannot be understood as completely "private" – after all, private property is in essence a public claim in the sense that it excludes all others to the thing in question. Private property only makes sense in that it is opposed to an otherwise public world. And it hardly needs to be said that the resolution of Indigenous land claims are matters of public concern. Moreover, recent events have demonstrated that the occupation of public property (or semi-public property) for protest or to house (or encamp) marginalized communities are controversies that are high on the public agenda. Along with intellectual property – certain to be pressured by the advance of artificial intelligence – we see a near future where a diverse group of social science scholars will be grappling with core issues of property law. Even those seeking new paradigms and dramatic reforms would be better served by understanding existing property law doctrines. We suspect that these centuries-old doctrines of property law will continue to prove resilient and shape outcomes even as circumstances radically change.

Even more than Chapter 8, the following two chapters – Chapter 9 on labour law and Chapter 10 on the environment – demonstrate the near impossibility of separating the private from the public. It is difficult to categorize labour law as public or private law. The relationship between a private employer and its employees is now always a matter subject to at least some public regulation; where there is a union, the "tripartite" arrangement requires even more state involvement to help achieve a collective outcome all parties can agree to. When the union is a public sector one, the state's facilitating role is complicated by its additional role as the employer. Once we add in the constitutional guarantee of freedom of association, now interpreted by the Court to include some degree of meaningful collective bargaining, the public aspects of what was once a strictly "private" employment relationship cannot be denied.

Similarly, the public interest in a clean and sustainable environment has made state action and enforcement a necessity, even against private property and private businesses. As Chapter 10 suggests, environmental laws clearly lay at the nexus of law and politics. With the constitutional division of powers not assigning the "environment" to any particular level of government, all Canadian governments tend to play some role in answering public demands for environmental action. This had led to a number of federalism controversies over the environment, including important Supreme Court precedents that are continuing to play out in Canadian politics to this day. As Chapter 10 notes, however, environmental legal action is not all a matter of public law: Strategic litigation to silence public interest groups using private law rules of defamation are themselves now restrained by new anti-SLAPP laws created by some provincial governments. Even though the "public" role of the government is often foremost of mind when we think about environmental regulation, we must be aware that the legal battles are often a mixture of private interests, groups advocating for public interests, and governments muddling their way between answering calls for environmental action but also accommodating the economic interests that are almost always at stake too.

While this text is about the law, its subtext is the state. Woven throughout the entire text is the notion that the law as we understand it today cannot exist without the active involvement and support of the state. This raises a number of questions that are beyond the scope of this book but have been the subject of a wide range of political science study: What is the state? How were states formed? How do states function? What happens when they fail? We don't deny that these are important questions, but (out of necessity) we have chosen to avoid essential questions about the state and largely restrict ourselves to the way the state uses law to achieve public ends. In some ways, this is can be quite perfunctory – state force ultimately backs up all laws, so even providing judicial enforcement of contract law means that all contracts are to some minimal degree "public." We have tried to show throughout – using a neo-institutional approach – that the interpenetration of the state and the law can be more complex: The state leveraging private law by creating a new cause of action to confront a public problem is a subtle government use of law that we don't see commented on much by political scientists or social scientists generally. Again, to do so is difficult because you need to see both the operation of legal doctrines and the public policy context they operate within and subsequently influence. It is towards these more complete understandings that this textbook aims.

After many years of studying it, we remain fascinated by law and legal phenomena. We hope our enthusiasm for the subjects presented in this text will prove contagious, and that a new generation of young scholars – whether headed to law school or careers in the social sciences – continue to explore and expand our knowledge of law. We hope those students, keeping this textbook in mind, will always strive for a robust understanding of law, engaging with legal doctrines on their own terms but also appreciating their political underpinnings and societal impacts.

# Glossary

**acceptance**   an essential element of a valid contract. Acceptance is demonstrated when both parties have agreed to the terms of the contract.

*actus reus*   a Latin term, meaning "guilty act." Used in criminal law to describe an action which warrants a criminal penalty. See also *mens rea* below.

**adjudication**   the process of deciding according to law, and the dispute resolution method employed by courts.

**adversarial legalism**   a form of policy-making policy implementation that relies primarily on legal rules and contestation by legal actors, as opposed to more bureaucratic or administrative means.

**alibi**   a Latin term, meaning "excuse." Generally refers to a criminal law defence grounded in evidence regarding one's whereabouts that casts doubt on the Crown's theory of the case.

**amber light theories**   an approach to administrative law that recognizes the importance of administrative agencies and tribunals as stand-alone entities, while also acknowledging the importance of judicial oversight in maintaining the integrity of decisions made by political actors.

**amending formula**   a specific procedure that needs to be followed to change the constitution.

**appellate jurisdiction**   the ability of a court to hear a case decided by a court below it in the judicial hierarchy.

**arbitration**   a dispute resolution method wherein parties agree to a decision-maker and with the understanding that the parties will be bound by the decision the arbitrator makes.

**balance of probabilities (BOP)**    the standard of proof, often applicable in private law cases, which requires the evidence provided to make the claim more likely than not (or, in other words, a more than 50 per cent probability of being true).

**beyond a reasonable doubt (BARD)**    the standard of proof used in most criminal matters, which is not met if there are any remaining doubts so long as those doubts are based on reason or logic. In a criminal case, this requires that the Crown must prove beyond a reasonable doubt that the accused is guilty of the crimes that have been committed. Otherwise, the standard of proof is not met, and the accused is not found guilty.

**bi–jural nation**    a nation which includes at least two general legal systems (e.g., Canada, which utilizes both the common law system and civil law system).

**binding arbitration**    a type of dispute resolution in which the parties agree upon the appointment of an arbitrator who, after hearing submissions from both sides, imposes a resolution on the parties deemed, in the arbitrator's eyes, to be fair, reasonable, and consistent with the collective agreement. Used often in labour law.

**bundle of rights**    an acknowledgement that some rights are best conceived of as a collection of several rights. Commonly used to describe property rights, where a single "right" to a thing might actually be a right of ownership, a right to possession, and a right to use.

**burden of proof**    is a rule of both criminal and private law according to which one party (usually the prosecution or plaintiff) has the obligation to provide evidence to substantiate their claim. In the *Canadian Charter of Rights and Freedoms* context (see Chapter 3), someone challenging a law bears the burden of first showing that the law infringes their rights; but, once established, the burden shifts to the government to prove that its law is a reasonable limit on that right. In the SLAPP context (see Chapter 10), it is the plaintiff's duty to demonstrate that there is a real case based on merit.

**cause of action (or cause)**    the grounds on which an individual or entity may file a lawsuit against another. A cause of action may be established by statute or a common law precedent.

**certification**    in labour law, commonly understood as the entire process of establishing a union, beginning when some of the employees seek to unionize. Certification is the final step, when the union becomes the exclusive bargaining representative of the employees.

**class action lawsuit**    often used in environmental law, these cases involve identifying a group of litigants who have suffered damages who then sue collectively under the name of a single (or several) representative plaintiff. Most jurisdictions have special legislation that allows such actions and prescribes the process and special rules for doing so (e.g., Ontario's *Class Proceedings Act*).

**collective bargain**   a negotiation between the employer and all the employees together as represented by their union (or association).

**commensurability**   the notion that all injuries recognized in law can be reduced to a definitive monetary value in losses.

**comparative negligence**   a concept in negligence law that allows for liability and damages to be proportioned according to the degree of fault when there are multiple tortfeasors.

**consideration**   an essential element of a valid contract. Each party to the contract must give something of value for the contract to be valid.

**constitutions**   enactments which are considered the supreme law in a state, made up of written documents and/or unwritten conventions (see Chapter 3).

**contract law**   the legal standards and rules that regulate legally binding agreements created between participants.

**conventions**   traditions representing a shared understanding, reinforced by established precedents, which constitute effective rules for political behaviour (some of which exist as part of the Canadian constitution).

**copyright**   granted in property law to protect the intellectual property of an idea.

**corrective justice**   an approach used to address a deprivation caused by wrongdoing, the goal being to return the affected party, as much as possible, to the state that they would have been in had the wrong not occurred.

**correctness**   a standard of review in administrative law that requires an agency or tribunal's determination to be the same as that which the reviewing court would have decided.

**costs**   in environmental law, during SLAPP cases there is a shift in costs in the trial. If the case is determined to be a SLAPP lawsuit, or the plaintiff loses, they will bear a larger share of the defendants' cost in the case.

**crimes against property**   a broad category of crimes which includes those such as breaking and entering, trespassing, and damage to property but also crimes like fraud and embezzlement.

**crimes against the person**   crimes of which danger or apprehension of danger is brought to another person.

**Crown immunity**   the common law doctrine that the state or sovereign cannot be sued or held liable in court.

**distributive justice**   an approach that suggests justice is better achieved by more equitably apportioning or dividing benefits or better distributing costs.

**due diligence**   a standard of proper care. In environmental law, it generally refers to the steps taken to ensure that the risks to the environment are minimized.

**duty of care**   a legal responsibility placed on parties making them responsible for taking steps to prevent injury to anybody whose activities they may affect.

**enabling legislation**    statutes enacted by the government that create, empower, and give purpose to administrative entities such as boards, agencies, and commissions.

**endowment effect**    an effect noted by Richard Thaler, relating to property, which states that once you possess something, it increases in value to you and you therefore may feel that you have a sort of "right" to it.

**environmental assessment**    an administrative process designed to evaluate the impact of development projects on the environment.

**error of law**    an error of law is made when the decision of an administrative tribunal is arrived at through a misinterpretation or improper application of statute or a legal rule.

**exclusive bargaining representative of all employees**    a concept in labour law establishing that, when a union becomes certified, all employees are represented by the union regardless of any individual employee's disposition towards the union.

**expedited review**    a speedier process; in the SLAPP context, it prevents parties from using delaying tactics to starve another party's resources.

**felonies**    a term used in the US legal system to denote serious criminal offences; it is not used in the Canadian criminal justice system (see instead "indictable offence").

**fiduciary relationship**    a relationship in which one party has the legal responsibility to act in the best interest of the other party (e.g., the legal relationship between the Crown and the Indigenous population in Canada, as established by s. 35 of the *Constitution Act,* 1982).

**general damages**    monetary compensation intended to address injuries that are subjective and often intangible (for "pain and suffering" in a personal injury suit, for example).

**green light theories**    an approach to administrative law that views administrative power as independent and shielded from judicial intervention. Green light theories prioritize good public administration, viewing it as a power not subjugated by, but instead equal to, courts.

**hearsay**    testimony about what someone else said. It is generally inadmissible as evidence if it is being offered to prove the truth of the statement.

**horizontal** *stare decisis*    the principle that calls for courts to follow their own precedents (on the same level of the judicial hierarchy, thus "horizontal").

**indictable offences**    the most serious offences found in the *Criminal Code of Canada*, including murder, robbery, and aggravated sexual assault. These offences proceed "by way of indictment" (which is a formal charging document).

**intervenor status**    a status granted by the court to parties that are not actual litigants to the case to lead evidence and present arguments in court on issues where they can offer the court perspectives that may not be presented by the named litigants.

**judicial decision**   the determination of an issue submitted to a court, usually accompanied by reasons for the judgment (also known as a "judicial opinion").

**jurisdiction**   the ability of a court to hear a case, by way of territory or subject matter, or through appellate review.

**jurisdictional error**   a subset of the possible errors of law that are recognized in administrative judicial review. Jurisdictional errors are those where an administrative board acts outside the powers laid out in its enabling legislation.

**legal identity**   a notion in law that that one might be considered a "person" in legal terms, even if it might not be true in other frames (e.g., the physical world). Sometimes also known as "legal personhood."

**lockouts**   in labour law, when employers prevent their unionized employees from working as part of the collective bargaining process (the employer power that parallels an employee "strike").

**mediation**   a dispute resolution method in the legal system wherein the parties agree on who the decision-maker will be, and any resolution the decision-maker proposes is only effective to the extent the parties agree to it.

***mens rea***   a Latin term, meaning "guilty mind." An aspect of criminal law that requires some degree of intentionality on the part of the accused to be found guilty; for most criminal offences, this means one cannot be found guilty of a criminal offence due to inadvertence or negligence.

**misdemeanors**   a term used in the US legal system to denote less serious criminal offences; it is not used in the Canadian criminal justice system (see instead "summary conviction offences").

**offer**   an essential component of a valid contract; an unmistaken proposition must be made regarding the exchange of something of value between parties.

**onus of proof**   the onus of proof is the obligation that one side has to offer substantial evidence for their claim.

**original jurisdiction**   the ability of a court to be the first to hear a case (sometimes referred to as "the court of first instance").

**ownership**   the broadest "bundle of rights" in property law, typically including the right to possess something, the right to use it, the right to manage it, and the right to transfer it to someone else.

**patent**   granted in property law to protect the intellectual property of an invention.

**personal property**   from property law; everything owned that is not attached to a particular location.

**possession**   a narrower set of property rights, related to immediate control and usage

**preliminary inquiry**   an early hearing in indictable offence proceedings. Here the Crown presents the evidence against the convicted and, depending on the sufficiency of the presented evidence, the judge will decide if there are grounds to proceed with a trial.

**presumption of innocence**    a core principle of our criminal justice system, the presumption of innocence principle requires that all accused of a crime must be considered innocent until proven guilty

**primacy of legal instruments**    refers to how legal instruments (i.e., constitutions, statutes, regulations) are authoritative over non-legal considerations (e.g., politics, convenience, customs, etc.).

**private law**    law which sets out expectations and rules for governing relationships between citizens, and which settles legal controversies that are citizen-versus-citizen.

**privative clauses**    from administrative law, special clauses incorporated into the enabling legislation of administrative boards or tribunals which attempt to preclude any judicial interference with the board or tribunal's decisions.

**procedural error**    from administrative law, procedural errors arise when the conduct of an administrative process does not meet the standard required of them. These errors could include a failure to produce a written decision including the reasoning for a decision or a failure to provide an oral hearing where the case required one.

**procedural fairness**    the set of principles required of administrative tribunals and agencies that ensure claimants are treated in accordance with appropriate rules and practices. Often this includes an individual's right to be heard before a decision is made and, once a decision has been made, to know the reasons for the outcome.

**procurement**    the formal process of obtaining something.

**public interest standing**    often used in environmental law, it allows groups or individuals to bring a case to the courts, even if they have no direct stake in the controversy.

**public law**    law which relates to issues of governance, and where the state is one of the parties to the case.

**public sector unions**    unions in which the employer is the state in some capacity.

**punitive damages**    damages that go beyond addressing the injury to the plaintiff and instead seek to deter the behvaiour of the defendant.

**quasi-judicial**    characteristic of entities, like administrative tribunals, that imitate processes used by a court even though the administrative body is established to perform a function related to expertise in a particular field.

**radical title**    from the English conception of property law, understanding the Crown to be the ultimate owner of the land. It allows the Crown to take private property if it has a compelling public reason to do so. If property owners die without a will, and there are no beneficiaries, the property goes to the Crown in recognition of its radical title.

**Rand formula**    used in labour law, a doctrine that holds that a dissenting employee can decline membership in the union in a formal sense but still must pay union dues and accept the union as their representative.

**real property**    property related to land and everything permanently attached to it.

**reasonable care**    a common law standard for actions that a reasonable person would take to prevent injury to someone the owe a duty of care.

**reasonable foreseeability**    a common law standard that limits liability to only those consequences that a reasonable person could predict would result from their wrongdoing.

**reasonableness**    a standard of review used in administrative law that means a court will be deferential to outcomes of an administrative decision-maker even if it is not the decision the court itself would have made but is one which might still be considered an appropriate outcome based on reason and given the decision-maker's expertise.

**red light theories**    an approach to administrative law that emphasizes the importance of judicial oversight and emphasize the primacy of law over the expertise of bureaucratic actors.

**reference cases**    cases heard by the Supreme Court of Canada regarding abstract legal questions submitted to it by governments.

**regulations**    orders made by competent officers or agencies, delegated to them by statutory authority.

**self-defence**    a criminal defence which concedes that the accused did commit an offence but did so as part of an act of self-protection, and they should therefore be excused.

**SLAPPS**    strategic litigation against public participation; private lawsuits where individuals, corporations, or even governments sue those who might object to their activities.

**special damages**    monetary compensation that addresses losses by the plaintiff where the amount is quantifiable, using actual receipts or projected metrics (like "loss of employment income").

**standard of care**    the standard of precautions that must be met for one to have properly fulfilled a duty of care.

**standard of proof**    a standard, which differs in civil and criminal law, that must be met by those carrying the burden of proof. See "beyond a reasonable doubt" and "balance of probabilities."

**standard of review**    the standards by which courts subject administrative decisions. See "correctness" and "reasonability."

**standing**    a term used to describe those entitled to appear before a court, normally because they have been directly affected by the legal matter at stake.

**statutes**    laws passed by Parliament, also known as acts of Parliament. Also applies to enactments of provincial legislatures (which are known by a variety of names).

**statutory right of appeal**    from administrative law, a clause that might be included in enabling legislation that facilitates judicial review by explicitly identifying the line of appeal to a particular court.

**strict liability**    where that the commission of an act is enough to establish culpability. Seen in aspects of criminal law related to environmental issues, such that the fact of an environmental spill can be the basis of the finding of guilt alone.

**strikes**    a concept in labour law where workers withhold their labour in an organized and collective manner.

**style of cause**    the name of a case, which also identifies the parties to the case. In criminal cases, the style of cause is typically "R v (Defendant)," and in civil disputes, "(Plaintiff) v (Defendant)".

**subject-matter jurisdiction**    the ability of a court to hear a case based on its subject matter; for instance, in Canada, issues related directly to federal laws are (as declared in the legislation itself) litigated in Canada's federal court system.

**summary conviction offences**    the least serious offences in the *Criminal Code of Canada*. Such offences proceed in an expedited fashion and where the penalty is capped at a fine of up to $5,000 and/or imprisonment for up to two years.

*terra nullius*    meaning "land of no one," a Western European legal concept that describes land that is not owned by any other European nation.

**textualism**    an approach to statutory interpretation which emphasizes the text of the statute itself.

**tort**    a legal wrong, as recognized in the common law.

**tort of family violence**    a specialized tort that recognizes the injuries stemming from a pattern of violent, threatening, or controlling behavior in the context of a family relationship.

**tort of negligent investigation**    a specialized tort that applies to police when their investigation is conducted in a manner that unintentionally falls short of what a reasonable police officer would have done.

**tortfeasor**    a term used for someone who has committed a tort (essentially, the defendant in private tort actions).

**trademark**    granted in property law to protect a name or "mark" that one does business under to differentiate it from competitors.

**trespass**    to infringe on property that belongs to someone else without adequate justification.

**tripartite**    a framework in labour law with three essential actors (representatives of employees, the employer, and the state) participating in a process to resolve employment disputes.

**unconscionable contract**    a contract that, due to the circumstances of its creation, cannot be considered to have been freely made and thus does not constitute a true "meeting of the minds," making it unenforceable.

**vertical** *stare decisis*    the requirement that courts lower in the judicial hierarchy are obligated to follow decisions made by courts above them.

# References

## Articles, Books, Chapters, and Reports

Alcantara, C., & Whitfield, G. (2010). Aboriginal self-government through constitutional design: A survey of fourteen aboriginal constitutions in Canada. *Journal of Canadian Studies*, *44*(2), 1–24. https://doi.org/10.3138/jcs.44.2.122

Arthurs, H. (1979). Rethinking administrative law: A slightly Dicey business. *Osgoode Hall Law Journal*, *17*(1), 1–45. https://doi.org/10.60082/2817-5069.2067

Arthurs, H., & Bunting, A. (2014). Socio-legal scholarship in Canada: A review of the field. *Journal of Law and Society*, *41*(4), 487–99. https://doi.org/10.1111/j.1467-6478.2014.00682.x

Atcheson, A., Smits, B., Parry, D., & Zanetti, J. (2019, October 5). *Penalty Creep: What is going on with Environmental Fines across Canada?* Ontario Bar Association. https://www.oba.org/Sections/Environmental-Law/Articles/Articles-2019/October-2019/penalty-creep-what-is-going-on-with-environmental

Atkey, R. (1972). The Statutory Powers Procedures Act, 1971. *Osgoode Hall Law Journal*, *10*(1), 155–75. http://digitalcommons.osgoode.yorku.ca/ohlj/vol10/iss1/6

Baker, D. (2010). *Not quite supreme: The courts and coordinate constitutional interpretation.* McGill-Queen's University Press. https://doi.org/10.1515/9780773580701

Baker, D. (2020). Criminal justice and criminal law. In H. Bakvis & G. Skogstad (Eds.), *Canadian federalism: Performance, effectiveness, and legitimacy* (4th ed., pp. 114–37). University of Toronto Press.

Baker, D. (2022, May 16). *Parliament can and should restore limits to the intoxication defence.* Toronto Star. https://www.thestar.com/opinion/contributors/parliament-can-and-should-restore-limits-to-the-intoxication-defence/article_e17dd8dd-578f-59df-be9e-80adb6a43a4e.html

Baker, D., & Janzen, B. (2013, May). *Is it time to overhaul the Criminal Code of Canada?* Macdonald-Laurier Institute Publication. https://www.macdonaldlaurier.ca/files/pdf/2013.05.25-Commentary-Criminal_Code_Overhaul-vFinal-web.pdf

Baker, D., & Knopff, R. (2014). *Daviault* dialogue: The strange journey of Canada's intoxication defence. *Review of Constitutional Studies*, *19*(1), 35–58.

Baker, D., & Sheldrick, B. (in press). Legal blindspots in Canadian political science. In E. Macfarlane & K. Puddister (Eds.), *Disciplinary divides in the study of law and politics*. University of Toronto Press.

Bateman, T. (1998). Rights application doctrine and the clash of constitutionalism in Canada. *Canadian Journal of Political Science*, *31*(1), 3–29. https://doi.org/10.1017/S000842 3900008660

Bateman, T. (2012). Human dignity's false start in the Supreme Court of Canada: Equality rights and the Canadian Charter of Rights and Freedoms. *International Journal of Human Rights*, *16*(4), 577–97. https://doi.org/10.1080/13642987.2011.621695

Baude, W., & Sachs, S. (2017). The law of interpretation. *Harvard Law Review*, *130*, 1079–147.

Beaulac, S., & Côté, P. (2006). Driedger's "modern principle" at the Supreme Court of Canada: Interpretation, justification, legimitization. *Revue juridique Thémis*, *40*, 131–72.

Bingham, T. (2010). *The rule of law*. Penguin Books.

Bhat, P.I. (2020). *Idea and methods of legal research*. Oxford University Press. https://doi.org /10.1093/oso/9780199493098.001.0001

Blackstone, W. (1893). *Commentaries on the Laws of England in Four Books* (Vol. 1). J.B. Lippincott. https://oll.libertyfund.org/titles/sharswood-commentaries-on-the-laws-of-england -in-four-books-vol-1

Blake, R. (2015). *Lions or jellyfish: Newfoundland-Ottawa relations since 1957*. University of Toronto Press. https://doi.org/10.3138/9781442622654

Borrows, J. (2010). *Canada's Indigenous constitution*. University of Toronto Press.

Borrows, J. (2015, October 1). The durability of terra nullius: *Tsilhqot'in Nation v. British Columbia. University of British Columbia Law Review*, *48*(3), 701–42.

Borrows, J. (2016). *Freedom and Indigenous constitutionalism*. University of Toronto Press.

Bradley, S. (2007, April 1). Conflict of interest, duress and unconscionability in Quebec civil law: Comment on "The origins of a coming crisis: Renewal of the 'Churchill Falls Contract.'" *Dalhousie Law Review*, *30*(1), 259–80.

Bresge, A. (2016, June 7). *Halifax collector wins legal battle with Canada Post over hockey card*. CTV News. https://atlantic.ctvnews.ca/halifax-collector-wins-legal-battle-with-canada -post-over-hockey-card-1.2935612

Calavita, K. (2016). *Invitation to law & society* (2nd ed.). University of Chicago Press. https:// doi.org/10.7208/chicago/9780226296616.001.0001

Cameron, A., Graben, S., & Napoleon, V. (2020). Introduction: The role of Indigenous law in the privatization of lands. In A. Cameron, S. Graben, & V. Napoleon (Eds.), *Creating Indigenous property* (pp. 1–38). University of Toronto Press. https://doi.org/10.3138 /9781487532116-002

Canadian Women's Foundation. (2024, April 5). *The facts about the gender pay gap*. https:// canadianwomen.org/the-facts/the-gender-pay-gap/

Chambers, R. (2021). *The law of property*. Irwin Law.

Cooper, C.J. (1988). Stare decisis: Precedent and principle in constitutional adjudication. *Cornell Law Review*, *73*(2), 401–10.

Crandall, E. (2022). Amendment by stealth of provincial constitutions in Canada. *Manitoba Law Journal*, *45*(1), 173–7. https://doi.org/10.29173/mlj1317

Dagan, H. (2021, March 4). *A liberal theory of property*. Cambridge University Press. https://doi.org/10.1017/9781108290340

Daly, P. (2018, May 11). Revisiting *Dunsmuir*: Food for thought. *Administrative Law Matters*. https://www.administrativelawmatters.com/blog/2018/05/11/revisiting-dunsmuir-food-for-thought/

Daly, P. (2022, May 31). *The ages of administrative law*. (Ottawa Faculty of Law Working paper no. 2022-16). https://doi.org/10.2139/ssrn.4124674

Dicey, A.V. (1982). *Introductory to the study of the law of the constitution*. LibertyClassics, Liberty Fund. https://oll.libertyfund.org/title/michener-introduction-to-the-study-of-the-law-of-the-constitution-lf-ed (Original work published 1885)

Dick, C. (2024, March). The ascent of the Canadian judicial council: Bill C-9 and the move towards judicialized governance. *Canadian Journal of Political Science, 57*(1), 195–214. https://www.cambridge.org/core/services/aop-cambridge-core/content/view/0D4357A9A6150E706CC261B86BA47733/S0008423923000793a.pdf

Do, M. (2022). Beyond consultation: A research agenda to investigate partnerships and comanagement in land governance. In K. Puddister & E. Macfarlane (Eds.), *Constitutional crossroads* (pp. 384–400). UBC Press. https://doi.org/10.59962/9780774867931-023

Dyzenhaus, D. (2010). *Hard cases in wicked legal systems: Pathologies of legality*. Oxford University Press.

Ellickson, R. (2011, September 1). Two cheers for the bundle-of-sticks metaphor, three cheers for Merrill and Smith. *Econ Journal Watch, 8*(3), 215–22.

Emon, A., & Ahmed, R. (Eds.). (2018). *The Oxford handbook of Islamic law*. Oxford University Press. https://doi.org/10.1093/oxfordhb/9780199679010.001.0001

Feehan, J., & Baker, M. (2007, April 1). The origins of a coming crisis: Renewal of the Churchill Falls contract. *Dalhousie Law Review, 30*(1), 207–57.

Flanagan, T. (2019). *First Nations? Second thoughts* (3rd ed.). McGill-Queen's University Press. https://doi.org/10.1515/9780773558540

Flynn, A. (2022). Parks as persons: Legal innovation or colonial appropriation? *Fordham Urban Law Journal, 50*(1), 1–25. https://commons.allard.ubc.ca/fac_pubs/715/

Fraser, W. (1997). Your place or mine? In C. Kolbert (Ed.), *The idea of property in history and modern times* (pp. 79–95). The Ian Mactaggart Trust and Churchill Press.

Froc, K.A. (2022, October 18). *What Parliament refused to hear about Canada's new extreme intoxication law*. The Conversation. https://theconversation.com/what-parliament-refused-to-hear-about-canadas-new-extreme-intoxication-law-191813

Gardner, J. (2011). Can there be a written constitution? In L. Green & B. Leiter (Eds.), *Oxford studies in the philosophy of law* (Vol. 1, pp. 162–94). Oxford University Press. https://doi.org/10.1093/acprof:oso/9780199606443.003.0005

Gordon, S. (2002). *Controlling the state: Constitutionalism from ancient Athens to today*. Harvard University Press.

Goudge, S., & Sheldrick, B. (1988). Privative clauses in 1987: Where do we stand? In I. Blue (Ed.), *Administrative law: Deflecting the glacier*. Law Society of Upper Canada.

Green, A. (2022). *Picking up the slack: Law, institutions and Canadian climate policy*. University of Toronto Press. https://doi.org/10.3138/9781487553319

Hall, P., & Taylor, R. (1996). Political science and the three new institutionalisms. *Political Studies, 44*(5), 936–57. https://doi.org/10.1111/j.1467-9248.1996.tb00343.x

Hamil, S.E. (2015). Common law property theory and jurisprudence in Canada. *Queen's Law Journal*, 40(2), 679–704.

Harding, M.S. (2021). *Judicializing everything? The clash of constitutionalisms in Canada, New Zealand, and the United Kingdom*. University of Toronto Press. https://doi.org /10.3138/9781487528492

Harlow, C. (1980, May). "Public" and "private" law: Definition without distinction. *Modern Law Review*, 43(3), 241–65. https://doi.org/10.1111/j.1468-2230.1980.tb01592.x

Harlow, C., & Rawlings, R. (2009). *Law and administration*. Cambridge University Press. https://doi.org/10.1017/CBO9780511809941

Hart, H.L.A. (1961). *The concept of law*. Clarendon Press.

Hausegger, L., Hennigar, M., & Riddell, T. (2025). *Canadian courts: Law, politics, and process* (3rd ed.). Oxford University Press.

Hausegger, L., & Riddell, T. (2020). Judges on judging in Canadian appellate courts: The role of legal and extra-legal factors on decision-making." *Ottawa Law Review*, 52(1), 1–30.

Heller, M., & Salzman, J. (2021). *Mine! How the hidden rules of ownership control our lives*. Doubleday.

Hennigar, M. (2002). Players and the process: Charter litigation and the federal government. *Windsor Yearbook of Access to Justice*, 21, 91–109.

Hennigar, M. (2010, December). Exploring complex judicial-executive interaction: Federal government concessions in Charter of Rights cases. *Canadian Journal of Political Science*, 43(4), 821–42. https://doi.org/10.1017/S0008423910000739

Hennigar, M. (2022). The most important Charter right? The rise and future of section 7. In K. Puddister & E. Macfarlane (Eds.), *Constitutional crossroads* (pp. 160–76). UBC Press. https://doi.org/10.59962/9780774867931-011

Hessey, K. (2021, October 21). *How a river in Quebec won the right to be a legal person*. Global News. https://globalnews.ca/news/8230677/river-quebec-legal-person/

Hiebert, J.L. (2002). *Charter conflicts: What is Parliament's role?* McGill-Queen's University Press. https://doi.org/10.1515/9780773570375

Hodgetts, Ted. (1973). *The Canadian public service*. University of Toronto Press. https://doi .org/10.3138/9781487599485

Hogg, P.W. (1973). The Supreme Court of Canada and administrative law, 1949–1971. *Osgoode Hall Law Journal*, 11(2), 187–223. https://doi.org/10.60082/2817-5069.2257

Hunt, C. (2021, March 30). Unconscionability in the Supreme Court of Canada: *Uber Technologies Inc. v. Heller*. *The Cambridge Law Journal*, 80(1), 25–8. https://doi.org /10.1017/S0008197321000209

Huscroft, G. (2004). "Thank God we're here": Judicial exclusivity in Charter interpretation and its consequences. *Supreme Court Law Review*, 25, 241–67. https://doi.org/10.60082 /2563-8505.1065

Hutchinson, T., & Duncan, N. (2012). Defining and describing what we do: Doctrinal legal research. *Deakin Law Review*, 17(1), 83–119. https://doi.org/10.21153/dlr2012 vol17no1art70

Johnstone, R. (2017). *After Morgentaler: The politics of abortion in Canada*. UBC Press. https://doi.org/10.59962/9780774834407

Kagan, R. (2019). *Adversarial legalism: The American way of law* (2nd ed.). Harvard University Press. https://doi.org/10.4159/9780674242678

Kelly, J.B. (2005). *Governing with the Charter: Legislative and judicial activism and framers' intent*. UBC Press. https://doi.org/10.59962/9780774851718

Knopff, R. (2003). How democratic is the Charter? And does it matter? In J.E. Magnet, G. Beaudoin, G. Gall, & C. Manfredi (Eds.), *The Charter of Rights and Freedoms: Reflections on the Charter after twenty years* (pp. 199–218). Butterworths.

Koch, A., and Peden, W. (Eds.). (2004). *The life and selected writings of Thomas Jefferson*. Modern Library, Random House.

Kozel, R.J. (2017). *Settled versus right: A theory of precedent*. Cambridge University Press. https://doi.org/10.1017/9781316412237

Kronman, A. (1994). Contract law and distributive justice. In J.L. Coleman (Ed.), *Private law theory*. Garland.

Lagassé, P. (2019). The Crown and government formation: Conventions, practices, customs, and norms. *Constitutional Forum*, 28(3), 1–18. https://doi.org/10.21991/cf29384

Lambert, B., & McInturff, K. (2016). *Making women count: The unequal economics of women's work*. Oxfam Canada.

Landry, N. (2010). From the streets to the courtroom: The legacies of Quebec's anti-SLAPP movement. *Review of European Community and International Environmental Law*, 19(1), 58–69. https://doi.org/10.1111/j.1467-9388.2010.00664.x

Laskin, B. (1952). Certiorari to labour boards: The apparent futility of privative clauses. *Canadian Bar Review*, 30, 986–1003.

Lasswell, H. (1936). *Politics: Who gets what, when, how*. McGraw-Hill.

Lawlor, A., & Crandall, E. (2023). The Canadian Charter's notwithstanding clause as an institutionalized mechanism of court curbing. *American Review of Canadian Studies*, 53(1), 1–21. https://doi.org/10.1080/02722011.2023.2180954

Leach, A. (2021). The no more pipelines act? *Alberta Law Review*, 59(1), 7–40. https://doi.org/10.29173/alr2662

Leyland, P., & Anthony, G. (2013). *Textbook on administrative law*. Oxford University Press.

Liston, M. (2011). Governments in miniature: The rule of law in the administrative state. In C. Flood & L. Sossin (Eds.), *Administrative law in context: A new casebook* (pp. 77–114). Emond Montgomery Publishing.

Locke, J. (2003). *Second treatise of government*. The Project Gutenberg. https://www.gutenberg.org/files/7370/7370-h/7370-h.htm (Original work published 1690)

Loughlin, M. (2000). *Sword and scales: An examination of the relationship between law and politics*. Bloomsbury.

Macfarlane, E. (2012). *Governing from the bench: The Supreme Court of Canada and the judicial role*. UBC Press. https://doi.org/10.59962/9780774823524

Macfarlane, E. (Ed.). (2016). *Constitutional amendment in Canada*. University of Toronto Press. https://doi.org/10.3138/9781442619005

Macfarlane, E. (2023). Studying judicial decision-making. In P. Daly & J. Tomlinson (Eds.), *Researching public law in common law systems* (pp. 136–49). Elgar Publishing. https://doi.org/10.4337/9781789904383.00013

Macpherson, C.B. (1978). *Property: Mainstream and critical positions*. University of Toronto Press.

Mandel, M. (1989). *The Charter of Rights and the legalization of politics in Canada*. Wall & Thompson.

March, J., & Olsen, J. (1983). The new institutionalism: Organizational factors in political life. *American Political Science Review*, 78(3), 734–49. https://doi.org/10.2307/1961840

Markham, L. (2021, August 29). *The man who filed more than 180 disability lawsuits*. The New York Times. https://www.nytimes.com/2021/07/21/magazine/americans-with-disabilities-act.html

Marland, A., Osborne, P., & Levesque, M. (2020). Suing Canadian governments: Core public policy and operational decisions. *Canadian Public Administration*, 63(4), 543–62. https://doi.org/10.1111/capa.12396

McLellan, M. (2020, July 2). Innocence compensation: The success rate of actions for negligent investigation. *The Canadain Bar Review*, 98(1), 34–69. http://doi.org/10.2139/ssrn.3402066

McNabb, D., & Baker, D. (2021). Ignoring implementation: Defect in Canada's "rape shield" policy cycle. *Canadian Journal of Law and Society*, 36(1), 23–46. https://doi.org/10.1017/cls.2020.35

Merry, S. (1988). Legal pluralism. *Law and Society Review*, 22(5), 869–96. https://doi.org/10.1093/oxfordhb/9780199542475.013.0034

Mikadze, K. (2016). Pipelines and the changing face of public participation. *Environmental Law and Practice*, 29, 83–109.

Monahan, P., Wright, W., & Chamberlain, E. (2024). *Hogg's liability of the Crown* (5th ed.). Thomson Reuters.

Morton, F.L., & Knopff, R. (2000). *The charter revolution and the court party*. Broadview Press.

Novick, S.M. (Ed.). (1995). *The collected works of Justice Holmes*. University of Chicago Press.

Oguamanam, C. (2004). Indigenous Peoples and International Law: The Making of a Regime, *Queen's Law Journal*, 30(1), 348–99.

Oxford English Dictionary. (n.d.). law, n.1. In *Oxford English Dictionary Online*. Retrieved March 1, 2022, from https://www.oed.com/view/Entry/106405

Paciocco, D.M. (2009). Unplugging jukebox testimony in an adversarial system: Strategies for changing the tune on partial experts. *Queen's Law Journal*, 34(2), 565–610.

Paine, T. (1994). *Common sense*. The Project Gutenberg. https://www.gutenberg.org/cache/epub/147/pg147-images.html (Original work published 1776)

Parker, S., & Wasylenchuk, K. (2021, April 29). Spot the trend: Increasing environmental penalties in Canada. *Assessing the Impact: Environmental and Resources Law Blog*. https://environmentalandresourcelawblog.blogspot.com/2021/04/spot-trend-increasing-environmental.html

Patzer, J., & Ladner, K. (2022). Indigenous rights and the Constitution Act, 1982: Forty years on and still fishing for rights. In K. Puddister & E. Macfarlane (Eds.), *Constitutional crossroads* (pp. 348–66). UBC Press. https://doi.org/10.59962/9780774867931-021

Pirie, F. (2021). *The rule of laws: A 4,000-year quest to order the world*. Basic Books.

Posner, R.A. (2009). *Law & literature* (3rd ed.). Harvard University Press. https://doi.org/10.4159/9780674054417

Priel. D. (2012). Jurisprudence between science and the humanities. *Washington University Jurisprudence Review*, 4(2), 269–324. https://doi.org/10.2139/ssrn.1566858

Pring, G. (1989). SLAPPs: Strategic lawsuits against public participation. *Pace Environmental Law Review*, 7(1), 3. https://doi.org/10.58948/0738-6206.1535

Pring, G., & Canan, P. (1986). *Getting sued for speaking out*. Temple University Press.

Puddister, K. (2019). *Seeking the court's advice: The politics of the Canadian reference power*. University of Toronto Press. https://doi.org/10.59962/9780774861120

Puddister, K. (2023, September). Oversight and accountability for serious incidents in Canada: Who polices the police? *Canadian Public Administration*, 66(3), 390–408. https://doi.org/10.1111/capa.12538

Rhodes, B. (2016, June 7). *Halifax man successfully sues Canada Post over mangled hockey card*. CBC News. https://www.cbc.ca/news/canada/nova-scotia/canada-post-lawsuit-connor-mcdavid-hockey-1.3620514

Roach, K. (2022). *Canadian policing: Why and how it must change*. Irwin Law.

Russell, P.H. (1987). *The judiciary in Canada: The third branch of government*. McGraw-Hill Ryerson.

Russell, P.H. (2004). *Constitutional odyssey: Can Canadians become a sovereign people?* (3rd ed.). University of Toronto Press.

Russell, P.H. (2019). *Canada's odyssey: A country based on incomplete conquests*. University of Toronto Press.

Said, D. (2023). Navigating entangled terrain: The Supreme Court's impact and the dismissal powers of human rights tribunals. *Canadian Public Administration*, 66(3), 409–25. https://doi.org/10.1111/capa.12540

Samuel, G. (1983, September). Public and private law: A private lawyer's response. *Modern Law Review*, 46(5), 558–83. https://doi.org/10.1111/j.1468-2230.1983.tb02534.x

Sanderson, D. (2018). The residue of *Imperium*: Property and sovereignty on Indigenous lands. *The University of Toronto Law Journal*, 68(3), 319–57. https://doi.org/10.3138/utlj.2017-0084

Savage, L., & Smith, C.W. (2017). *Unions in court: Organized labour and the Charter of Rights and Freedoms*. UBC Press. https://doi.org/10.59962/9780774835404

Schauer, F. (2009). *Thinking like a lawyer: A new introduction to legal reasoning*. Harvard University Press. https://doi.org/10.2307/j.ctvjk2x3k

Schauer, F. (2015a, November 15). Is law a technical language? *San Diego Law Review*, 52(3), 501–13.

Schauer, F. (2015b). *The force of law*. Harvard University Press.

Schauer, F. (2018). On treating unlike cases alike. *Constitutional Commentary*, 33(3), 437–50.

Schauer, F., & Spellman, B. (2017). Analogy, expertise, and experience. *The University of Chicago: Law Review*, 84(1), 249–68.

Scheuerman, W.E. (2020). *The end of law: Carl Schmitt in the twenty-first century*. Rowman & Littlefield International.

Schmunk, R. (2023, January 20). *Decades after the infamous "hot coffee" case, McDonald's is being sued over another scalding spill*. CBC News. https://www.cbc.ca/news/canada/british-columbia/mcdonalds-hot-coffee-lawsuit-burnaby-bc-1.6719467

Sedley, S. (2015). *Lions under the throne: Essays on the history of English public law*. Cambridge University Press. https://doi.org/10.1017/CBO9781316402863

Segal, J., & Spaeth, H. (2002). *The Supreme Court and the attitudinal model revisited*. Cambridge University Press. https://doi.org/10.1017/CBO9780511615696

Sharpe, R. (2018) *Good judgment: Making judicial decisions*. University of Toronto Press.

Sheldrick, B. (2009). Administrative law and public governance: An overlooked dimension of governance. In O.P. Dwivedi, T. Mao, & B. Sheldrick (Eds.), *The evolving physiology of government: Canadian public administration in transition* (pp. 353–74). University of Ottawa Press.

Sheldrick, B. (2014). *Blocking public participation: The use of strategic litigation to silence political expression*. Wilfrid Laurier University Press. https://doi.org/10.51644/9781554589302

Sheldrick, B. (2021). Balancing freedom of expression and access to the courts: Assessing Ontario's anti-SLAPP legislation. In E. Macfarlane (Ed.), *Dilemmas of free expression* (pp. 168–84). University of Toronto Press. https://doi.org/10.3138/9781487529314-011

Sherry, S. (2011). Foundational facts and doctrinal change. *University of Illinois Law Review, 2011*(1), 145–86.

Shklar, J. (1986). *Legalism: Law, morals, and political trials*. Harvard University Press.

Sigalet, G. (2023). Legislated rights as trumps: Why the notwithstanding clause overrides judicial review. *Osgoode Hall Law Journal, 61*(1), 63–97. https://doi.org/10.60082/2817-5069.3978

Sigalet, G., & Woodfinden, B. (2021, June 15). *Opinion: Doug Ford's use of the notwithstanding clause stands up for democracy*. National Post. https://nationalpost.com/opinion/opinion-doug-fords-use-of-the-notwithstanding-clause-stands-up-for-democracy

Sims, Jane. (2017, May 7). Harry Kraemer has successfully fought back against enforcers of smoking laws. *The London Free Press*. https://lfpress.com/2017/05/07/harry-kraemer-has-successfully-fought-back-against-enforcers-of-smoking-laws

Slattery, B. (2005). Paper empires: The legal dimensions of French and English ventures in North America. In J. McLaren, A.R. Buck, & N.E. Wright (Eds.), *Despotic dominion: Property rights in British settler societies* (pp. 50–78). UBC Press.

Slinn, S. (2005). The limitations of pieces of paper: A role for social science in labour law. *Canadian Labour and Employment Law Journal, 12*, 291–312. https://digitalcommons.osgoode.yorku.ca/scholarly_works/2270

Small, T. (2022). Policing partisan self-interest? The Charter and election law. In K. Puddister & E. Macfarlane (Eds.), *Constitutional crossroads* (pp. 143–59). UBC Press. https://doi.org/10.59962/9780774867931-010

Smith, R.M. (1988). Political jurisprudence, the "New Institutionalism" and the future of public law. *The American Political Science Review, 82*(1), 89–108. https://doi.org/10.2307/1958060

Snow, D. (2023, October). *When rights clash: The notwithstanding clause and Saskatchewan's pronoun policy*. Macdonald-Laurier Institute. https://macdonaldlaurier.ca/wp-content/uploads/2023/10/20231003_When-Rights-Clash-Snow_PAPER-v6.pdf

Statistics Canada. (2022, May 30). Quality of employment in Canada: Pay gap, 1998–2021. https://www150.statcan.gc.ca/n1/en/pub/14-28-0001/2020001/article/00003-eng.pdf?st=1v8ksbIC

Stratas, D. (2018, March 8). A decade of *Dunsmuir*: Please no more. *Administrative Law Matters*. https://www.administrativelawmatters.com/blog/2018/03/08/a-decade-of-dunsmuir-please-no-more-hon-david-w-stratas/

Sullivan, R. (2007, June 12). *Statutory interpretation* (2nd ed.). Irwin Law.

Sunstein, C.R. (1997). *Legal reasoning and political conflict*. Oxford University Press. https://doi.org/10.1093/oso/9780195100822.001.0001

Tamanaha, B. (2004). *On the rule of law: History, politics, theory*. Cambridge University Press. https://doi.org/10.1017/CBO9780511812378

Thaler, R. (1980). Toward a positive theory of consumer choice. *Journal of Economic Behaviour and Organization, 1*(1), 39–47.

Tollefson, C. (1994). Strategic lawsuits against public participation: Developing a Canadian response. *Canadian Bar Review, 73*(2), 200–33.

Tollefson, C. (1996). Strategic lawsuits and environmental politics: *Daishowa Inc. v. Friends of the Lubicon. Journal of Canadian Studies, 31*(1), 119–32. https://doi.org/10.3138/jcs.31.1.119

Tucker, E. (2012). The malling of property law? The Toronto Eaton Centre cases, 1984–1987, and the right to exclude. In E. Tucker, J. Muirs, & B. Ziff (Eds.), *Property on trial: Canadian cases in context* (pp. 303–51). Irwin Law.

Vago, S., & Barkan, S.E. (2021). *Law and society* (12th ed.). Routledge. https://doi.org/10.4324/9781003024194

Valinsky, J. (2023, September 21). *McDonald's once again sued after customer burns herself on hot coffee.* CNN Business. https://www.cnn.com/2023/09/21/business/mcdonalds-hot-coffee-lawsuit/index.html

Verdun-Jones, S. (2020). *Criminal law in Canada: Cases, questions and the code* (7th ed). Emond.

Waddams, S. (1992). *Introduction to the study of law* (4th ed.). Carswell.

Waldron, J. (1999). *The dignity of legislation.* Cambridge University Press. https://doi.org/10.1017/CBO9780511621987

Watson Hamilton, J. (2021). Cautious Optimism: *Fraser v. Canada (Attorney General). Constitutional Forum, 30*(2), 1–14. https://doi.org/10.21991/cf29418

Weber, M. (1970). Politics as a vocation. In H.H. Gerth and C.W. Mills (Eds.), *From Max Weber: Essays in sociology* (pp. 77–128). Routledge. (Original work published 1919)

Weiler, P.C. (1971). The "slippery slope" of judicial intervention: The Supreme Court and Canadian labour relations 1950–1970. *Osgoode Hall Law Journal, 9*(1), 1–79.

Weinrib, E.J. (2012). *Corrective justice.* Oxford University Press. https://doi.org/10.1093/acprof:oso/9780199660643.001.0001

Yowell, P. (2018). Constitutional rights and constitutional design: Moral and empirical reasoning in judicial review. Hart Publishing.

Ziff, B. (2019). The Supreme Court, fundamental principles of property law, and the shaping of Aboriginal title. In P. Daly (Ed.), *Apex courts and the common law* (pp. 385–404). University of Toronto Press. https://doi.org/10.3138/9781487530167-015

## Cases and Statutes

*Ahluwalia v Ahluwalia*, 2022 ONSC 1303, vard 2023 ONCA 476.

*Alberta (Education) v Canadian Copyright Licensing Agency*, 2012 SCC 37.

*Americans with Disabilities Act of 1990*, 42 USC, s 12101.

*Andrews v Grand & Toy Alberta Ltd*, [1978] 2 SCR 229, 1978 CanLII 1.

*Andrews v Law Society of British Columbia*, [1989] 1 SCR 143, 1989 CanLII 2.

*Anisminic Ltd v Foreign Compensation Commission*, [1969] 2 AC 147 HL.

*Assisted Human Reproduction Act*, SC 2004, c 2.

*Bell Express Vu v R*, 2002 SCC 42.

*British Columbia Teachers' Federation v British Columbia*, 2016 SCC 49.

*British Columbia v Imperial Tobacco Canada Ltd.*, 2005 SCC 49.

*British North America Act, 1867*, SS 1867, c 3.

*Burnet v Coronado Oil & Gas Co*, 285 US 393 (1932).

*Calder v Attorney-General of British Columbia*, [1973] SCR 313, 34 D.L.R. (3d) 145.

*Canada (Attorney General) v Bedford*, 2013 SCC 72.

*Canada (Attorney General) v Federation of Law Societies of Canada*, 2015 SCC 7.

*Canada Elections Act*, SC 2000, c 9.

*Canada Evidence Act*, RSC 1985, c C-5.

*Canada (Human Rights Commission) v Taylor*, [1990] 3 SCR 892, 1990 CanLII 26.

*Canada (Minister of Immigration and Citizenship) v Vavilov*, 2019 SCC 65.

*Canada National Parks Act*, SC 2000, c 32.

*Canada Post Corporation Act*, RSC 1985, c C-10.

*Canada v Schmidt*, [1987] 1 SCR 500, 1987 CanLII 48.

*Canada Wildlife Act*, RSC 1995, c. W-9.

*Canadian Environmental Assessment Act*, SC 1992, c 37, as amended by SC 2012, c 19.

*Canadian Environmental Protection Act*, SC 1999, c 33.

*Canadian Environmental Enforcement Act*, SC 2009, c 14.

*Canadian Impact Assessment Act*, SC 2019, c 28.

*Capelas Homes Ltd*, [1998] OLRD No 3121.

*Carlill v Carbolic Smoke Ball Co*, [1893] 1 QB 256 (CA).

*Caron v Alberta*, 2015 SCC 56.

*Carter v Canada (Attorney General)*, 2015 SCC 5.

*Christie v The York Corporation*, [1940] SCR 139, [1940] 1 D.L.R. 81.

*Churchill Falls (Labrador) Corp v Hydro-Québec*, 2018 SCC 46.

*Clark v Canada Post*, 2016 NSSM 18.

*Committee for the Commonwealth of Canada v Canada*, [1991] 1 SCR 139, 1991 CanLII 119.

*Competition Act*, RSC 1985, c C-34.

*Constitution Act, 1867*, 30 & 31 Vict, c 3.

*Constitution Act, 1982*, Schedule B to the *Canada Act 1982*, (UK), 1982, c 11.

*Copyright Act*, RSC 1985, c C-42.

*Copyright Modernization Act*, SC 2012, c 20.

*Criminal Code*, RSC 1985, c C-46.

*Crown Liability and Proceedings Act*, RSC 1985, c C-50.

*Delgamuukw v British Columbia*, [1997] 3 SCR 1010, 1997 CanLII 302.

*Delisle v Canada*, [1999] 2 SCR 989, 1999 CanLII 649.

*Dickson v Vuntut Gwitchin First Nation*, 2024 SCC 10.

*Donoghue v Stevenson*, [1932] AC 562.

*Doré v Barreau du Québec*, 2012 SCC 12.

*Dunmore v Ontario (Attorney-General)*, 2001 SCC 94.

*Dunsmuir v New Brunswick*, 2008 SCC 9.

18 USC, s 1751.

*Egan v Canada*, [1995] 2 SCR 513, 1997 CanLII 302.

*Environmental Protection Act*, RSO 1990, c E.19.

*Evidence Act*, RSO 1990, c E.23.

*Fraser v Canada (Attorney General)*, 2020 SCC 28.

*Globe and Mail v Canada (Attorney General)*, 2010 SCC 41.

*Harper v Canada (Attorney General)*, 2004 SCC 33.

*Harvard College v Canada (Commissioner of Patents)*, 2002 SCC 76.

*Hazardous Products Act*, RSC 1985, c H-3.

*Health Services and Support – Facilities Subsector Bargaining Assn v British Columbia*, 2007 SCC 27.

*Hill v Church of Scientology*, [1995] 2 SCR 1130, 1995 CanLII 59.

*Hill v Hamilton-Wentworth Regional Police Services Board*, 2007 SCC 41.

*Hunter Engineering Co v Syncrude Canada Ltd*, [1989] 1 SCR 426, 1989 CanLII 129.

*Individual's Rights Protection Act*, SA 1972, c 2.

*Interpretation Act*, RSC 1985, c I-21.

*Irwin Toy Ltd v Quebec (Attorney General)*, [1989] 1 SCR 927, 1989 CanLII 87.

*Jones v Tsige*, 2012 ONCA 32.

*Lavoie v Canada*, 2002 SCC 23.

*Leonard v Pepsico, Inc*, 88 F. Supp. 2d 116 (SDNY 1999), aff'd 210 F.3d 88 (2d Cir. 2000).

*Liebeck v McDonald's Restaurants*, 1995 WL 360309 (Bernalillo County, N.M. Dist. Ct. 1994).

*Lochner v New York*, 198 U.S. 45 (1905).

*M v H*, [1999] 2 SCR 3, 1999 CanLII 686.

*Mattel, Inc v 3894207 Canada Inc*, 2006 SCC 22.

*Meredith v Canada*, 2015 SCC 2.

*Monsanto Canada Inc v Schmeiser*, 2004 SCC 34.

*Montréal (City) v 2952–1366 Québec Inc*, 2005 SCC 62.

*Mounted Police Association of Ontario v Canada (Attorney General)*, 2015 SCC 1.

*Mustapha v Culligan of Canada Ltd*, 2008 SCC 27.

*Nelson (City) v Marchi*, 2021 SCC 41.

*Nevsun Resources Ltd v Araya*, 2020 SCC 5.

*Newfoundland (Attorney General) v Churchill Falls (Labrador) Corp*, [1988] 1 SCR 1085, 70 Nfld. & P.E.I.R. 126.

*Newfoundland (Treasury Board) v N.A.P.E.*, 2004 SCC 66.

*Nicholson v Haldimand Norfolk Police Commrs Bd.*, [1979] 1 SCR 311, 1978 CanLII 24.

*O'Connor v Oakhurst Dairy*, No. 16–1901 (1st Cir. March 13, 2017).

*Ontario (Attorney General) v Working Families Coalition (Canada) Inc.*, 2025 SCC 5.

*Patent Act*, RSC 1985, c P-4.

*Personal Information Protection and Electronic Documents Act*, SC 2000, c 5.

*Physical Activities Regulations*, SOR/2019–285.

*People v Simpson*, No. BAO97211, 1995 WL 704381 (Cal. Super. Ct. 1995).

*Pierson v Post*, 3 Caines 175 (1805).

*Prince George (City) v Stewart*, 2021 BCSC 2089.

*Prohibitions del Roy*, 1607 12 Co. Rep. 63.

*Protecting Elections and Defending Democracy Act*, SO 2021, c 31.

*R v Baldree*, 2013 SCC 35.

*R v Bryan*, 2007 SCC 12.

*R v Butler*, [1992] 1 SCR 452, 1992 CanLII 124.

*R v Chan*, 2004 SCC 57.

*R v Comeau*, 2018 SCC 15.

*R v Daviault*, [1994] 3 SCR 63, 1994 CanLII 61.

*R v DB*, 2008 SCC 25.

*R v Desaultel*, 2021 SCC 17.

*R v Guignard*, 2002 SCC 14.

*R in right of Newfoundland v Commission Hydro-Electrique de Quebec*, [1982] 2 SCR 79, 1982 CanLII 28.

*R v Keegstra*, [1990] 3 SCR 697, 1990 CanLII 24.

*R v Khan*, [1990] 2 SCR 531, 1990 CanLII 77.

*R v Khelawon*, 2006 SCC 57.

*R v Kirkpatrick*, 2022 SCC 33.

*R v Lifchus*, [1997] 3 SCR 320, 1997 CanLII 319.

*R v Mapara*, 2005 SCC 23.

*R v Marshall*, [1999a] 3 SCR 456, 1999 CanLII 665.

*R v Marshall*, [1999b] 3 SCR 533, 1999 CanLII 666.

*R v Martineau*, [1990] 2 SCR 633, 1990 CanLII 80.

*R v Mohan*, [1994] 2 SCR 9, 1994 CanLII 80.

*R v Morgentaler*, [1988] 1 SCR 30, 1988 CanLII 90.

*R v National Post*, 2010 SCC 16.

*R v Oakes*, [1986] 1 SCR 103, 1986 CanLII 46.

*R v Safarzadeh-Markhali*, 2016 SCC 14.

*R v Sharma*, 2022 SCC 39.

*R v Somerset*, [1995] 1 All ER.

*R v Sparrow*, [1990] 1 SCR 1075, 1990 CanLII 104.

*R v Sullivan*, 2022 SCC 19.

*R v Vaillancourt*, [1987] 2 SCR 636, 47 D.L.R. (4th) 399.

*Ramsden v Peterborough*, [1993] 2 SCR 1084, 1993 CanLII 60.

*Re BC Motor Vehicle Act*, [1985] 2 SCR 486, 1985 CanLII 81.

*Re Public Service Employees Relations Act (Alta)*, [1987] 1 SCR 313.

*Re Resolution to Amend the Constitution*, [1981] 1 SCR 753, 125 D.L.R. (3d) 1 [*Patriation Reference*].

*References re Greenhouse Gas Pollution Pricing Act*, 2021 SCC 11.

*Reference Re Impact Assessment Act*, 2022 ABCA 165.

*Reference Re Impact Assessment Act*, 2023 SCC 23.

*Reference Re Milgaard (Can.)*, [1992] 1 SCR 866, 90 D.L.R. (4th) 1.

*Reference Re Remuneration of Judges of the Provincial Court (PEI)*, [1997] 3 SCR 3, 1997 CanLII 317.

*Reference re Secession of Quebec*, [1998] 2 SCR 217, 1998 CanLII 793 [*Secession Reference*].

*Reference Re Steven Murray Truscott*, [1967] SCR 309, 62 D.L.R. (2d) 545.

*Reference Re Validity of Section 5 (a) Dairy Industry Act*, [1949] SCR 1, 1948 CanLII 2.

*Regional Municipality of Waterloo v Persons Unknown and to be Ascertained*, 2023 ONSC 670.

*Resolution to Amend the Constitution*, [1981] 1 SCR 753, 125 D.L.R. (3d) 1.

*Rizzo & Rizzo Shoes Ltd (Re)*, [1998] 1 SCR 27, 1998 CanLII 837.

*Rodriguez v British Columbia (Attorney General)*, [1993] 3 SCR 519, 1993 CanLII 75.

*Roe v Wade*, 410 U.S. 113 (1973).

*Roncarelli v Duplessis*, [1959] SCR 121, 1959 CanLII 50.

*Sale of Goods Act*, RSO 1990, c S.1.

*Saskatchewan Federation of Labour*, 2015 SCC 4.

*Saskatchewan (Human Rights Commission) v Whatcott*, 2013 SCC 11.

*Sattva Capital Corp v Creston Moly Corp*, 2014 SCC 53.

*Singh v Minister of Employment and Immigration*, [1985] 1 SCR 177, 1985 CanLII 65.

*Smoke-Free Ontario Act, 2017*, SO 2017, c 26, sch 3.

*Society of Composers, Authors and Music Publishers of Canada v Bell Canada*, 2012 SCC 36.

*South West Terminal Ltd v Archer Land & Cattle Ltd*, 2023 SKKB 116.

*St. Catharines Milling and Lumber Co v R*, 1887, 13 SCR 577.

*SY v FGC* (1996), 78 BCAC 209 (CA), 128 WAC 209.

*Ter Neuzen v Korn*, [1995] 3 SCR 674, 1995 CanLII 72.

*Tercon Contractors Ltd v British Columbia (Transportation and Highways)*, 2010 SCC 4.

*Thomson Newspapers Co v Canada (Attorney General)*, [1998] 1 SCR 877, 1998 CanLII 829.

*Tinker v Des Moines School Dist*, 393 US 503 (1969).

*Trademarks Act*, RSC 1985, c T-13.

*Tranchemontagne v Ontario (Director, Disability Support Program)*, 2006 SCC 14.

*Trump v United States*, 603 US No. 23-939 (2024).

*Tsilhqot'in Nation v British Columbia*, 2014 SCC 44.

*Uber Technologies Inc v Heller*, 2020 SCC 16.

*Vriend v Alberta*, [1998] 1 SCR 493, 1998 CanLII 816.

*Whiten v Pilot Insurance Co*, 2002 SCC 18.

# Index

Note: Page numbers that include an *italicized t* denote a table reference.